The Bilingual Child

RESEARCH AND ANALYSIS OF EXISTING EDUCATIONAL THEMES

Edited by

António Simões, Jr.

SCHOOL OF EDUCATION
BOSTON UNIVERSITY
BOSTON, MASSACHUSETTS

ACADEMIC PRESS   New York   San Francisco   London   1976

A Subsidiary of Harcourt Brace Jovanovich, Publishers

ACADEMIC PRESS, INC.
111 Fifth Avenue, New York, New York 10003

United Kingdom Edition published by
ACADEMIC PRESS, INC. (LONDON) LTD.
24/28 Oval Road, London NW1

Library of Congress Cataloging in Publication Data

Main entry under title:

The Bilingual child.

    (Educational psychology series)
    1.   Education, Bilingual–Addresses, essays, lectures.
I.   Simões, António.
LC3715.B54   371.9'7   76-2948
ISBN 0–12–644050–6

For
Teresa, Ann-Christine, and Jean-Paul

Contents

PART II
PROGRAMS IN BILINGUAL–BICULTURAL EDUCATION: AN ANALYSIS
OF TOTAL OR PARTIAL IMMERSION PROGRAMS

4 The Case for Partial or Total Immersion Education 65

Andrew D. Cohen

**5 Bilingual Education for the English Canadian:
Recent Developments** 91

Merrill Swain and Henri C. Barik

**6 Attending a Primary School of the Other Language
in Montreal** 113

John Macnamara, Joyce Svarc, and Sharon Horner

PART IV
GENERAL TOPICS AND REVIEW OF THE LITERATURE

List of Contributors

Numbers in parentheses indicate the pages on which the authors' contributions begin.

Henri C. Barik (91), The Ontario Institute for Studies in Education, Toronto, Ontario, Canada

Richard E. Baecher[1] (41), Division of Curriculum and Teaching, School of Education, Fordham University at Lincoln Center, New York, New York

Chester C. Christian, Jr. (17), Department of Modern Languages, Texas A & M University, College Station, Texas

Andrew D. Cohen (65), Centre for Applied Linguistics, Hebrew University, Jerusalem, Israel

Karl C. Diller (145), Department of English, and Interdepartmental Committee on Linguistics, University of New Hampshire, Durham, New Hampshire

Joan C. Dye (173), Department of Curriculum and Teaching, Division of Programs in Education, Hunter College of the City University of New York, New York

Joshua A. Fishman (229), Ferkauf Graduate School, Yeshiva University, New York, New York

John F. Greene (3), University of Bridgeport, Bridgeport, Connecticut

Judith T. Guskin[2] (237), Kenosha, Wisconsin

Sharon Horner[3] (113), Department of Psychology, McGill University, Montreal, Quebec, Canada

Thomas M. Iiams (253), Educational Research Associates, New York, New York

Sally Kaminsky (155), Faculty of Educational Studies, Richmond College of the City University of New York, Staten Island, New York

John Macnamara (113), Department of Psychology, McGill University, Montreal, Quebec, Canada

Alice Neundorf (133), Navajo Reading Study, The University of New Mexico, Albuquerque, New Mexico

John Read (133), Navajo Reading Study, The University of New Mexico, Albuquerque, New Mexico

Bernard Spolsky (133), Department of Linguistics, The University of New Mexico, Albuquerque, New Mexico

Joyce Svarc (113), Department of Psychology, McGill University, Montreal, Quebec, Canada

Merrill Swain (91), The Ontario Institute for Studies in Education, Toronto, Ontario, Canada

Darryl R. Townsend (189), Texas Area Learning Resource Center, The University of Texas at Austin, Austin, Texas

Perry A. Zirkel (3), College of Education, University of Hartford, West Hartford, Connecticut

[1] Present address: 113 West 60th Street, New York, New York 10023.

[2] Present address: 4116 12th Street, Kenosha, Wisconsin 53140.

[3] Present address: McGill–Montreal Children's Hospital Learning Center, 3640 Mountain Street, Montreal, Quebec, Canada H3G 2A8.

Preface

As a curriculum specialist with an interest in bilingual–bicultural education, I have found educational research in the areas of bilingualism and biculturalism scattered and sometimes contradictory. It is true that in the domain of the social sciences, especially in comparative education, the literature is rich about differences and similarities in our adult cultures. Unfortunately, the research in the area of bilingualism with a special emphasis on children and school programs is just now commencing with a serious note.

This volume was conceived and written to help find a focus and indicate trends of research on bilingual children and their educational needs. The authors of these chapters are dedicated researchers and practical innovators; hence, the book deals as much with basic research as with applications in existing situations. We believe this volume will be of seminal import.

Perry Zirkel and John Greene present a statistical interpretation on developing cultural attitude scales. This chapter is extremely important for the bilingual teacher because it explores the equation between bilingualism and biculturalism. This problem is significant for field evaluators who are attempting to improve bilingual programs. For the educators who are not grounded in statistical analysis, the authors carefully explain different statistical concepts, which simplifies the analysis of the cultural attitude scales.

The next chapter concerns itself with early and indefinitely continuing literacy in a minority home language, plus literacy in another language learned in school. The emphasis is on social and psychological implications for the bilingual child. Chester Christian's unique approach to social and psychological problems of the young bilingual person is analyzed by a descriptive study, especially in the domain of sociology of knowledge. Self-concept, significant others, the pre-school period, the school environment, and other important themes are studied in detail. Early parental training is one of many conclusions of bilingual literacy.

Bicognition is now a topic of interest for most urban educators, be it in the bilingual field or in the analysis of social class. Richard Baecher describes cognitive style as the consistent manner in which an individual comes to know the world and its relationships. The author uses the educational sciences as a vehicle to research and develop classroom prescriptions for the bilingual student. Some of the major conclusions are: (1) Bilingual–bicultural education can benefit from the common language and conceptual framework of the educational sciences; (2) educational cognitive style analysis offers the teacher an effective diagnostic–prescriptive strategy; (3) educational cognitive style "maps" can be generated for bilingual students; (4) teacher-aides, peer-tutors, and volunteers, along with materials and media, can be matched with a student's cognitive style.

The bilingual field is still in controversy with relation to partial or total immersion education. Andrew Cohen's chapter attempts to resolve some of the conflicting issues. His immersion model is convincing and should be carefully read. He explores the differences among young children and older children in immersion programs. An interesting analysis is made between immersion and submersion programs. Some conclusions made about submersion programs are: (1) Students are grouped indiscriminately with native English speakers; (2) the students are not permitted to speak their native language in school; (3) the teachers had low expectations for the success of the students, especially those from certain ethnic groups.

The Canadian experience in bilingualism is now a serious endeavor. Merrill Swain and Henri Barik describe some recent developments for the English Canadian. This chapter is very useful for the educator in that the authors show how a battery of tests can be useful in bilingual research. Immersion programs are examined with great care and the chapter supplements and legitimates the previous chapter on immersion programs.

This section on submersion programs and the Canadian experience would not be complete without another view on submersion programs. John Macnamara, Joyce Svarc, and Sharon Horner researched the experiences of children attending a primary school of another language in Montreal. The questions are: Can an immersion program be successful for a *second* language? What are the social effects of attending a school where initially one does not know the language? These and other questions are reviewed in this chapter.

A book on bilingualism should have a chapter on the American Indian. The study of the Navajo bilingual programs illustrates the need for quality education. The social and economic importance for bilingual programs are discussed in some detail. As implied by the authors, John Read, Bernard Spolsky, and Alice Neundorf, our commitment to the native American has been neglected since the birth of the United States. This chapter is an important contribution in the field of bilingualism.

Karl Diller's contribution centers on some new trends for applied linguistics and foreign language teaching in the United States. He carefully describes different approaches to foreign language teaching. Any teacher in bilingual education or in teaching English as a second language should be familiar with this chapter.

Bilingualism and learning to read is still an unresolved issue in the field. There are many variables in learning how to read, one variable being the school environment. Sally Kaminsky describes this variable from the psycholinguistic point of view. Her sensitivity for the bilingual child who is learning to read is dealt with in a professional manner. Standardized testing, social class, prediction in reading, and other important issues are discussed by the author.

The next chapter is a highly practical description of classroom management. Taking "life-space" and aggression as a primary domain, Joan Dye gives many practical examples for the classroom teacher. The ordering of time, furniture arrangement, color and design of the classroom, objects for display, storage and maintenance, and other day-to-day problems of classroom management are suggested for the educator.

Many studies have been completed in the area of interaction analysis. As teaching becomes more of a science, educators must know the kinds of interactions that are meaningful for successful teaching. The bilingual field is no exception. Darryl Townsend presents a bilingual interaction analysis instrument for the researcher and the classroom teacher. This instrument is highly useful to better the quality of the bilingual classroom. The research possibilities for different ethnic groups are limitless.

What is the future of the bilingual field? Why is bilingual education different from teaching English as a second language? Does bilingual education legitimize ethnic identity? Joshua Fishman explores these issues and arrives at some interesting conclusions. Basically, is the American public mature enough to accept bilingual education as an integral part of the school system?

Community and school expectations are sometimes in conflict. Judith Guskin's chapter attempts to describe what children bring to school and what the school expects from them. Her specific analysis and recommendations should be part of any curriculum guide.

How can one really assess the effects of bilingualism and bilingual education on pupil achievement and cognitive development? Thomas Iiams' chapter is enlightening. He has carefully researched this problem from an historical perspective, and it is surprising to note that this problem has been around for the past several decades.

It is my hope that this book will diminish the talk in the political arena and generate a regard for bilingual–bicultural education as a serious educational endeavor. I believe that bilingual–bicultural programs may present an alternative to schooling as it now exists in the United States.

Part I

COGNITIVE AND AFFECTIVE STUDIES IN
BILINGUAL–BICULTURAL EDUCATION

Cultural Attitude Scales: A Step toward Determining Whether Programs Are Bicultural as Well as Bilingual

PERRY A. ZIRKEL, University of Hartford, Connecticut
JOHN F. GREENE, University of Bridgeport, Connecticut

Introduction

Efforts to evaluate and enhance the cultural attitudes of the pluralistic population of the American public schools are relatively recent phenomena (Cooke, 1973). The recent growth of bilingual programs have been extended to include bicultural components as well as linguistic and cognitive elements. Yet teaching methodology and program assessment have been confined generally to the linguistic and cognitive areas. While programs propose to enhance ethnic identity and cross-cultural understanding, few efforts are expended in acquiring associated measurements. Consequently, a pressing need exists for appropriate instrumentation and psychometric studies in this area.

The *Cultural Attitude Scales* (*CAS*)[1] represent an initial approach in the measurement of cultural attitudes and knowledge with respect to the Puerto Rican, Anglo-American, and Black-American cultures. Its component scales are applicable to programs that propose to enhance ethnic identity or cross-cultural understanding among any one or more of these three ethnic groups. These scales do not require reading ability; rather, they are based on pictorial stimuli and response options. The directions are particularly appropriate for elementary-school programs involving children who may differ culturally as well as linguistically.

The stimuli for the component scales of the *CAS* are graphic illustrations of the dress, sports, foods, and popular symbols of the Puerto Rican, Anglo-American, and Black-American cultures. The child reacts to these pictorial stimuli by marking one of five faces on a happy–sad Likert scale. There is also a separate response option indicating that the child has no knowledge of the particular cultural referent of the item.

[1] The *Cultural Attitude Scales* are available from Learning Concepts, 2001 North Lamar, Austin, Texas 78705.

The purpose of this chapter is to describe the development and validation of the *CAS*. After a review of the related instruments and a description of the item development procedures in the next section, substudies pertaining to the reliability and validity of the *CAS* will be presented.

In light of the technical aspects of the measurement topics to be discussed, a general review of related terms follows. This review should be regarded as optional, depending on the technical interest and expertise of the reader. The term *correlation coefficient* (r) is often used in the field of measurement. This statistic indicates the degree to which two variables are related. While correlation coefficients may range from -1.00 to $+1.00$, they usually are positive and typically fall between $+.30$ and $+.90$ when applied to measurement data. Stronger relationships are associated with higher coefficients. For example, a stronger relationship between weight and height is reflected in the high correlation coefficient of .85. On the other hand, a weak relationship between weight and IQ would probably be expressed by a coefficient near .00.

The term *level of significance* (p) as applied to correlation coefficients reveals the probability or chance that a given coefficient could have occurred by chance alone, and that no relationship exists between the variables in the population despite the fact that the sample under consideration yielded a high value. Because of the conservative nature of research, the level of significance or chance of committing an error is usually set very low. Typical values are .05 (5%) and .01 (1%).

The term *analysis of variance* denotes a statistical procedure employed to compare the averages or means of several groups. The resulting statistic is referred to as an *F*-ratio. At the risk of oversimplifying, it may be said that high *F*-ratio values are associated with greater differences between the means. Level of significance as applied to analysis of variance represents the chance that significant differences were found in the samples under consideration as a result of random chance, and that no differences exist in the population.

The term *test reliability* refers to the consistency of the measure. The internal consistency of the test reflects the degree to which the test items are homogeneous, and the internal consistency is determined by analyzing the item responses based on one testing date. The procedure consists of calculating two half-score subtotals, and correlating these two values across all subjects. Because this procedure involves only half-scores, the resulting correlation is statistically adjusted for length by the Spearman–Brown formula to yield an estimated internal consistency coefficient for the full score. The stability of a test across time is determined by a test–retest correlation coefficient. This procedure necessitates administering the instrument to the same subjects on different dates. Usually, as the interval between the dates increases, the stability decreases.

The *validity* of a test estimates the degree to which the test actually measures the construct or variable under consideration. Test validity is primarily an estimate of the accuracy of the instrument. Validity may be classified into two domains: content validity and empirical validity. Content validity is determined by comparing the item content with the variable being measured. Content validity includes both objective and subjective procedures. Conversely, empirical validity requires hard data. The most common statistic associated with empirical validity is the correlation coefficient. Measurement experts further categorize empirical validity into such terms as *construct validity, criterion-related validity, concurrent validity,* and *predictive validity.* While formal definitions of these terms are beyond the scope of this section, it should be noted that empirical data serve as the foundation in each instance. The procedure usually illustrates the existence of an empirical relationship between the test and a theoretically logical external criterion, but factor validity con- stitutes an exception to this generality. Factor validity examines the internal structure of multidimensional scales.

A procedure called *item analysis* is used during the development of a scale. Decisions pertaining to the deletion or retention of specific items are rendered through item analysis. In the affective domain, item analysis consists of examining the distribution of the response to certify that the item is capable of discrimination. Next, the directionality of the discrim- ination is considered by correlating the item scores with the total scores (less the specific item's contribution to the total score) across all sub- jects. A strong relationship (high correlation) is expected. That is, high item scores should be associated with total scores if the item is dis- criminating in the appropriate direction. The analysis is conducted for each item separately, and the resulting correlation coefficient is referred to as an *item validity.*

Review of related instruments

The earliest and most extensive source of research data concerning cultural attitudes has been verbal instruments. Bogardus' (1925, 1933) *Social Distance Scale* is probably the best known. It represents a verbal continuum of seven social situations ranging from intimate acceptance (e.g., "Would marry") to active rejection ("Would have to live outside my country"). Bogardus developed his instrument by having 100 judges, consisting of college faculty members and students, rate each of 60 statements according to the extent of social distance it reflected. According to the original form of the instrument, subjects were asked to indicate the statement(s) that expressed their reaction to each of 40 nationalities, 30 occupations, and 30 religions. This scale has revealed rather consistent results in the several years of its use with college students (Bogardus, 1933). Newcomb (1950) reported split-half reliability coefficients for the Bogardus scale up to .90, indicating high internal consistency. Moreover, researchers (e.g., Smith, 1969) have modified the instrument so that the ethnic stimuli and social statements correspond to the locale of their study and so that the mode of response reflects a range of intensity for each statement. Finally, other researchers (Miller & Biggs, 1958; Zeligs, 1948) have adapted Bogardus' methodology for use with adolescent students. There are no data available regarding the psychometric properties of this adapted form of Bogardus' instrument. However, its impracticability with respect to elementary school pupils seems clear, particularly where linguistic differences become a significantly limiting or intervening factor.

A second common verbal technique for assessing cultural attitudes is the semantic differential. Developed by Osgood, Suci, and Tannenbaum (1957), the semantic differential consists of pairs of bipolar adjectives (e.g., good–bad, strong–weak, fast–slow) typically demarcating a seven-point scale. Jenkins, Russell, and Suci (1957) found high reliability coefficients for the semantic differential mean ratings, although not for the individual ratings of American undergraduate students. Rosen (1959) found evidence of the predictive validity of this technique. However, he noted the conceptual and linguistic limitations of this technique with respect to pupils in the lower grades.

Sedlacek, Brooks, and Chaples' (1971) *Situational Attitude Scale* represents an interesting technique for assessing cultural or ethnic attitudes, which incorporates elements of both Bogardus' and Osgood's methodologies. The subject is presented with statements describing various socially sensitive situations in two alternate forms: one with a culturally neutral protagonist and an otherwise identical statement except for an ethnically identified protagonist; for example:

> *Someone on our street was raped by a tall man.*
> *Someone on our street was raped by a tall black man.*

The subject is asked to respond to each statement by selecting among polar adjectives (e.g., afraid–unafraid, happy–sad). Although limited by its high verbal factor and redundancy restraints, this technique seems suggestive of possible use for secondary, if not elementary, school pupils. (An example of a possible statement is: "A new student just entered the class today.")

Another instrument worthy of mention is a multiple-choice bicultural measure developed by Seelye (1969). Although applied to highly literate Americans living in Guatemala, for which application it appeared highly reliable and valid, Seelye's instrument exemplifies an enlightening empirical technique based on contrastive analysis of target cultures. The range of cultural situations reflected in its items include recreation, food consumption, clothing, and religious practices specific to the target cultures.

Yousef's (1968) study supported the effectiveness, in eliciting cultural attitudes, of everyday situational stimuli as compared with objectives and impersonal generalizations. Radke and Sutherland (1949) employed an open-ended, written questionnaire approach to try to elicit underlying cultural values and attitudes. However, both approaches are too verbal and abstract to be used alone in measuring the cultural attitudes of primary school children.

Several other verbal instruments measuring attitudes toward minority groups are presented and discussed by Shaw and Wright (1967). All of these scales were developed prior to World War II. Most of them focus on interracial attitudes among black and white Americans. Although they were carefully developed, these instruments cannot be applied directly to the current assessment of attitudes among elementary school students toward specific cultural groups, because of recent social–political developments such as the Civil Rights movement, Black Pride movement, and the emergence of Hispanic groups.

Since verbal instruments are limited, researchers have turned to non-verbal forms of stimuli or response modes for assessing the cultural attitudes of elementary school students. Several studies have elicited data regarding the ethnic attitudes among black and white American pupils through the use of dolls (Clarke & Clarke, 1955; Goodman, 1964; Radke & Trager, 1950). Despite the significance of these studies, their stimulus and scoring techniques are not practicable for assessing the attitudes among groups of elementary school children toward specific cultural groups.

Related nonverbal instruments are based on the use of photographs, drawings, or cutout figures. Horowitz (1939) used photographs of individual black and white American children as choices for "preferred playmates." Johnson (1950a,b) employed selected photos as the basis of a projective measure to assess the racial attitudes of Anglo- and Mexican-American subjects. Koslin (1970) used photographs of segregated and integrated classroom scenes as well as movable cutout figures in simple social settings as indicators of interracial attitudes. The *Self-Social Symbols Tasks* (Ziller, Hagey, Smith, & Lang, 1969) also used gummed cutout figures to elicit racial attitudes as well as self-perceptions. The *Preschool Racial Attitude Measure* (Thompson, Friedlander, & Oskamp, 1967) includes elements of the previously mentioned verbal and nonverbal instruments. The child is presented 12 brief stories, each of which portrays a protagonist along an evaluative dimension in a social situation. After hearing each story, the child is asked to choose between two drawings of the protagonist, which differ only in skin color (e.g., "Here are two girls. Everyone says that one of them is pretty. Which is the pretty girl?"). Although these creative techniques have been used successfully with young children, they are basically limited to black–white stereotypes.

Schmeidler and Windholz (1972) used an unusual nonverbal response method in a study comparing university students from Thailand and the United States. The students were asked to draw a line of any shape to express the meaning of each word in a list. Each drawing was scored for such variables as pressure, closure, complexity, direction, and size. Farber and Schmeidler (1971) employed the same technique in comparing attitudinal differences to "black" and "white" among Anglos and Black-American adolescents. The scoring system, as well as conceptual basis, would seem of limited applicability to the purpose of the present study.

The *Cross-Cultural Attitude Inventory*, a forerunner of the present instrument, was developed by Jackson and Klinger (1971) to assess attitudes toward Mexican-American and Anglo-American cultures among elementary school pupils. It consists of drawings of various popular symbols in these two cultures, to which the child is asked to respond by marking one of five faces on a sad–happy dimension. Jackson (1973) reported test–retest correlations for the Mexican-American and Anglo-American items of .57 and .76 for a 15-day period ($n = 92$), and of .49 and .58 for a 30-day period ($n = 83$). McCallon (1972) judged these reliability coefficients to indicate a relatively good degree of stability, considering the difficulties of measurement in this area.

Development of item content

In an effort to maximize content validity, *CAS'* original item pool was derived from informal interviews and discussions with pupils, parents, and teachers of each of the target cultural groups, respectively. These sources were asked to suggest possible items, representing the way of life of their cultural group, that could be evoked easily by a simple illustration and a typical verbal expression. This broad-based procedure generated 40–60 items for each culture. The item pool for each subtest was then reduced to 25–35 items by a representative committee of the particular cultural group. Eliminations were based on preliminary considerations only. Subsequently, each committee selected an artist of its own cultural background to prepare the simple line drawings of each item.

Selection of appropriate items

Students representing each cultural group served directly as "judges" to screen the prototype item illustrations and terms. Because of the probable difficulty presented by this task for at least some pupils in the elementary grades, students on the junior high school level were selected to serve as judges. Each group of judges consisted of 50–56 students in grades 7–10 from a metropolitan area in the Northeast representing the cultural group of the target prototype items they were asked to judge. There were an approximately equal number of males and females in each judging group. In addition to the mainland judging groups for the Black-American, Anglo-American, and Puerto Rican cultures, a group of Puerto Rican adolescents in Puerto Rico was secured to complement the screening process for the Puerto Rican items.

Each group of judges was asked to rate the prototype item illustrations in terms of their culture on a questionnaire developed in parallel English and Spanish forms. The items were presented visually and orally in the prototype forms. The judges rated each prototype item of their culture according to its representativeness on a four-point scale ranging from 0 (not at all) to 3 (excellent) and on a two-point valence scale (positive or negative). Items were rejected if the mean representativeness score was 1.7 or less, or if the positive percentage level was 66% or less. As a result, six items were deleted from the Anglo-American subtest, four items were deleted from the Black-American subtest, and three items were deleted from the Puerto Rican subtest.

The remaining items were then compiled into test booklets. The illustrations were revised and refined according to the judging group's comments. A pictorial response model was selected, consisting of a "wondering" (no knowledge) face separated from five "feeling" faces, ranging from a pronounced frowning face to a pronounced smiling face (scored as "1" and "5," respectively). A sample item is illustrated in Figure 1.1.

The test booklets were administered to 336 pupils in Grades 1 through 6 of a large school system for item analysis purposes. The sample consisted of 201 Puerto Ricans, 100 Black-Americans, and 35 Anglo-Americans. The levels for item retention were operationally established as (1) a distribution of 80% or less for any response category, and (2) a correlation with total score of .30 or above.

As a result of the item analysis, 4 items were eliminated from the

FIGURE 1.1. Sample page from the Puerto Rican scale of the Cultural Attitude Scales. (*From* Puerto Rican Cultural Attitude Scale, *copyright* © *1973 by Perry A. Zirkel. Reprinted by courtesy of author and of Learning Concepts, Austin, Texas.*)

Anglo-American subtest and 2 items were eliminated from the Black-American subtest. In the Puerto Rican subtest, all items met the criteria for item retention.

From the set of remaining items, 15 items were selected for each scale so as to provide a balanced distribution of cultural referents throughout the instrument. The item validities for the items selected for the Anglo-American ranged from .34 to .61. The item validities for the Black-American scale were bounded by .31 and .65. In the Puerto Rican subtest, the item validities were between .36 and .65. All item validities were significant beyond the .01 level.

Thus, the process employed to develop the *Cultural Attitude Scales* (*CAS*) included two stages. In the initial stage, the original item pool was derived from informal interviews and discussions with pupils, parents, and teachers from each of the target cultural groups. The second stage consisted of an extensive item-selection procedure in which the judges noted the appropriateness of each item. Subsequently, the items were administered to 336 subjects and exposed to item analysis. The resulting set of 15 items in each subscale constituted the final form of the *CAS*.

In light of the development procedure employed, the content validity of the *CAS* has been established, and the *CAS* is deemed to be a promising instrument for measuring cultural attitudes and knowledge. The extent to which the potential of the *CAS* will be realized, however, remains to be seen. Consequently, empirical studies focusing on other validity and reliability attributes are considered in subsequent sections.

Reliability

Split-half reliability coefficients adjusted by the Spearman–Brown formula for length were obtained from a sample of 330 Anglo-American, Black-American, and Puerto Rican pupils in Grades 1–6. The coefficients for the Anglo-American and Puerto Rican scales were .77 and the coefficient for the Black-American scale was .68. Each coefficient was significant at the .001 level. Thus, in light of the construct being measured, the scales are deemed to be internally consistent.

The test–retest reliability coefficients obtained over a 3-week interval with a sample of Anglo-American, Black-American, and Puerto Rican students distributed across Grades 1–6 are reported in Table 1.1. As may be seen by viewing this table, the test–retest reliability coefficients ranged from .52 to .61 and were statistically significant at the .01 level. Hence, the stability of the measure across time is established.

Validity

Evidence of the empirical validity of the CAS is revealed in Table 1.2. As this table shows, the most knowledgable and favorable cultural group for each measure was generally the one represented by that measure. For example, consider the attitude domain of the Puerto Rican scale. Note that the score of the Puerto Rican subjects (4.34) surpassed the average of the Anglo-American subjects (3.55) and the Black-American subjects (3.85). The corresponding F-ratios emanating from analysis of variance procedures indicate that the means were significantly different at the .01 level.

Moreover, the highest attitude and knowledge score for any one group generally coincided with the respective measure. For example, the highest Anglo-American attitude, of 4.58, was found in the Anglo-American scale, surpassing the other Anglo-American means of 3.76 and 3.85 for the Black-American and Puerto Rican scales.

In order to assess further the validity of the CAS, data were collected reflective of the relationship between the results of the instrument and

TABLE 1.1. TEST–RETEST RELIABILITY COEFFICIENT

	Black-American pupils ($n = 39$)	Puerto Rican pupils ($n = 56$)	Total, including 12 Anglo pupils ($n = 107$)
Black-American scale	.61	.60	.59
Puerto Rican scale	.52	.58	.53
Anglo-American scale	.57	.61	.60

TABLE 1.2. ATTITUDE AND KNOWLEDGE SCORES FOR EACH GROUP

Scale	Domain	Subjects			F-ratio
		A-A	B-A	PR	
Anglo-American	Attitude	4.58	4.20	4.37	8.62[a]
	Knowledge	14.84	11.00	9.14	14.07[a]
Black-American	Attitude	3.76	4.24	3.67	37.07[a]
	Knowledge	14.54	13.96	12.54	37.84[a]
Puerto Rican	Attitude	3.85	3.85	4.34	20.34[a]
	Knowledge	13.77	11.43	13.43	37.21[a]

[a] $p < .01$.

those of the following external criteria: (1) a teacher rating scale, (2) a sociogram, and (3) a verbal attitude scale.

In Substudy 1, the teachers of 330 Anglo-American, Black-American, and Puerto Rican pupils in Grades 1–6 were asked at the end of the school year to rate the attitude of each of their pupils toward each of the three cultures on a 1 (very negative) to 5 (very positive) Likert-type scale. At the same time, and independent of teachers' ratings, the pupils were tested by outside examiners with the CAS scales. The correlation coefficients between the teacher ratings and test results for each target culture are given in Table 1.3.

As can be seen in Table 1.3, the results of the teacher ratings and the CAS results were statistically significant beyond the .01 level for each of the three target cultural groups. Although the correlations were lower than expected, some support for the CAS is realized.

Substudy 2 was designed to explore the relationship between the CAS scores and the results of a sociogram in terms of ethnicity. A sample of 102 pupils in five multiethnic classrooms (Grades 2–4) were asked to indicate their sociometric choices according to a technique described by Cohen (1969). Each of the pupils is given a number that is clearly visible. After arranging their seats in a large circle, the examiner directs the children in a game that results in listing their two preferred choices for "playing with," "working with," and "sitting with." The responses

TABLE 1.3. RELATIONSHIP BETWEEN TEACHER RATINGS AND TEST RESULTS[a]

Black-American	.23[b]
Puerto Rican	.15[b]
Anglo-American	.34[b]

[a] $N = 330$.
[b] $p < .01$.

TABLE 1.4. CORRELATION
COEFFICIENTS BETWEEN
SOCIOGRAM SCORES AND CAS
RESULTS WITH RESPECT TO
ETHNICITY[a]

Black-American	.18
Puerto Rican	.28[b]
Anglo-American	.21[c]

[a] $N = 102$.
[b] $p < .05$.
[c] $p < .01$.

are analyzed according to ethnicity so as to generate Anglo-American
and Puerto Rican socio-values for each subject.

The same subjects are tested the following day with the CAS. The
correlation analysis between the sociogram scores and the CAS scores
are reported in Table 1.4. It was hypothesized that a significant relationship would emerge between the pupils' ethnic choices on the sociogram
and their ethnic attitudes as reveaed by the CAS.

As shown by Table 1.4, the relationship between the sociometric criterion and the CAS instrument approached significance with respect to
the Black-American culture and attained significance with respect to the
Anglo-American and Puerto Rican cultures beyond the .05 and .01 levels,
respectively. Although sociometric choices within multiethnic classrooms
certainly entail a complex of individual factors, of which ethnicity is
only one, the relationship between the ethnic choices of the sociogram
and the cultural attitudes from the CAS provides further evidence of
the validity of the instrument's scales.

In Substudy 3, the results of each scale were compared with those of
a verbal criterion measure of cultural attitudes. The criterion measure
selected for this substudy was based on Zeligs' (1948) and Miller and
Biggs (1958) adaptation of Bogardus' techniques for use with adolescent
students. The subject consisted of 87 pupils in Grades 6 and 7 ($n = 29$ for
each group). This upper limit of the grade range for the CAS was selected
to attain a practicable level for administering the criterion instrument.
Moreover, the criterion instrument was presented bilingually to assure
comprehension and uniformity in the verbal stimuli. The correlation
coefficients obtained between the *Cultural Attitude Scales* and the
verbal criterion are given in Table 1.5 for each ethnic group.

As revealed by Table 1.5, the relationship between the verbal criterion
and the attitude scale for each culture attained significance beyond the
.01 level. These resules provide further evidence of the concurrent
validity of the *Cultural Attitude Scales*.

TABLE 1.5. CORRELATION COEFFICIENTS BETWEEN CAS AND VERBAL CRITERION

Black-American scale	.46[a]
Puerto Rican scale	.32[a]
Anglo-American scale	.39[a]

[a] $p < .01$.

The relationship between the scores of the CAS and the organismic variables—sex, age, and grade—were examined for the first substudy's sample of 330 pupils. In contrast to the criterion variables, these variables should be independent of the test's results. The relationships are reported in Table 1.6.

As hypothesized, the relationship between the CAS and the organismic variables were generally low and not statistically significant, indicating the relative independence of the test instrument.

As a final support of the validity of the CAS, the intercorrelations between the three scales were generated (Table 1.7). Although the intercorrelations are independent measures, one would expect a moderate interrelationship between them as a reflection of the generality of the psychological constructs of "culture" and of "attitude." As shown in Table 1.7, the intercorrelations indicated a moderate degree of commonality.

Summary and conclusions

Various substudies have provided general evidence of the validity and reliability of the CAS. The development process provided evidence of the content validity of the CAS. The test–retest and split-half reliability coefficient reflected a moderate degree of stability and internal consistency for each modular measure, especially when compared to previous instruments in this area. The degree and directionality of the means of

TABLE 1.6. CORRELATION COEFFICIENTS BETWEEN CAS SCORES AND ORGANISMIC VARIABLES[a]

	Sex	Age	Grade
Black-American	.06	.02	.13[b]
Puerto Rican	− .03	.02	− .06
Anglo-American	.12[b]	.03	− .06

[a] $N = 330$.
[b] $p < .05$.

TABLE 1.7. INTERCORRELATIONS BETWEEN
THE THREE SCALES[a]

	Black-American	Puerto Rican
Puerto Rican	.14	—
Anglo-American	.33[b]	.55[b]

[a] $N = 330$.
[b] $p < .01$.

the three scales supported the claim of construct validity. Evidence of
the criterion validity of the CAS was revealed in the statistically significant correlation coefficients between its results and external teacher
ratings, sociometric choices, and verbal measures of cultural attitudes.
Thus, the CAS should be regarded as a promising instrument, but
additional efforts certainly must be expanded in the quest for an adequate measure of cultural attitudes.

References

Bogardus, E. S. Measuring social distance. *Journal of Applied Sociology*, 1925, 9, 299–308.

Bogardus, E. S. Racial distance changes in the U.S. during the past thirty years. *Sociology and Social Research*, 1958, 43, 127–134.

Bogardus, E. S. Social distance scale. *Sociology and Social Research*, 1933, 17, 265–271.

Clarke, K. B., and Clark, M. K. Skin color as a factor in racial identification of Negroes by pre-school children. *Journal of Social Psychology*, 1955, 11, 159–169.

Cohen, B. Title VII sociogram. Report presented in *Bilingual Newsletter* of Dunlap Associates, Darien, Conn., 1969.

Cooke, M. Social psychology and foreign language teaching. *Foreign Language Annals*, 1973, 7, 215–223.

Farber, R., and Schmeidler, G. Race differences in children's responses to black and white. *Perceptual and Motor Skills*, 1971, 33, 359–363.

Goodman, M. E. *Race awareness in young children*. New York: Collier Books, 1964.

Horowitz, R. E. Racial aspects of self-identification in nursery school children. *Journal of Psychology*, 1939, 7, 91–99.

Jackson, S. The Cross-Cultural Attitude Inventory: A report of item validity and stability. Paper presented at the annual meeting of the American Educational Research Association, New Orleans, 1973. ERIC Document Reproduction Service ED 073 885.

Jackson, S., and Klinger, R. *Cross-Cultural Attitude Inventory: Test Manual*. Austin, Texas: Urban Research Group, Inc., 1971.

Jenkins, J. J., Russell, W. A., and Suci, C. J. An atlas of semantic profiles for 360 words. In *Studies on the role of language in behavior*. Minneapolis: University of Minnesota, 1957.

Johnson, G. An experimental projective technique for the analysis of racial attitudes. *Journal of Educational Psychology*, 1950, 41, 257–278.

Johnson, G. The origin and development of the Spanish attitude toward the Anglo and the Anglo attitude toward the Spanish. *Journal of Educational Psychology,* 1950, *41,* 423; 439. (b)

Koslin, S. Classroom racial balance and students' interracial attitudes. Paper presented at annual meeting of American Educational Research Association, Minneapolis, 1970. (ERIC Document Reproduction Service ED 040 266)

McCallon, E. An analysis of cross-cultural scores. Report of the Center for Research and Evaluation, North Texas State University, Denton, 1972.

McCandless, B. R., and Marshall, H. R. A picture sociometric technique for preschool children and its relation to teacher judgments of friendship. *Child Development,* 1957, *28,* 139–147.

Miller, K. M., and Biggs, J. B. Attitude change through undirected group discussion. *Journal of Educational Psychology,* 1958, *49,* 224–228.

Newcomb, T. M. *Social psychology.* New York: Holt, 1950.

Osgood, C. E., Suci, G. T., and Tannenbaum, P. H. *The measurement of meaning.* Urbana, Ill.: University of Illinois, 1957.

Radke, M. J., and Sutherland, J. Children's concepts and attitudes about minority and majority American groups. *Journal of Educational Psychology,* 1949, *46,* 449–468.

Radke, M. J., and Trager, H. G. Children's perception of the social roles of Negroes and Whites. *Journal of Psychology,* 1950, *29,* 3–33.

Rosen, E. A cross-cultural study of semantic problems and attitude differences: Italy. *Journal of Social Psychology,* 1959, *49,* 137–144.

Schmeidler, G., and Windholz, G. A nonverbal indicator of attitudes: Data from Thailand. *Journal of Cross-Cultural Psychology,* 1972, *3,* 383–394.

Sedlacek, W. E., Brooks, G. C., and Chaples, E. A. Problems in measuring racial attitudes: An experimental approach. Report submitted to the Cultural Study Center for the University of Maryland, College Park, 1971. (ERIC Document Reproduction Service ED 058 330)

Seelye, H. N. An objective measure of biculturation: Americans in Guatamala, a case study. *Modern Language Journal,* 1969, *53,* 503–514.

Shaw, M. E., and Wright, J. M. *Scales for the measurement of attitudes.* New York: McGraw–Hill, 1967.

Smith, M. W. Measuring ethnocentrism in Hilo, Hawaii: A social distance scale. *Sociology and Social Research,* 1969, *54,* 220–236.

Thompson, K. S., Friedlander, P., and Oskamp, S. PRAM: A change in racial attitude of preschool children. Report conducted at the Claremont Graduate School, Claremont, Calif., 1967. (ERIC Document Reproduction Service ED 037 510)

Yousef, F. S. Cross-cultural testing: An aspect of its resistance reaction. *Language Learning,* 1968, *18,* 227–234.

Zeligs, R. Children's group attitudes. *Journal of Genetic Psychology,* 1948, *72,* 101–110.

Ziller, R. C., Hagey, J., Smith, M., and Lang, B. H. Self-esteem: A self-social construct. *Journal of Consulting and Clinical Psychology,* 1969, *73,* 84–95.

Zirkel, P. A. Self-concept and the "disadvantage" of ethnic group membership. *Review of Educational Research,* 1971, *41,* 211–225.

Social and Psychological Implications of Bilingual Literacy

CHESTER C. CHRISTIAN, JR., Texas A & M University

Introduction: Bilingual literacy and bilingual education

The type of bilingual literacy of principal concern in this study is early and indefinitely continuing literacy in a minority home language, accompanied by literacy in a second language learned in school. The ideal pattern would consist of learning to read and write the home language during the preschool years, continuing to learn in and through it together with the school language during the entire period of formal education, and of developing maximum skills in both languages throughout the lifetime, with the nature and complexity of skills varying with the professional and personal needs of the individual. This pattern occurs infrequently in the United States, but it does occur, and could become more common with the development of appropriate techniques of bilingual education.

Theodore Andersson, one of the first and most effective contemporary supporters of bilingual schooling in this country, recently has given much of his attention to "biliteracy" for those whose native language is not English (Andersson, 1975). He is convinced that children whose parents speak Spanish in the home, for example, can and should be taught to read in Spanish, beginning between the ages of 18 and 30 months, so that they may be literate in their home language when they enter kindergarten and are first exposed systematically to a second language. He believes that they could then learn to read English quickly and effectively. The practicality of these suggestions has been demonstrated in the experience of the present writer (Christian, in press), and their theoretical validity is supported by a review (Callaway, 1970) of relevant research.

Where the language spoken in the home is different from that spoken at school, literacy in the home language is usually promoted as a tool for the acquisition of literacy in the school language. Once this tool is developed, the school rarely continues to be interested in the first language. The question of concern to most government officials, educators, and even family members is whether literacy in the home language is more effective than initial literacy in the school language as a basis for continuing education in the latter. Research on this question has been reviewed (Engle, 1975) and is inconclusive.

Particularly where literacy in the home language is delayed until children start to school, and where the objective is transition from the home language to the school language for all further educational purposes once literacy in the latter is attained, it seems to be implicitly accepted that most of those who do not speak the school language at home, in comparison with those who do, will remain permanently retarded in education. The home language is used at school only to reduce the degree of retardation—and perhaps also to encourage those who speak the minority language to feel better about their deficiencies.

Early and continuing literacy in the home language might have much more beneficial social and psychological results than acculturation and assimilation through the oral use of the home language in school. Such literacy could provide a form of creative cultural pluralism that would offer both individual and social alternatives not now readily available to most citizens of the United States. It might produce the amalgamation of academic and folk bilingualism suggested by Gaarder (1975) for the increased enrichment of both. And, more than any other possible result of bilingual education, the development of skills to be used permanently in reading and writing two languages potentially could magnify the personal and social benefits of learning in more than one language—from enhancement of the self-concept through improvements in intercultural and even international relations.

Failure of any program in bilingual education to develop bilingual literacy implies, no matter what objectives are stated, a process of assimilation to the majority, and a discriminatory view of the minority language and culture. This process necessarily acts negatively on the pupil who is less than exclusively exposed to the dominant language, and almost assures him a continuing position of psychological and social inferiority. The irony is that he or she is the heir to the "language resources" (Fishman, 1966, p. 15) of the United States, and is thus often better prepared for what has been called "elite" as opposed to "compensatory" education (Gaarder, 1975, p. 8) than are most other children in the public schools.

Literacy and the self-concept

For most children, literacy is delayed until the child has completed the primary stage of socialization, for which the family is usually the principal agent. By the time the secondary socialization process begins, in which the school and the written word play a major role, the self-concept is considered to have been formed in a manner and to a degree that it will not be changed fundamentally thereafter. During the period of primary socialization, the child internalizes the world of family members and friends not as "one of many possible worlds. . . . but as *the* world, the only existent and only conceivable world, the world *tout court*" (Berger and Luckmann, 1967, p. 134). It is for this reason that the language spoken by family and friends is of such transcendent significance in the creation of the child's identity during this period. "Language not only serves for purposes of communication but also to indicate a person's reference group; his language is inexorably tied to his image of himself" (Modiano, 1972, p. 187).

The extent to which written language affects the child's self-image depends largely on the use his parents make of it, and on whether he associates their language with writing at all. He is almost inevitably exposed to many written words in the outdoor environment and on television, and becomes aware of the fact that these words either do or do not represent the language of his parents. If written language is not associated with his home language, either within or without the home, the result may be a greater than normal differential between the functions of *significant others* and the *generalized other* in the formation of the self-concept. These terms, used by George Herbert Mead (1934) in a classic analysis of the formation of the self-concept, contrast the role played in the child's development by those most significant to the child in his self-evaluation and acceptance of social constraints with the role played by others outside the primary group and with the more general concept of their expectations and attitudes. For bilingual persons, the division often is linguistic as well as social; the oral use of the home language is identified with significant others, and the formal use of the school language, *as well as the processes of reading and writing,* is identified with the generalized other.

The degree to which significant others are associated with reading and writing is highly important in the development of the self-concept, and *therefore* to the acquisition of literacy. Children whose parents spend much time reading learn to see themselves potentially in the role of readers. I have observed a child less than 1 year old look fixedly at an encyclopedia page with no pictures, and go through all the motions of reading, including the gesture of "Don't interrupt me; I'm busy." Her concept of herself as a "reader" led to her ability to recognize and name in Spanish 23 letters of the alphabet before she was 2 years old (Christian, in press); she began to read words shortly thereafter. By the time she entered kindergarten, she was reading books in Spanish, and 3 months thereafter was reading books (by Dr. Seuss, for example) in

English for her own pleasure. The positive emotional association of reading with the self is attributed to the identification of the process with parents and with their language during the primary socialization process.

The possibility of enabling the child to read at a much earlier age than children in general now learn to read has many direct implications for the formation of the self-concept. Discussions of the process have concentrated on technical procedures and results, however, rather than on the psychological implications. The importance of such implications is indicated by the remark of Söderbergh's daughter at the age of 2½ years: "Mother, I get so frightened when it says *frightful* on the reading card" (Söderbergh, 1971). Later, Söderbergh notes (p. 125) that the child's experiences in real life seemed much more intense when they represented something she had read about than when they did not. When written words are associated with preschool experiences during the period of primary socialization, when the self-concept of the child is being formed, they may be expected to have a stronger and longer-lasting impact than at any other part of the life cycle.

FORMATION OF THE SELF-CONCEPT DURING THE PRESCHOOL PERIOD

The development of the concept of the self in early childhood was analyzed early in this century by Charles H. Cooley (1902) and George Herbert Mead (1934), both of whom emphasized the role of language in the social processes by means of which the child comes to conceive his own existence in terms of the existence of others. Cooley spoke of the *looking-glass self* in referring to the manner in which the child comes to view himself through the eyes of others; Mead used the terms *I* and *me* to differentiate between the individual and social aspects of the self. In each case, language is considered one of the most important mediating factors in the development of the self-concept. And in each, it is assumed that significant variation would result from exposure of the child regularly to more than one language, but Mead and Cooley, as do most other social theorists, seem to assume that the child will be exposed predominantly if not exclusively to one language, that of the family, the community, the school, and the nation.

The implications of bilingualism and bilingual literacy for the early development of the self-concept in terms of these analyses can only be suggested briefly here. An analysis in greater depth of the general implications of these theories, and one that is systematically related to the social and psychological functions of language as well as to variations in ethnic group identity, may be found in a treatise on the sociology of knowledge by Berger and Luckmann (1967). The relations of symbolic to social phenomena is a central theme in the sociology of knowledge, which is concerned with the manner in which all perceived reality, including the self, is conditioned by linguistic and other symbols on the one hand, and by social reality on the other. The process begins, of course, in early childhood. It is discussed by these authors as the "internalization of reality" (pp. 129–163).

As Berger and Luckmann point out, the child has no choice of significant others; neither does he have a choice of the first language he will hear. This lack of choice will create in the child a "sense of inevitability" and "however much the original sense of inevitability may be weakened in subsequent disenchantments, the recollection of a never to be repeated certainty—the certainty of the first dawn of reality—still adheres to the first world of childhood" (p. 135).

The influence of the parent's language on the formation of personal identity may begin with birth or even before. Condon and Sander (1974), through films of infant movements, have shown that rhythmic bodily responses to the rhythm of specific speech structures occur in the first day of life, and state that it may be possible that such responses occur even in the womb. Their evidence indicates that responses vary with different languages, and that there is no such regular response to nonlinguistic sound stimuli. Thus the "mother language" seems to be internalized in a profound sense from the beginning, long before the meaning of specific words and concepts is perceived.

At a later stage, the child develops a "looking-glass self"—beliefs about the way others perceive him, perceptions of their judgments of him, and feelings about those judgments. Most of the evidence from which he constructs this image is linguistic, and contact with another language at this stage may be felt as destructive: "The appearance of an alternative symbolic universe poses a threat because its very existence demonstrates empirically that one's own universe is less than inevitable" (Berger and Luckmann, p. 108).

The child develops, between the "I" and the "me," a system of communication that is normally monolingual, representing a relatively coherent and consistent system of concepts, but this situation may change rapidly when the "me" starts speaking another language. This change implies a new set of social rules for the "I," a new and different type of conversation between the "I" and the "me," and a new self-concept for the person.

EFFECTS ON THE SELF-CONCEPT OF CONTACT WITH THE SCHOOL ENVIRONMENT

For the child whose parents do not speak the language of the school, the first step in the alteration of his self-concept, and a step closely associated with the beginnings of literacy, is the change of name. In a so-called bilingual program I visited not long ago, for example, a girl's name was written on a paper attached to the table in front of her: *Rosie*. I asked, "¿Así es que te llamas Rosie?" ('So your name is Rosie?'; literally, 'So you call yourself Rosie?'). She looked at me very deliberately and said, "Yo me llamo Rosa" ('My name is Rosa'; literally, 'I call myself Rosa'). And a little boy at the same table, with the name "Joe" written on the paper in front of him, quickly added, "Y yo me llamo José" ('And my name is José'; literally, 'And I call myself José'). The irony here is that neither the teacher nor any other pupil in the first-grade class would have had any difficulty in pronouncing any Spanish name; the only apparent reason for the change was that the school environment seemed to demand it.

Berger and Luckmann emphasize the psychological and social significance of the name: "The child learns that he *is* what he is called . . . . To be given an identity involves being assigned a specific place in the world" (p. 132). The name establishes the child's identity even if it is not a part of a family tradition, related to the home language, or even chosen by his parents, because the effect on the child is as though it were. And usually the name does fit neatly into one language and culture, but not into others. In one such case, a friend from Mexico who attended school in Colorado told me that when his teacher called the roll, she always called his name as "Almost–Jesus." His name is Jesús Olmos. This given name is common in Hispanic culture, but of course it is almost invariably changed in the United States, because the only alternative is to pronounce it correctly.

The child, called repeatedly by his name in the first years of his life, learns to perceive it as, for himself, the central element in a system of sounds that defines his identity; variations in the pronunciation may indicate for him the difference between a family member or friend and a stranger. Our daughter came home from kindergarten saying, "At school they call me Raquel [English pronunciation /rəkéəl/], but my name is Raquel [Spanish pronunciation /rrakel/]."

Two months later, Raquel wrote a letter to Santa Claus in English and signed it *Rachel*. When I asked why she had written her name that way, she answered, "Porque escribí la carta en inglés y no me gusta mezclar los idiomas" ('Because I wrote the letter in English and I don't like to mix my languages'). "¿Pero no te llaman Raquel /rrakel/ en la escuela?" ('But don't they call you Raquel at school?'), I asked. "No," she replied, "me llaman Raquel [English pronunciation], y me gusta más Rachel que eso" ('No, they rall me Raquel /rəkéəl/, and I like Rachel better than that').

The change in name is important because it symbolizes other changes which are imposed less obviously; in Cooley's (1902) terms, the child finds a different reflection of self, a different looking-glass self, and finds it necessary to become either a different person or a divided person. An unusual illustration, which nevertheless represents the process, is that of Johnny, a black boy I observed in a bilingual kindergarten several years ago. His family lived in a part of the community occupied largely by Mexican-Americans; his playmates usually spoke Spanish and he spoke Spanish with them. One day in kindergarten, some of the other children came upon a picture in a book of a black boy on a tricycle, and exclaimed, "There's Johnny, there's Johnny." Johnny went over to look at the book, seemed puzzled, and said distainfully, "That's not me; that's a little colored boy." At that time, he was happy and outgoing in his play with the other children; when I visited the program the next year, he was much more withdrawn and isolated. I asked the teacher why, and she said that she thought he had finally come to realize that he *was* the little boy on the tricycle.

Two important influences that the child encounters in school if not before are (1) the collective out-group perceptions of his in-group, applied to him as a person, and (2) symbolic representation of social reality in writing. The two are interrelated; the perceptions of the out-group, and the social ranking that results, depend in part on the relative prestige of any minority language spoken by the child. This prestige, in turn, seems to be closely related to the extent and depth of the literary tradition in that language, and the degree of literacy of those in the minority group who speak the language.

Even where the language represents a distinguished literary tradition, its use by a specific group may be considered to have nothing to do with that tradition—not even, in fact, to be "the same language." The possibility of its providing a basis for literacy is therefore ignored, and the child is taught to read and write in and through a language he does not understand, which is unrelated to his self-concept and to the sense of inevitability characteristic of that concept and of the language in which it was formed.

PROBLEMS RESULTING FROM ACQUISITION OF A WRITTEN LANGUAGE DIFFERENT FROM THAT WHICH IS SPOKEN AT HOME

The social and psychological implications of literacy for the child whose parents do not speak the school language are closely associated with the myriad technical problems of learning to read and write a language one does not speak. These problems are too numerous and complex to be treated in detail here, but I will attempt to give some indication of their nature.

The process of learning to use any given language and to become a member of the culture of those who speak it involves learning to accept

certain possibilities—in terms of sound, structure, meaning, and so on—
and to reject other possibilities. The child learns to identify with those
possibilities he has been taught to accept as valid and significant, and to
treat all others as meaningless. If at school he is taught in a language
consisting in great part of sounds he has learned to regard as meaningless, arranged in structures he has been taught to reject, in terms of
meanings he must consider invalid if he is to maintain the sense of reality
he has acquired, it is no wonder that he develops psychological problems and has difficulty adjusting to the social world represented by the
school. And if the only language he is taught to read and write further
denies the validity of his own system and robs him of its meanings, it is
no wonder that literacy, so far as he is able to attain it, is not integrated
into his self-concept as an aspect of his own personal reality.

The written language should be a means of expanding personal reality
into time and space, and of integrating into the personal reality that of
other persons who are distant in time and space. But it is difficult to do
so when the means of doing so itself represents a reality that is alien to
the person, a reality he has learned to reject in order to achieve the
identity he has.

Let us take an example that may seem trivial, but, when multiplied
thousands of times, in terms of structures and meanings as well as
sounds, is highly significant because of its psychological and social implications.

The sound of the *i* as in English *sit* does not exist in Spanish, so the
person who has heard only Spanish has not learned either to hear or to
produce the sound, and will not distinguish between *sit/seat, bit/beat,
ship/sheep, lip/leap, fit/feet,* and so on. When he learns to write English,
however, he not only must become able to distinguish the sound, but
also must know when to represent it by *i, y, ie, e, ee, o, u,* or *ui* (Lado,
1957, p. 100). In Spanish, on the other hand, there is only one way to
represent each of the vowel sounds.

Matluck and Mace (1973) have discussed the interrelation of phono-
logical and grammatical problems for Mexican-American children that
result in increasing educational retardation, as long as the child remains
in school, as compared with monolingual speakers of English. My own
experience (12 years teaching classes composed of 85% to 95% native
speakers of Spanish) indicates that these problems rarely occur for students who have learned to read and write Spanish competently before
learning to read and write English. This effect may be attributed, I
believe, to psychological and social, as well as to technical, factors, and
each factor is both cause for and effect of the other. Literacy in two
languages clarifies the technical contrasts between one system and the
other. For example, differences between sounds that tend to be heard

the same way may be learned through their written representation, as when the student who speaks Spanish earns that *sh* and *ch* represent different sounds and meanings in English, but learns that the former does not occur in Spanish in terms of spelling, sound, or meaning. The person who does not read or write his home language, on the other hand, but is forced to read and write another, may become confused even about the sounds in his first language as he learns new sounds and learns their representation in the second. He is put into a world in which he feels unsure of himself and of the attitudes and judgments of others in reference to him. Literacy in the language of his parents makes their world at least comparable to that of the school.

Identification of literacy with the dominant language and culture of the United States

Literacy in English in the schools of the United States is the principal instrument used by government in the secondary socialization process. When instruction in any other language occurs, that language is treated almost inevitably as an object of learning rather than a medium of socialization. Literacy for the serious purposes of life is therefore confined almost exclusively to English.

Popenoe speaks of the dangers of "cultural and especially linguistic pluralism," pointing out that "if we had many different basic values and were committed to different goals it would be difficult for any state or government to maintain its authority" (1971, p. 295). The provision of literacy only through English assures that only folk values are maintained by other languages, and that the literate society, which includes almost all those who have any authority, is dominated by Anglo traditions and values.

More specifically, the identification of literacy with English is assured by the publication of textbooks only in English, and the representation of "appropriate" values by the content of textbooks is controlled by the government by the process of textbook selection. The extent to which these values differ from those of other cultures and languages is indicated by the difficulty of finding "suitable" materials in Spanish, for example, even though every school in 20 other countries has and uses such materials.

In recent years, the possibility of going, as Glazer and Moynihan suggested (1963), "beyond the melting pot," has been taken ever more seriously. They cite a proposal, made by William H. Seward in 1840, that children of immigrants be taught in their language by members of their faith. A recent article (Eisele, 1975) calls attention to statements by John Dewey indicating at least limited approval of cultural pluralism —for example, his statement that children of immigrant families "are too rapidly, I will not say Americanized, but too rapidly denationalized. They lose the positive and conservative value of their own native traditions, their own native music, art, and literature" (p. 70). Dewey does not suggest maintaining the language of immigrants by public education, much less providing, through literacy in that language, the possibility of deep and regular contact with the sources traditions, music, art, and literature that it represents.

So long as literacy is provided and developed by the public schools only in English, it seems clear that any variety of "cultural pluralism" that might be developed would be very limited, and that the underlying goal even of bilingual education is, under those conditions, assimilation.

TRADITIONS OF ASSIMILATION

The concept of the United States as a melting pot of languages and cultures, in which all become "American" and speak only English, is, as Glazer and Moynihan have pointed out, "as old as the Republic" (1963, p. 288). They describe how the terminology originated with a play, first performed in 1908, entitled *The Melting Pot*, which represented an idealistic view of an amalgamation of races, resulting in the creation of a "superman" (p. 289).

Assimilation of minority group members is in harmony with an expressed ideal of United States culture to "forget the past" and "begin again." Although many of the early settlers undoubtedly found this idea attractive, another reason for immigration was to escape an environment hostile to one's particular traditions and to preserve them more nearly intact in the New World. This reason involved insistence on control over the education of children, which many minority group members still find highly desirable.

Still, the dominant tradition in the United States is for the parents to have principal control only over primary socialization processes, and for the state to take charge of most of the elements in secondary socialization when the child enters school. One of the most basic social issues brought into focus by the existence of groups whose members do not speak the official, national, or school language at home is that of the relative privileges and responsibilities of parents and the state in the creation of the identity, potential, limitations, and social functions of each member of each new generation. Traditionally, the privileges and responsibility pass in large part from the parents to the state at the age when most children begin to read and write. And it is principally through literacy in the language of the school that the state exercises its influence on what and whom the child is to become.

LITERACY IN ENGLISH AS A MEANS OF ASSIMILATION

For the child who, before entering school, has become familiar with materials written in the language of his parents, even though he may not have learned to read, the school experience may easily be felt as an extension of the home experience, and the transition from primary to secondary forms of socialization may be experienced with a minimum of trauma. For children who speak a different language, or even a different dialect, from that used in the schools, this transition is much more difficult. As Bernstein has expressed it, "The child is expected, and his parents as well, to drop his social identity, his way of life and its symbolic representation, at the school gate" (1971, p. 138).

Even in bilingual programs, literacy in the home language has not been a major concern thus far. Bilingual schooling (Andersson and Boyer, 1970) has been organized as a compensatory program to enable children who are viewed as linguistically, culturally, socially, educationally, and economically "deprived" to narrow the gap between themselves and the "more fortunate" pupils who have been exposed only to English during the preschool years. If assimilation is the final objective, and literacy in English the means, of education in the schools, less than exclusive exposure to English is appropriately defined as a deficiency.

Bernstein has observed that compensatory education "distracts attention from the deficiencies in the school itself and focuses upon deficiencies within the community, family, and child" (1971, p. 138). Fishman suggests that a non-English mother tongue is generally viewed as a "disease of the poor" in discussing bilingual and compensatory education, and ironically states that such education is used "to enable the patient to throw off the mother tongue entirely and to embrace all-American vim, vigor, and vitality" (1975, p. 6). Compensatory education assumes that literacy in English and assimilation are the exclusive goals of such education, each of which leads to the other.

Both Fishman (1975, pp. 5–8) and Gaarder (1975, pp. 8–11) suggest elitist forms of bilingual education as a substitute for the compensatory forms it necessarily takes when the final objective is literacy in English for assimilation and vice versa. Elitist forms cultivate literacy in the home language and in a second language, to a level suitable for professional as well as for personal purposes. This type of education at present is provided least often for those who have the best background for taking advantage of it. If they are expected to maintain their home language at all, it is as a personal means of communication with a limited number of others in narrowly restricted circumstances—a means of placing both psychological and social limits on them.

Psychological effects of monolingual literacy for a bilingual person

Children who are expected by teachers and other official representatives of the state within or outside the school to consider their language only as an oral means of communication, not to be read or written as is the language of the school and that of the government, may also be expected to consider their language and that of their parents inferior. When they learn to read and write only the language of the school—even though they may be instructed orally in their home language for as long as is felt necessary—and do not even learn that science, literature, mathematics, geography, and all the transcendent subjects of school attention exist in their home language, that language must almost inevitably be considered a second-rate means of communication. It is not far from that conclusion to the conclusion that those who speak the home language are second-rate people.

For those who speak a minority language, this conclusion may have been found inescapable even before they entered school, because of attitudes in the community toward the language and those who speak it. Once when I spoke in Spanish to a 3-year-old child, she asked if I were a maid. Such attitudes may be found in the minority language community itself as well as the majority language community.

IDENTIFICATION WITH SELECTED HISTORICAL PROCESSES

Through both imaginative and factual literature, the person learns to view himself in relation to real and fictional events and persons, and to interpret his own character as well as the social reality in which he lives in relation to them. What he reads may imply that his existence, feelings, and experiences are important or may imply that they are insignificant.

When what he reads is in a language not associated with significant others, the later implication may be derived, no matter what the content, from the initial reading experience. It is further indicated by the selection of persons, both fictional and historical, to be represented in writing and pictures, from the Pollyanna-ish Anglos in the beginning readers to the heroes of history and literature studied in high school and college. More important still, but also more difficult to define (and therefore to escape), are the values implied by what is represented. Even when names associated with a minority language and culture are found in textbooks, the context and interpretation may be so distorted by what are, in terms of that language and culture, alien values and judgments, that the minority language student would not identify with the persons represented, or would do so negatively.

Thus, for example, many of the traditions interpreted as heroic in Hispanic contexts—the search for the Fountain of Youth, El Dorado, the great individual, personal adventures of the *conquistadores*—may be interpreted as irrational, frivolous, and immoral in terms of Puritan traditions. And the type of sexual contacts that produced the mestizos of Spanish America and the Southwest—the racial heritage of most Spanish-speaking children in the United States—is of course ignored almost completely, both in history and in fiction.

The type of judgment on Hispanic values that is implicit in most history and literature written in English is presented explicitly by Clough (1960, pp. 99–116) in a discussion of variations on the basic values of Western civilization. He disparages the egocentrism of the "Latin" cultures, for example, pointing out that "all social enterprises require a certain amount of negation of self" and that "no automobile would ever get assembled if workers did not go to the factories at appointed times" (p. 105). It seems highly probable, however, that without this cultural characteristic among Spaniards. Spanish America would never have existed. Although it may be that the existence of Spanish America is, on some scale of values, as important as the production of automobiles. Puritan modesty, with its own brand of egocentrism, is so important nowadays that hardly anyone wants to identify with the Spanish.

Spanish-speaking persons have, on occasion, chosen to identify themselves with the unwritten languages and cultures of Indian groups, as the children of Aztlán or of Montezuma (Ortego, 1970), and to ignore the fact that it was their Spanish ancestors who gave them their language, family system, religion, and all the other important institutions through which psychological and social realities are created.

Many persons of Mexican descent, both in the United States and in Mexico, attempt to reject their Hispanic heritage and adopt what they suppose to be the culture of the Aztecs because Spaniards are viewed as conquerors and exploiters of the Indians, and the latter have been presented as morally superior to the former, with a great pre-Colombian culture. They ignore the fact that there were many pre-Colombian Indian cultures in Mexico, and that presently they are represented by those Indian groups who conserve the more than 30 Indian languages spoken there, not by those whose language is Spanish.

My experience has been, however, that when the latter come into contact with the written forms of the historical reality of Spain and Spanish America, they recognize in these forms both their family and their personal heritage. The classical realities created in Spanish writing evoke the original reality to which they were introduced in early childhood by their parents.

Monolingual literacy does not permit this type of contact for bicultural groups, nor, therefore, the growth of roots established by the family and its language. Education then represents a graft onto those roots, and produces a plant not as healthy as it might have been.

IDENTIFICATION WITH MEMBERS OF THE DOMINANT SOCIETY

Children who do not learn to read and write the language of their parents are, after entering school, subject to constant pressures to identify with members of the dominant society as a condition for personal and social "success," even when they continue to speak the minority language. Under these circumstances, they may consider identification with family and friends as secondary in importance to identification with members of the majority society.

There are many degrees and varieties of equilibrium between the two forms of identity, related systematically to language usage. These variations are discussed by Fishman (1971, pp. 286–299) as forms of *diglossia,* or the use of two or more languages or language varieties for different personal and social functions. Two of the most common functions are the use of a vernacular in informal, especially primary group, contacts, and of a formal language, often distinguished by its use in reading and writing, especially in institutional contexts such as education, religion, and government. Fishman describes how industrialism tends to increase the role of the school and work language in the family, and to break down the differentiation between language forms as well as functions.

In the absence of literacy in the home language, the user may become progressively less convinced of its validity as a language and at the same time, because of increasing literacy in the school language and contacts with those who speak it, allow it more and more to take over the functions of the home language. The final result may be complete assimilation through identification with those who speak only the official language.

DISAPPEARANCE OF THE SELF AS GENERATED BY
PARENT IDENTIFICATION

In spite of the accuracy and the importance of Berger and Luckmann's previously cited statement regarding the "never-to-be-repeated certainty . . . of the first world of childhood" (p. 135), the identity provided by the parents for the child does seem often to be lost, at least for all practical purposes. Some parents accept this loss willingly, and even insist on it; some regret it but regard it as inevitable; others struggle to maintain the child's family identity at least outside formal institutional contexts; and still others want their children to live within the frame of reference of their culture as fully and completely as possible, through study in their language and even in their country of origin.

Reactions of children seem just as varied as attitudes and desires of parents. In the first place, these is some resistance, apparently varying widely in degree with both individuals and cultures, to the processes of socialization per se. "The little animal fights back, so to speak" (Berger and Luckmann, p. 182). Dennis Wrong has discussed some of the implications of not recognizing this fact in a paper on "the oversocialized conception of man" (1961), pointing out that modern sociology has developed a concept of humanity that ignores individual personal and biological realities.

This variety in character and temperament, coupled with the appearance in the social environment of discrepant ways of being, create conditions in which every person is a potential "traitor to himself" (Berger and Luckmann, p. 170). For example, when parent and peer group value systems differ, the person may act out those of one system while identifying himself with the other. Or he may become an "individualist" capable of taking on whatever identity is required by the situation (p. 171). Berger and Luckmann also discuss the results of discrepancies between the worlds of primary and of secondary socialization, stating that the individual may choose the world of secondary socialization as a reality within which to operate—to manipulate others for specific purposes—without being identified in his own mind as a part of it (p. 172).

In these and other kinds of cases, the person may suppress even his own consciousness of his identity as a function of the language and culture of his parents. He may maintain a personal relationship with them, but does so, insofar as possible, out of the view of others with whom he considers it desirable to identify. Berger and Luckmann (p. 173) indicate the profound implications of this situation—where the person not only plays at not being himself but also plays at being someone else —for any person or society. People become actors, divorced from ethnic and familial realities. The prevalence of these phenomena makes Goffman's (1959) theatrical analogies appropriate for the analysis of modern societies.

SIGNIFICANCE OF OCCUPATIONAL IDENTIFICATION

A characteristic of modern bureaucracy is that members are expected to take on an identity that is characteristic of any given position they occupy. A change of position usually implies a change of identity. This characteristic is the principal reason for the appropriateness of the view Goffman (1959) has presented of everyday life as a series of roles in which the actor attempts to impress each of his audiences in a given way. As societies become more complex, more urbanized, and more industrialized, it becomes socially dysfunctional for individuals to retain familial identities that may interfere with geographic, occupational, or even ideological mobility.

The person who speaks a minority language at home, then, may find it more difficult than others do to play the expected role at work, especially as he changes from manual labor to technical, white-collar, and professional positions. These positions require not only that he use English, but that the self be represented through language in given specific ways appropriate to each situation and function. Karabel and Astin (1975, p. 381) point out that this type of white-collar position is increasingly dominant in the labor market, and that its means of attainment, higher education, demands sophisticated and acceptable types of skills in English.

In view of this situation, it is not surprising that parents who speak minority languages at times demand the suppression of their own language by their children in exchange, as they conceive it, for maximum education and socioeconomic mobility. Some parents who are bilingual speak a minority language to each other, but only English to their children. In one case that recently came to my attention, the parents of two boys had even themselves stopped speaking Spanish for twenty years while their sons grew up. Now that their children are young men in college, the parents are speaking Spanish to each other, and their sons are learning the language. Other parents insist on the exclusive use of the minority language at home, and teach their children to read and write it. The great variety of parental attitudes and policies with respect to children may itself exercise pressure toward the acceptance by the children of identification with classmates and co-workers, of identification with the social role at all stages of life rather than with family origins, language, and culture.

Since those who speak minority languages in the United States only rarely possess the degree of literacy necessary for employment in occupations where such knowledge is needed or necessary, occupational identification is almost always in terms of the dominant language and culture. Even among teachers in bilingual programs, Gaarder (1975) found that illiteracy in the minority language was prevalent.

Social and psychological significance of the development of bilingual literacy

Bilingual literacy as defined at the beginning of this paper is uncommon in the United States, but a recent study indicates the basis for its development does exist in some communities. Patella and Kuvlesky (1975) asked high school sophomores in four counties of South Texas about their ability to read and write Spanish; 88% of males and 88% of females said that they could read the language, and 69% of males and 82% of females said that they could write it—this in spite of the fact that only 56% of males and 62% of females had ever taken a course in Spanish in school. A fairly high proportion (11–36%) had used their abilities to read and/or to write Spanish on the job.

The social and psychological significance of highly developed bilingual literacy would be much greater than what is implied by practical abilities to read and write two languages, however. The importance of language in the processes of socialization, the relations between family and school, the understanding of fundamental processes of human interaction, and the manner in which psychological and social reality are formed by language are all factors that make bilingualism more profoundly significant than it appears superficially.

PROVISION FOR PREVIOUSLY NONEXISTENT PERSONAL ALTERNATIVES

Bilingual literacy provides an increase in personal alternatives ranging from work location to manner of being. Bilingualism without biliteracy provides, in comparison, a very restricted range of alternatives, the principal one of which is escape into a personal folk reality and out of the manipulated urban-industrial and commercial reality (Christian and Sharp, 1972) dominant in United States society. This alternative may be rationale enough for the maintenance of folk bilingualism as deliberate policy, but it does not recognize the great potential of native bilingual children educated in the elite traditions.

Persons educated only in the folk traditions of their family language do not themselves recognize this potential, because they reflect the views of others toward them. They have internalized the self together with, and even emphasizing, its limitations as conceived by those who do not speak their language or have *only* received formal training in it. During my past twenty years of almost daily contact with Mexican-Americans, for example, I have observed constantly the contrast between abilities and potential, on the one hand, and their inaccurate concept of their limitations as a reflection of perceived attitudes toward them, on the other.

There is a widespread notion, for example, that folk Spanish is so different from "Castilian" Spanish (which many believe, inaccurately, is the Spanish of educated people in Spanish America) that Mexican-Americans are not able to communicate in Spanish with people from other countries. However, neither my wife, who is Peruvian, nor any of the members of her family, have had any difficulty communicating in Spanish with any Mexican-American they met in Texas from their first moment of arrival in the United States, in spite of their contacts with a range of persons from those illiterate in both Spanish and English to others highly literate in both. Recently, for example, I came home to find my wife in animated conversation in Spanish with a woman I thought at first might be from a Spanish American country. After about 15 minutes, the woman used the term "asina" (an archaic form of *así*) and I concluded that she was Mexican-American. When she discovered that I am a professor of Spanish, however, she apologized for her use of Spanish and began to use English, in spite of the fact that there had been complete and instantaneous communication in Spanish.

On my first visit to a bilingual program, administrators told me they were not sure the children spoke "real" Spanish; after 15 minutes speaking Spanish with the children, I assured the administrators that the children's Spanish was as real as the Spanish I spoke. Similarly, after my most recent visit to such a program, the teacher exclaimed, "I didn't know these children could speak that much Spanish!"

One of the major problems in developing a broader range of alternatives for most speakers of minority languages in the United States is that they have had little contact either with the written language, which usually constitutes a standard of usage for speech at least in formal situations, or with those who are literate; therefore they have little feeling for the authenticity of the language they use. For example, a Spanish instructor who recently asked her Mexican-American students to make a list of "Chicano" words was provided with 42 words, 38 of which are used in other countries, and 30 of which are standard forms acceptable at any level of social usage. And these students *had* had contact with written Spanish.

In terms of employment, the area of greatest demand for speakers of foreign languages is that which requires other skills and knowledge in addition to language abilities, including reading and writing. In general, foreign language specialization is designed to prepare students only to teach language and literature, and other professional skills are not developed, so that there are few psychologists, sociologists, social workers, doctors, and so on who speak the language of minority groups or who are able to work in other countries. Early and continuing bilingual literacy for those who speak a minority language could provide this type of opportunity for them.

Jobs, travel, friendship, and other practical benefits of speaking foreign languages are important to the person and to his society, but the most profound social and psychological influences of bilingual literacy might appear in less visible and tangible form, affecting basic psychological and social structures subtly but deeply, enriching the sociocultural environment, developing intercultural understanding, mitigating provincial attitudes and values, and increasing personal and social flexibility in many areas of United States society.

ENRICHMENT OF THE SOCIOCULTURAL ENVIRONMENT

Each language implies a specific structuralization of reality and a particular mode of being, manifest in a set of subcultures associated with that language. This fact does not necessarily imply the validity of all the conclusions that have been derived from the Whorf–Sapir hypothesis (Whorf, 1956; Sapir, 1958). But it does seem clear that the two facets of the hypothesis, linguistic determinism and linguistic relativity, as described by Dale (1972, p. 204), result from the process of language learning simultaneous with and forming the basis for socialization, at least to some degree. When more than one language is involved in this process, opportunities as well as problems are created.

Hertzler (1965) describes some of the problems associated with the use of two languages. One problem is that the person "lives with two different sets of cultural perspectives" (p. 429). He must therefore "always be socioculturally and psychologically oriented in two different worlds" and as a result is a "divided man."

But it is precisely this type of division that creates alternatives for the individual, for social groups, and even for the society as a whole. Without these alternatives, a much narrower range of cultural perspectives is imposed, and individual and social choices are limited. The increase in types of choice permitted seems particularly important in view of the pressures toward conformity and uniformity created by mass communications and mass culture as well as by technology, commerce, and urbanization (Christian and Sharp, 1972).

DEVELOPMENT OF INTERCULTURAL UNDERSTANDING

Bilingual literacy permits the comparison of two cultural perspectives on similar cognitive, affective, and imaginative levels and minimizes the distortions inherent in the invidious distinctions that result from the exclusively oral use of one language and from the use of both oral and written forms of the other. It therefore offers the potential for a high level of intercultural understanding, both nationally and internationally.

For most people, the cultural identity of another group is visible only in written form. Even when personal and social contacts occur between groups, they are usually so brief and so infrequent that understanding is not developed, and in fact minor but highly visible differences may foster misunderstanding. The "inappropriate" use of even a single word during such contacts, for example, may create a stereotype of vulgarity, pretentiousness, or other undesirable characteristics, and may thus impede communication and understanding such as could result from deeper commonalities. The written language, on the other hand, allows a breadth of contact through time in a context that is minimally threatening, and therefore provides a medium for understanding in perspective of contacts that may occur.

For example, I am convinced that there are deep and permanent cultural meanings in common between Spanish-speaking groups in the United States and the citizens of Spanish American countries, but that these are obscured by minor lexical differences and by the relatively narrow focus of the culture of the former group on personal and familial life—limits imposed by lack of contact with writing in the home language. My Mexican-American students who have overcome these limitations have always seen themselves in, for example, contemporary novels of Spanish-American countries. They recognize their culture there.

MITIGATION OF PROVINCIAL ATTITUDES AND VALUES

The type of linguistic ethnocentricity that exists at all intellectual and social levels seems at times incredible. Recently, in conversation with an uneducated country woman, she remarked, "I just love the way they spoke English in Jesus' time." That this ethnocentricity is not limited to the uneducated is indicated by an experience in a university Latin class, where a teacher read from the Bible in Latin, and the response of a graduate student (majoring in music) was, "But I didn't know the Bible was ever written in any language but English." And, from my point of view, the remark of a prominent professor of political science was equally provincial. In a faculty discussion of the possibility of teaching a class in political science in Spanish, he asked seriously, "But if students were taught in Spanish, how could we ever find out if they had learned anything?"

These and many other examples could be used to demonstrate that for most people the reality provided by their parents in their language is the only possible valid reality and their system of values is the only logical one in existence. This reality is thought, felt, and argued in different ways by taxi drivers and doctors of philosophy, but we all share this type of provincialism. Literacy in more than one language seems the only effective way to mitigate it.

INCREASE IN PERSONAL AND SOCIAL FLEXIBILITY

Those persons who have learned more than one language in childhood and who have continued to develop each through reading and writing as well as speaking, seem to have been prepared in the best possible way for dealing with situations where personal and social flexibility is required. In the modern world, these situations are being multiplied—from busing pupils out of their communities to flying Kissinger around the world. There is now a level of sophistication with respect to the relativity of values—if not with respect to its source in language differences—that makes increasingly more difficult the imposition of one set of values on persons with different traditions.

The person who has learned the relativity of his own culturalinguistic values to one other set is thereby prepared to respond more realistically to any further set that may be presented. Early and continuing bilingual literacy therefore seems to provide the best possible preparation for the cultural confrontations that are increasing in the nation and in the world. With this view in mind, speakers of minority languages should be regarded as *advantaged* rather than *disadvantaged,* and education for them should be modified so that they can take advantage of their potential through bilingual literacy.

At the time bilingual literacy is offered to children whose native language is not English, it would be possible for these children to help others whose home language is English to acquire a second language, and for the two groups to become able to understand each other in either of the two languages, resulting in psychological, social, and educational benefits for both. A program in which this was done very effectively was established 12 years ago in the Laredo United Independent School District of Texas. Children whose home language was English, as well as those whose home language was Spanish, learned to read and write both languages in the first and second grades, and to use dictionaries and encyclopedias. The program continues under the direction of Mrs. Dolores Earles, an enthusiastic supporter of bilingualism for both groups, but federal government support has been withdrawn from Nye School, where the program originated, because of the high proportion of children who "do not need" bilingual education. Thus, bilingual education is still viewed officially as compensatory education.

Summary and conclusions

Compensatory education involving a transition from family use of a minority language to literacy exclusively in the school language can never be fully satisfactory because of the role of the former in establishing the permanent identity of the child in his first few years of life. This form of education implies an attempt to change rather than to develop the child's identity through literacy, with the family and the state providing divergent directions. Linguistic and educational problems, with negative psychological and social consequences, are the usual result.

Early and continuing bilingual literacy could provide a form of psychological development and of social potential generally associated with elite rather than with disadvantaged groups. The ability to function in a literate tradition and/or in a professional capacity in more than one language could create personal and professional alternatives now rarely offered by the educational system of the United States to anyone. Citizens educated in more than one culturalinguistic tradition could provide valuable services to the community, the state, and the nation, from facilitating administration of government services for minority and foreign groups, to increasing awareness of the nature and significance of language and cultural differences in general.

There is evidence that literacy in the home language could be provided at a much earlier age than that at which reading is conventionally taught, and it seems possible to teach children to read languages such as Spanish, which has a much closer correspondence between the sound and writing systems, more quickly and easily than to teach them to read English. However, some intervention of the state in early childhood education would seem necessary for this to be accomplished, and such intervention might signify a dimunition in the autonomy of the family and increasing determination by the state of the identity and potential of minority group children. Such intervention could be interpreted as an infringement on the rights of parents to have children "of their own."

One possible solution would be to provide materials and train parents, no matter what their degree of literacy, to use letters, words, and books in playing with their young children in such a way as to associate literacy with their language, if not to read it. Then children could be taught to read the home language in kindergarten (as is done in Edinburgh, Texas, for example). Materials and instruction could be provided thereafter in that language at every grade level, with English supplementing rather than substituting for the home language in the processes of secondary socialization as well as education.

However it may be attained, the uses as well as the psychological and social implications of bilingual literacy are many, complex, and profound, especially for those who have learned a minority language in the home before coming into regular contact with a national school language. Literacy in the home language can be expected to influence such persons' concepts of themselves, the attitudes of others toward them, the development of their abilities in the school language and of their academic preparation in general, and their adult roles in society. In an important sense, the education of those who speak two languages can never be "equal" to the education of monolinguals; it must be inferior or superior. Whether it will be one or the other depends heavily on whether literacy is provided in only one or in both languages.

References

Andersson, T. A proposed investigation of preschool biliteracy. Austin, Tex.: Author, 1975.

Andersson, T., and Boyer, M. *Bilingual schooling in the United States*. Washington, D.C.: U.S. Government Printing Office, 1970.

Berger, P. L., and Luckmann, T. *The social construction of reality: A treatise in the sociology of knowledge*. Garden City, N.Y.: Doubleday, 1967.

Bernstein, B. *Class, codes, and control* (2 vols.). London: Routledge and Kegan Paul, 1971.

Callaway, W. R. Modes of biological adaptation and their role in intellectual development. *PCD Monograph Series, 1*. Beverly Hills, Calif.: The Galton Institute, 1970.

Christian, C. C., Jr. Development of skills in a minority language before age 3: A case study. In T. Andersson and W. Mackey (Eds.), *Early childhood bilingualism*. Quebec: Laval University, in press.

Christian, C. C., Jr., and Sharp, J. M. Bilingualism in a pluralistic society. In D. L. Lange and C. J. James (Eds.), *Foreign Language Education: A Reappraisal*. Skokie, Ill.: National Textbook, 1972.

Clough, S. B. *Basic values of Western civilization*. New York and London, Columbia University Press, 1960.

Condon, W. S., and Sander, L. W. Neonate movement is synchronized with adult speech: Interactional participation and language acquisition. *Science*, 1974, *183*, 99–101.

Cooley, C. H. *Human nature and the social order*. New York: Charles Scribner's Sons, 1902.

Dale, P. S. *Language development: Structure and function*. Hinsdale, Ill.: Dryden Press, 1972.

Eisele, J. C. John Dewey and the immigrants. *History of Education Quarterly*, 1975, *15*, 67–85.

Engle, P. Language medium in early school years for minority language groups. *Review of Educational Research*, 1975, *45*, 283–325.

Fishman, J. A. (Ed.) *Advances in the sociology of language*. Vol. 1. The Hague: Mouton, 1971.

Fishman, J. A. Bilingual education and the future of language teaching and language learning. *ADFL Bulletin of the Association of Departments of Foreign Languages*, 1975, *6*, 5–8.

Fishman, J. A., (Ed.), *Language loyalty in the United States*. The Hague: Mouton, 1966.

Gaarder, A. B. Linkages between foreign language teaching and bilingual education. *ADFL Bulletin of the Association of Departments of Foreign Languages*, 1975, *6*, 8–11.

Glazer, N., and Moynihan, D. P. *Beyond the melting pot*. Cambridge, Mass.: MIT Press, 1963.

Goffman, E. *The presentation of self in everyday life*. Garden City, N.Y.: Doubleday, 1959.

Hertzler, J. *A sociology of language*. New York: Random House, 1965.

Karabel, J., and Astin, A. W. Social class, academic ability, and college "quality." *Social Forces*, 1975, *53*, 381–398.

Lado, R. *Linguistics across cultures*. Ann Arbor, Mich.: University of Michigan Press, 1957.

Matluck, J., and Mace, B. Language characteristics of Mexican-American children: Implications for assessment. *Journal of School Psychology*, 1973, *2*, 365–386.

Mead, G. H. *Mind, self, and society*. Chicago: University of Chicago Press, 1934.

Modiano, N. Bilingual education for children of linguistic minorities. In S. K. Ghosh (Ed.), *Man, language, and society*. The Hague: Mouton, 1972, pp. 179–189.

Ortego, P. *Children of Montezuma*. New York: Publications of the Center for the Study of Democratic Institutions, 1970.

Patella, V. M., and Kuvlesky, W. P. Bilingual patterns of nonmetropolitan Mexican-American youth: Variations by social context, language use, and historical change. College Station, Tex.: Authors, 1975.

Popenoe, D. *Sociology*. New York: Appleton–Century–Crofts, 1971.

Sapir, E. *Selected writings of Edward Sapir*. Edited by David G. Mandelbaum. Los Angeles: University of California Press, 1958.

Söderbergh, R. *Reading in early childhood: A linguistic study of a Swedish preschool child's gradual acquisition of reading ability*. Stockholm: Almqvist & Wiksell, 1971.

Whorf, B. *Language, thought, and reality*. Cambridge, Mass.: MIT Press, 1956.

Wrong, D. The oversocialized conception of man in modern sociology. *American Sociological Review*, 1961, *26*, 183–193.

Bilingual Children and Educational Cognitive Style Analysis

RICHARD E. BAECHER, Fordham University at Lincoln Center

Bilingual–bicultural education needs a coherent framework

In 1960 (p. 148), Manuel stated: "The bilingual situation is so complicated with linguistic and other factors that results of studies are hard to interpret and sometimes seem to lead to conflicting conclusions." Manuel's observation is equally valid today.

For instance, a recent study (Engle, 1975, p. 26) comparing the advantages of the Direct Method and the Native Language Approach concluded that 24 reports on these methods varied in every way conceivable. The majority of these reports lacked convincing evidence as to which instructional approach was more effective. In the light of her findings, Engle recommends a more careful research plan. Among the various factors to be controlled in future studies are the cultural and linguistic contexts of learning in the community, appropriate assessment techniques for both languages, and the use of adequate instructional methods and materials.

Saville-Troike (1973, pp. 1–2) has emphasized how important it is for teachers to accept and use bilingual students' cultural and linguistic experiences as bases on which to build goals for bilingual programs. This approach requires an appreciation and understanding of the nature of language as well as of specific languages, of how children acquire their first and second languages, and of specific cultural attitudes that influence their cognitive and socialization growth.

Another issue demanding the attention of practitioners in bilingual education is "bicognitive development." Ramirez, Herold, and Castañeda (1974, pp. 3–4) maintain that although children are entitled to linguistic and cultural diversity at school, this diversity is still inadequately supplied by multicultural–bilingual programs. These authorities argue that if these students are to live comfortably and successfully in the mainstream culture and in their own ethnic communities, they need to achieve cognitive flexibility. By cognitive flexibility or "bicognitive

41

development" of children is meant that they are equipped to operate effectively in diverse intellectual and social contexts, and that they at the same time retain and develop those cognitive abilities that were fostered by their unique home and community experiences.

In addition to the complexity of bilingual–bicultural education caused by the bicognitive, cultural, and linguistic factors already mentioned, dissatisfaction with the goals of bilingual programs is increasingly evident. Steinberg (1974) reported the following major findings on bilingual education in New York City: (1) systematic methods to assess the educational needs of pupils with limited English-speaking ability have not been devised; (2) the Central Board of Education and local community school boards have not established guidelines for bilingual programs; and most important, (3) educators cannot agree on the objectives of bilingual education and the best methods of teaching bilingual pupils.

Rivera (1973) accurately described the bilingual situation when he referred to the "quick fix solutions" that have absorbed the attention of bilingual teachers for the past several years. He claims that a "crisis–crash syndrome" has distorted the problems facing bilingual–bicultural education. He proposes that the phenomenon of bilingual education be studied from a scientific position (Rivera, 1973, p. 70). In other words, the educational practitioner now simply a maintainer of institutionalized approaches, methods, and techniques, must become more of a "scientist."

Vasquez (1974) decries the fact that bilingual education is not viewed as a collective effort for the communication of sound teaching strategies for the bilingual student. Moreover, since it is now primarily concerned with the linguistic performance of the pupil, bilingual education has neglected the "implementation of a coherent conceptual system" that seriously considers the ways in which such a student relates to the world around him.

In view of these statements, the purpose of this chapter is:

1. To introduce the reader to a conceptual framework identified as the educational sciences. Particular attention will be given to the relationship between educational cognitive style analysis and those factors deemed important by authorities in the educational development of bilingual children.
2. To illustrate the application of educational cognitive style analysis within a bilingual–bicultural setting. The components of an effective diagnostic–prescriptive strategy based on educational cognitive style "mapping" will be outlined for teachers of bilingual students.

The purpose of this chapter will have been realized if the reader becomes more sensitive to the interactions in the educational setting, to the conditions of the educational task, and to what Gagné and Briggs (1974, p. 9) refer to as the "previously learned capabilities" of the individual, i.e., his or her educational cognitive style.

As employed in this chapter, the phrase *bilingual children* includes both those students who have already mastered two language systems and those who will become bilingual, i.e., will be introduced to English as a new language. Furthermore, bilingualism necessarily implies *biculturalism* indicating the individual's cultural awareness of two social systems and the capacity to function in two cultural environments.

The educational sciences and bilingual–bicultural education

The complexity of the bilingual situation and the need for a conceptual framework is characteristic of American education in general. Historically, American education has presented an image of conflict and confusion. This spectacle arises from the lack of commonly agreed on goals, practices, and concepts. Educators lack a common language and a common framework; they cling to an amorphous collection of ideas, concepts, and methods borrowed from a variety of other disciplines (Radike, 1973, Intro.).

Joseph E. Hill (1972a) has offered an insight into the function of education by making a distinction between the "fundamental disciplines" and "the applied fields of knowledge." According to Hill (pp. 1–2), a fundamental discipline is a body of knowledge such as biology and psychology. Academic scholars are responsible for producing these areas of knowledge. They communicate about phenomena that they study through pure and distinctive forms of information.

An example of a pure and distinctive form of information generated by academic scholars is the construct of "code-switching." Increasingly employed by sociolinguists, a group of academic scholars concerned with the linguistic diversity and performance of bilingual communities, "code-switching" has come to mean the bilingual's ability to "switch" language codes effectively in response to selected characteristics of a transaction. Other illustrations are the constructs of "phoneme," used by linguists, and of "transfer," used in the fundamental discipline of psychology. Figure 3.1 shows the relationship between the fundamental disciplines and applied fields of knowledge.

Complementing the fundamental disciplines are the applied fields of knowledge. Since human progress is not restricted solely to the knowledge generated by academic scholars, groups of individuals concerned with certain practical considerations in the human situation have bor-

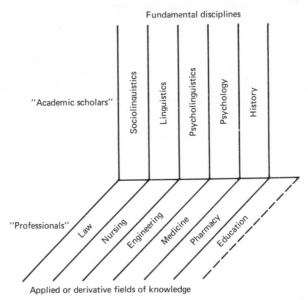

FIGURE 3.1 Relationship between fundamental disciplines and applied fields of knowledge. (*Adapted from Radike, 1973, p. 3.*)

rowed methods and terms of inquiry from the fundamental disciplines and integrated them into new areas of inquiry, the "applied fields." Not concerned with producing pure and distinctive forms of knowledge, practitioners or "professionals" of the applied fields seek to explain phenomena and solve problems in the practical aspects of the human situation. Medicine, pharmacy, engineering, and law are examples of applied fields that have achieved conceptual frameworks and agreed on languages. Figure 3.1 indicates this complementary relationship by means of a two-dimensional representation of a three-dimensional model in which the lines would run perpendicular to each body of knowledge.

Educators, however, in their endeavors to solve problems related to instruction, have exhibited serious difficulty in communication primarily because they lack an exact language representing a conceptual framework. The broken line under *Education* in Figure 3.1 symbolizes this dilemma. Education has drawn its definitions and concepts from numerous fundamental disciplines and applied fields. In other words, the information that constitutes education today is in the form of a loose, disconnected collection of methods and materials. It is evident that a conceptual framework and corresponding language are necessary ingredients toward the systematic solution of practical problems confronting educators. A similar situation faces the educator working in bilingual education and the teacher of English as a new language.

Hill (1972a) suggests that there are seven educational sciences. Each includes its own factual descriptions, concepts, and principles. These sciences are:

1. Symbols and their meanings.
2. Cultural determinants of the meanings of symbols.
3. Modalities of inference.
4. Educational memory.
5. Cognitive styles of individuals.
6. Student, teaching, administrative, and counseling styles.
7. Systemic analysis decision making.

It is not our aim to examine each of the educational sciences in depth. Instead, only that material included in the fifth educational science—cognitive styles of individuals—that is pertinent to teachers of bilingual children will be considered. The reader should note that the educational science of cognitive style entails the first four sciences. Moreover, because of the speculative nature of educational memory—the fourth educational science—this science will not be described in this chapter. For a more intensive study of the sciences, the reader should consult the bibliography offered by Berry and Sutton (1973), Hill (1975), and other materials noted in the reference list.

Equipped with the language and concepts of the educational sciences, practitioners can begin to answer the central question, "How do bilingual children come to know?"

Educational cognitive style helps teachers identify the strengths of bilingual children

Before the process of educational cognitive style is described, assumptions essential to the conceptual framework of the educational sciences must be stated. It will be shown that these assumptions correspond with the recent thinking of authorities in bilingual–bicultural education.

BASIC ASSUMPTIONS

The following basic assumptions are stated:

1. *Education is the process of searching for meaning.* The term *cognitive style* means the consistent manner in which an individual comes to know the world and its relationships. Simply, *educational cognitive style* refers to the way a student tends to seek meaning. This process can be attained through formal schooling with the help of other persons, or informally, through an individual's self-initiated and self-directed energies.

The distinction between informal and formal education clarifies the goals of bilingual–bicultural education and the function of the school.

Bilingual–bicultural education is the development and use of two languages—one of which is English, in the United States—as media of instruction by the school on behalf of the student. It involves the incorporation of two cultures—one of which is the culture of the child from a non-English background—into the school curriculum. Thus, students from linguistic and ethnic minorities are not linguistically and culturally deprived, for they have mastered all the basic phonology and major grammatical structures of their language by 5 years of age. Before entering the school, they have been learning about themselves and the world around them. In school, they too are ready to begin acquiring the various concepts and skills necessary for success. These concepts and skills are learned in the child's native language (Swanson, 1973, pp. 75–76).

Given the distinction between formal and informal instruction, bilingual–bicultural education is the school's effort to develop and help students from varied backgrounds in their search for meaning.

2. *Thought is different from language.* This assumption means that while concepts and thoughts may find their expression in language, i.e., in vocabulary and syntax, this is not to say that thought is equivalent to language. This assumption agrees with the findings of Piaget (1959), who views the relationship between thought and language as complex and dynamic.

If thought is defined as structuring reality, or "making sense" out of the quality of events and continuous stimulations to which the individual is submitted by virtue of being equipped with senses and proprioceptors, then thinking is an active process (Willink, 1973, p. 81). For the individual can mediate not just one but two types of symbols into meaning, the "theoretical" and the "qualitative" (Dewey, 1960 [1898]). Briefly, the individual acquires meaning not only through words and numbers, but also through such meaningful events as smiles, gestures, and other non-linguistic symbols. (See "A Brief Guide to Cognitive Style Mapping" for definitions and distinctions between the two types of symbols).

3. *A human being is a social creature with a unique capacity for deriving meaning from his environment and personal experiences through the creation and use of symbols.* Reference has already been made to the fact that the individual mediates symbols. A human being, indeed, is the only creature that searches for meaning and knowledge through symbols.

For example, the child's earliest contact with the world is made through the senses. The child mediates symbols of the sensory type. A baby's tactile experiences provide him with a set of qualitative symbols. Through these symbols, the child senses the social and physical world in which he finds himself. The child's theoretical symbolic ability develops with the acquisition of language. Then, he is able to read, write, hear, and talk about the qualitative events experienced (Wasser, 1971, p. 4–5).

Recent investigations by authorities in bilingual–bicultural education have been uncovering the various sources of the bilingual child's ability to create and use symbols (Nine-Curt, 1973; Bernal, 1974; Sueiro-Ross, 1974).

4. *Not content with biological satisfactions alone, a human being seeks meaning.* This assumption is essential if one is to avoid viewing the child as a passive, receptive organism. It differentiates the educational science of cognitive style from the stimulus–response reinforcement theory of Skinner and associates. Their position views the child as basically a creature of the environment, responding primarily to stimuli to initiate behavior and reinforcement to guarantee its repetition. Briefly, reinforced behavior is repeated, uninreinforced behavior is not repeated. This perspective sets the stage for behavior modification approaches, token reward systems, and other motivational devices, thereby overlooking the individual's tendency to seek meaning beyond biological satisfactions. Palomares (1972), in his description of the psychological state of being an individual trying to live in two cultures simultaneously, argues strongly that the bilingual is continually seeking meaning within two cultures.

These four assumptions, then, are primary considerations in focusing on the strengths of the bilingual child or in employing educational cognitive style analysis.

EDUCATIONAL COGNITIVE STYLE ANALYSIS

The term *educational cognitive style* refers to how an individual seeks meaning. A bilingual student's educational cognitive style describes the way he tends to acquire meaning from the context in which he finds himself. Initial steps in determining, or analyzing, the educational cognitive style of a bilingual pupil includes such questions as:

1. How does the bilingual take note of his environment?
2. What symbols does the individual prefer to use in solving problems?
3. Is the bilingual student characteristically a "listener" or a "reader" for information?
4. To what extent is the individual capable of understanding concepts and comfortable in his native language?

A Brief Guide to Cognitive Style Mapping*

I. SYMBOLS AND THEIR MEANINGS

Two types of symbols, theoretical (e.g., words and numbers) and qualitative (e.g., sensory, programmatic, and codes), are created and used by individuals to acquire knowledge and derive meaning from their environments and personal experiences. Theoretical symbols differ from their qualitative symbols in that the theoretical symbols present to the awareness of the individual something different from that which the symbols are. Words and numbers are examples of theoretical symbols. Qualitative symbols are those symbols which present and then represent to the awareness of the individual that which the symbol is. (Feelings, commitments and values are some examples of the meanings conveyed by the qualitative symbols.)

T(VL)—**Theoretical Visual Linguistics**—ability to find meaning from words you see. A major in this area indicates someone who reads with a better than average degree of comprehension.

T(AL)—**Theoretical Auditory Linguistics**—ability to acquire meaning through hearing spoken words.

T(VQ)—**Theoretical Visual Quantitative**—ability to acquire meaning in terms of numerical symbols, relationships, and measurements.

T(AQ)—**Theoretical Auditory Quantitative**—ability to find meaning in terms of numerical symbols, relationships, and measurements that are spoken.

The five qualitative symbols associated with sensory stimuli are:

Q(A)—**Qualitative Auditory**—ability to perceive meaning through sense of hearing. A major in this area indicates ability to distinguish between sounds, tones of music, and other purely sonic sensations.

Q(O)—**Qualitative Olfactory**—ability to perceive meaning through the sense of smell.

Q(S)—**Qualitative Savory**—ability to perceive meaning by the sense of taste. Chefs should have highly developed qualitative olfactory and savory abilities.

Q(T)—**Qualitative Tactile**—ability to perceive meaning by the sense of touch, temperature, and pain.

Q(V)—**Qualitative Visual**—ability to perceive meaning through sight.

The qualitative symbols that are programmatic in nature are:

Q(PF)—**Qualitative Proprioceptive (Fine)**—ability to synthesize

Q(PTF)—**Qualitative Proprioceptive Temporal (Fine)**—ability to synthesize a number of symbolic mediations into a performance demanding the use of fine musculature while monitoring a complex physical activity involving timing.

Q(PTG)—**Qualitative Proprioceptive Temporal (Gross)**—ability to synthesize a number of symbolic mediations into a performance demanding the use of gross musculature while monitoring a complex physical activity involving timing.

The remaining ten qualitative symbols associated with cultural codes are defined as:

Q(CEM)—**Qualitative Code Empathetic**—sensitivity to the feelings of others; ability to put yourself in another person's place and see things from his point of view.

Q(CES)—**Qualitative Code Esthetic**—ability to enjoy the beauty of an object or an idea. Beauty in surroundings or a well-turned phrase are appreciated by a person possessing a major strength in this area.

Q(CET)—**Qualitative Code Ethic**—commitment to a set of values, a group of principles, obligations, and/or duties. This commitment need not imply morality. Both a priest and a criminal may be committed to a set of values although the "values" may be decidedly different.

Q(CH)—**Qualitative Code Histrionic**—ability to exhibit a deliberate behavior, or play a role to produce some particular effect on other persons. This type of person knows how to fulfill role expectations.

Q(CK)—**Qualitative Code Kinesics**—ability to understand, and to communicate by, non-linguistic functions such as facial expressions and motions of the body (e.g., smiles and gestures).

Q(CKH)—**Qualitative Code Kinesthetic**—ability to perform motor skills, or effect muscular coordination according to a recommended, or acceptable, form (e.g., bowling according to form, or golfing).

Q(CP)—**Qualitative Code Proxemics**—ability to judge the physical and social distance that the other person would permit, between oneself and that other person.

Q(CS)—**Qualitative Code Synnoetics**—personal knowledge of oneself.

Q(CT)—**Qualitative Code Transactional**—ability to maintain a positive communicative interaction which significantly influences the goals of the persons involved in that interaction (e.g., salesmanship).

II. CULTURAL DETERMINANTS

There are three cultural determinants of the meaning of symbols: 1) individuality (I), 2) associates (A), and 3) family (F). It is through these "determinants" that cultural influences are brought to bear by the individual on the meanings of symbols.

I—Individuality—Uses one's own interpretation as an influence on meanings of symbols.

A—Associates—Symbolic meanings are influenced by one's peer group.

F—Family—Influence of members of the family, or a few close personal friends, on the meanings of symbols.

III. MODALITIES OF INFERENCE

The third set of the cartesian product indicating cognitive style includes elements which indicate the individual's modality of inference, i.e., the form of inference he tends to use.

M—Magnitude—a form of "categorical reasoning" that utilizes norms or categorical classifications as the basis for accepting or rejecting an advanced hypothesis. Persons who need to define things in order to understand them reflect this modality.

D—Difference—This pattern suggests a tendency to reason in terms of one-to-one contrasts or comparisons of selected characteristics or measurements. Artists often possess this modality as do creative writers and musicians.

R—Relationship—this modality indicates the ability to synthesize a number of dimensions or incidents into a unified meaning, or through analysis of a situation to discover its component parts. Psychiatrists frequently employ the modality of relationship in the process of psychoanalyzing a client.

L—Appraisal—is the modality of inference employed by an individual who uses all three of the modalities noted above (M, D, and R), giving equal weight to each in his reasoning process. Individuals who employ this modality tend to analyze, question, or, in effect, appraise that which is under consideration in the process of drawing a probability conclusion.

K—Deductive—indicates deductive reasoning, or the form of logical proof used in geometry or that employed in syllogistic reasoning.

monitoring or a complex task involving small, or fine, musculature (e.g., playing a musical instrument, typewriting); or into an immediate awareness of a possible set of interrelationships between symbolic mediations, i.e., dealing with "signs."

Q(PG)—Qualitative Proprioceptive (Gross)—ability to synthesize a number of symbolic mediations into a performance demanding monitoring of a complex task involving large, or gross, musculature (e.g., throwing a baseball, skiing).

Q(PDF)—Qualitative Proprioceptive Dextral (Fine)—a predominance of right-eyed, right-handed and right-footed tendencies (a typically right-handed person) while synthesizing a number of symbolic mediations into a performance demanding monitoring of a complex task involving small, or fine, musculature (e.g., writing right-handed).

Q(PDC)—Qualitative Proprioceptive Dextral (Gross)—a predominance of right-eyed, right-handed and right-footed tendencies (a typically right-handed person) while synthesizing a number of symbolic mediations into a performance demanding monitoring of a complex task involving large, or gross, musculature (e.g., throwing a baseball with the right hand).

Q(PKF)—Qualitative Proprioceptive Kinematics (Fine)—ability to synthesize a number of symbolic mediations into a performance demanding the use of fine musculature while monitoring a complex physical activity involving motion.

Q(PKG)—Qualitative Proprioceptive Kinematics (Gross)—ability to synthesize a number of symbolic mediations into a performance demanding the use of gross musculature while monitoring a complex physical activity involving motion.

Q(PSF)—Qualitative Proprioceptive Sinistral (Fine)—a predominance of left-eyed, left-handed and left-footed tendencies (a typically left-handed person) while synthesizing a number of symbolic mediations into a performance demanding monitoring of a complex task involving small, or fine, musculature (e.g., writing left-handed).

Q(PSG)—Qualitative Proprioceptive Sinistral (Gross)—a predominance of left-eyed, left-handed and left-footed tendencies (a typically left-handed person) while synthesizing a number of symbolic mediations into a performance demanding monitoring of a complex task involving large, or gross, musculature (e.g., throwing a baseball with the left hand).

* From Bowman et al., 1974. Courtesy Barbara Bowman, Betty Burch, Joseph E. Hill, and Derek Nunney.

5. In what way does the bilingual seek consensus with peers, make up his own mind, or rely on the judgments of the members of his or her family?
6. Does the bilingual child tend to reason in categories as does a mathematician; in contrasts, as does the artist; or in relationships, as does a social scientist?

These are only a few of the important questions that one might ask in observing how the bilingual student relates to his surroundings. Educational cognitive style analysis is as effective as the sensitivity and originality of the person(s) employing it. These questions provide a basis for "mapping" the numerous elements that make up an individual's cognitive style. The style of the individual encompasses various elements that have been defined by Hill (1972a) and that form the basic structures of the first five educational sciences. (See "A Brief Guide to Cognitive Style Mapping" for a listing of these elements and their definitions.)

The elements that form an individual's cognitive style are displayed in a cognitive style "map." Figure 3.2 contains the elements of cognitive style presently under consideration in the educational sciences.

For present purposes, the first three sets from Figure 3.2 will be briefly described. Through questioning and observations, a teacher can begin to explore these areas of a bilingual student's educational cognitive style. The first area of exploration is entitled *Symbols and Their Meanings*.

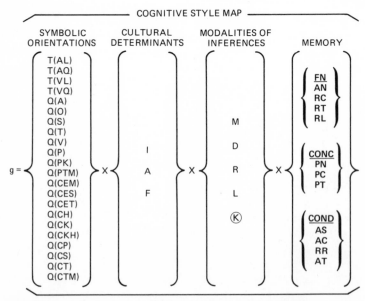

FIGURE 3.2 Cognitive style map. (*Adapted from Radike, 1973, p. 15.*)

The teacher, trained in behavioral descriptions, looks for indicators of the bilingual pupil's use of symbols. An indicator is an overt behavior that the teacher can perceive in some manner and that leads one to conclude that an element is present in the pupil's cognitive style. Specific rules for ascertaining the degree of presence of such elements follow this heading.

For example, the teacher may discover that a bilingual child is more successful in listening tasks employing the child's native language; the pupil prefers oral directions to visual ones. The student who asks to have stories read to him possesses a strong tendency to seek information from listening. Additionally, the teacher's attention may be drawn to the fact that the bilingual child excels in the use of mathematical symbols expressed in the child's second language. Furthermore, the observant teacher may note how often the pupil relies on his sense of hearing and touch in completing educational tasks, how readily he senses what others feel, how well he can draw according to a prescribed form, and even how capable he is of "reading" another's gestures. These elements, or symbols, provide clues to the strengths of bilingual students. They are indicators of the ways in which meaning is realized and of the feelings, commitments, and values of the bilingual child.

As the individual interprets symbols, his perceptions influence and are influenced by his culture. The second area of exploration, *Cultural Determinants,* can guide the teacher in finding out the degree of influence that social groups have on the perceptions of the bilingual. The main cultural influences on the meaning of symbols are exercised by an individual's *family, associates,* and *individuality.* These three "determinants" constitute the stable social networks that significantly influence one's perceptions. They define the social role that individuals play.

A teacher may note that a bilingual child frequently talks about home and family experiences and prefers to have the teacher, rather than classmates, explain things. The teacher, in such an instance, is viewed as a surrogate family member. These patterns indicate the presence of a strong "family" influence in the child's cognitive style. If the individual is not influenced by family, his associates or peers, may contribute significantly to how he perceives the world. For example, he may like to work in groups and follow the suggestions of his friends. In contrast, the pupil with a strong "individuality" determinant may prefer to work alone, is aware of the factors that make him different from other pupils, and decides for himself without consulting others. Cultural determinants, therefore, can offer the teacher of bilingual children an effective means to understand their world of human relationships.

The third area, *Modalities of Inference,* involves the processes employed by individuals in reaching decisions. The mode (pattern) of inference (reasoning) also influences meaning. The bilingual child who is receiving messages of words, pictures, numbers, and the like is engaged in the process of sorting, testing, and synthesizing before internalizing such messages.

A teacher may observe that some bilingual children are quick to place items in classes or categories according to obvious similar properties, and prefer specific directions and rules in completing educational tasks. Other pupils may be observed to use differences in their reasoning patterns; they are prone to compare things on the basis of a single feature, such as size or shape. Still others may look for multiple relationships in what they perceive; such children probably do well on inferential-comprehension tests. Some children have the tendency to combine all of these methods of thinking in arriving at conclusions. They may ask questions such as, "How is it different?" "How are they alike? and "What's the rule?" Finally, a few pupils may exhibit a deductive inferential reasoning pattern similar in many respects to that of the mathematician.

These three areas of exploration, "Symbols and their Meanings," "Cultural Determinants," and "Modalities of Inference," constitute the educational cognitive style of bilingual students. They assist and guide the teacher in what to look for in bilingual children. These three "sciences" indicate the variety of profiles such students show in achieving success at educational tasks. Analyzing the educational cognitive style of an individual results from the process called *cognitive mapping*.

COGNITIVE MAPPING

This process involves attempting to find out if a certain element is present in a bilingual pupil's style. Cognitive mapping involves discovering ways to observe, listen to, and elicit cognitive style elements. The use of standardized instruments, various observational techniques, and interviews are some methods that can be employed in the process of mapping.

Mapping occurs only after the teacher has tried to find out if an element is present in the bilingual student's style, has determined whether the element has a major, minor, or negligible rank, and has recorded the element on a form. To illustrate certain aspects of cognitive mapping, suppose that a teacher is mapping a student's cognitive style. The teacher includes in each set of information comprising the student's style those elements that the teacher knows to be present, having observed defined behaviors exhibited by the pupil. The following map is thus recorded.

Symbolic orientations	*Cultural determinants*	*Modalities of inference*

$$\left\{ \begin{matrix} T \overset{3}{(VL)} & T' \overset{2}{(AL)} \\ Q \underset{s}{(CEM)} & \end{matrix} \right\}_e \quad X \quad \left\{ \begin{matrix} I \\ F' \end{matrix} \right\} \quad X \quad \left\{ \begin{matrix} M \\ R' \end{matrix} \right\}$$

Without defining at this point what these symbols mean, the following rules in "mapping" are important (Radike, 1973, pp. 16–18).

1. The first set—"Symbolic Orientations"—contains "theoreticals" (T's) in the top row, and "qualitatives" (Q's) under each T, thereby forming two columns in the first set. The subscripts, e and s, mean that these elements were probed by Spanish and English instruments, respectively. The numerals above the "theoreticals" refer to the grade level of educational development in that specific element. This level is expressed in terms of composite grade levels involving measured abilities in vocabulary, language usage, and reading and listening comprehension in home Spanish and in English (Baecher, 1973, pp. 64–73).

2. In the second and third sets, elements are placed in a column. Therefore,

$$\left\{ \begin{array}{c} I \\ F' \end{array} \right\} \qquad X \qquad \left\{ \begin{array}{c} M \\ R' \end{array} \right\}$$

In the examples shown above, the prime mark ($'$) next to certain elements denotes a minor orientation for an element of a given set. A major orientation in an element is written in capital letters only, e.g., T (VL), while a minor orientation in an element has a prime mark ($'$) after the notation, e.g., T' (AL).

Educational cognitive style elements can be observed and determined as manifesting varying degrees of strength. These can be ranked on a 1–9-point scale as shown in Figure 3.3 (Nunney, 1975, p. 20). A teacher can ascertain the presence of a cognitive style element under consideration by employing this 9-point scale and the following principles (Baecher, 1973, pp. 77–79; Radike, 1973, p. 18).

Principle I. If the bilingual student whose style is being mapped demonstrates an element to the extent that the teacher is willing to place that student in the 50–99 percentile range, i.e., in the top half of the population exhibiting such an element, then a *major* orientation in the element under consideration could be assigned to that pupil.

Principle II. If the degree of presence of the element is of such a nature that the teacher could only place it in the 26–49 percentile range of the population, a *minor* orientation is assigned.

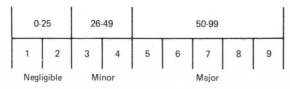

FIGURE 3.3 Percentile ranges for major, minor, and negligible orientations. (*From Nunney, 1975.*)

Principle III. If the teacher is willing to place the pupil in the 0–25 percentile range of the distribution, i.e., in the lowest quarter of the distribution, then the student would receive a negligible orientation in this element. It must be noted that a negligible orientation does not mean nonexistent, but rather that the element lacks significant strength in the style of the bilingual student.

Cognitive mapping, therefore, entails the use of a common language and concepts, a set of principles and rules, and a variety of instruments and techniques, the most important being the sensitivity and originality of the teacher. Radike (1973, p. 42) asserts that "anyone who has critically observed children in a classroom, examined their work, listened to their remarks, and pondered on the interactions of students has much of the professional training necessary to map students." The common language that describes the areas of "Symbols and their Meaning," "Cultural Determinants," and "Modalities of Inference" takes the form of an algebraic, visual shorthand.

Illustrated cognitive style maps of bilingual students

Application of the first three educational sciences can be shown by illustrating the cognitive style maps of bilingual pupils, based on research conducted by the author (Baecher, 1973). These maps serve to demonstrate the potential of educational cognitive style analysis as an effective and powerful diagnostic–prescriptive approach in assisting bilingual children.

For instance, bilingual student Number One (Figure 3.4), a fourth grader reading below grade level in English and Spanish, is a proficient "listener." He is successful in educational tasks that require listening in English and Spanish, respectively, as indicated by fourth- and fifth-grade levels of educational development in the element of T (AL), "theoretical auditory linguistic" capability. The element of T (AL) has been identified by the teacher as a major strength in this student's style. Moreover, this bilingual pupil works hard at educational tasks, Q (CET); is an individualist, (I); and reaches decisions through a form of categorical reasoning, (M). This map or profile shows the strengths that the teacher should incorporate in an educational context.

The cognitive style map of bilingual pupil Number Two (Figure 3.5) is that of a fourth grader reading above grade level in English and one grade level below in Spanish. At this stage of development, he can derive meaning effectively from oral and visual materials expressed in English.

Present grade: Sex: Age: Ethnic origin: 5.0 Reading grade
     4th   M   9 yrs. 10 mos.   Mexican Am.   (English)

                                             2.7 Reading grade
                                                (Spanish)

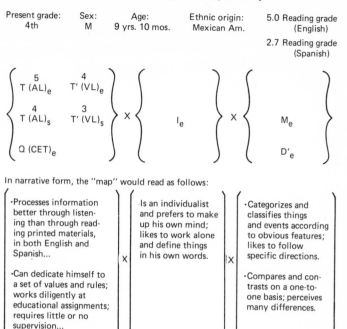

In narrative form, the "map" would read as follows:

$$
\left\{
\begin{array}{l}
\text{·Processes information} \\
\text{better through listen-} \\
\text{ing than through read-} \\
\text{ing printed materials,} \\
\text{in both English and} \\
\text{Spanish...} \\[4pt]
\text{·Can dedicate himself to} \\
\text{a set of values and rules;} \\
\text{works diligently at} \\
\text{educational assignments;} \\
\text{requires little or no} \\
\text{supervision...}
\end{array}
\right\}
\times
\left\{
\begin{array}{l}
\text{·Is an individualist} \\
\text{and prefers to make} \\
\text{up his own mind;} \\
\text{likes to work alone} \\
\text{and define things} \\
\text{in his own words.}
\end{array}
\right\}
\times
\left\{
\begin{array}{l}
\text{·Categorizes and} \\
\text{classifies things} \\
\text{and events according} \\
\text{to obvious features;} \\
\text{likes to follow} \\
\text{specific directions.} \\[4pt]
\text{·Compares and con-} \\
\text{trasts on a one-to-} \\
\text{one basis; perceives} \\
\text{many differences.}
\end{array}
\right\}
$$

FIGURE 3.4   Bilingual student Number One. (*Adapted from Baecher, 1973, p. 158.*)

Additionally, this individual is capable of identifying with the feelings of others, $Q\ (CEM)$; of completing specific educational tasks, $Q\ (CET)$; and can follow the directives of someone representing an authority figure, (F). He perceives multiple relationships among things and finds it easy to complete assignments if given ample illustrations and examples, (R).

Figure 3.6 shows that bilingual student Number Three is strongly influenced by associates, (A), in his behavior. He prefers to work in groups with his peers, instead of by himself. In addition, his map or profile exhibits an inference pattern that employs differences and contrasts and shows such other strengths as the ability to empathize with others and to work diligently at educational activities. An area in which this pupil needs immediate assistance is in receptive communication skills as indicated by the low levels of educational development in $T\ (AL)$ and $T\ (VL)$, i.e., in acquiring meaning from printed and spoken words and sentences in English and Spanish, respectively.

For additional cognitive style maps of bilingual pupils, the reader is referred to Baecher (1973).

In summary, a cognitive style map should not be viewed as fixed and static; it represents a dynamic and growing search for meaning on the

Present grade: Sex: Age: Ethnic origin: 5.1 Reading grade
    4th   M   9 yrs. 11 mos. Puerto Rican   (English)

                                                        3.1 Reading grade
                                                            (Spanish)

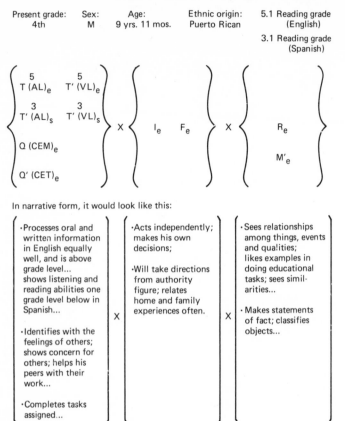

In narrative form, it would look like this:

| •Processes oral and written information in English equally well, and is above grade level... shows listening and reading abilities one grade level below in Spanish...

•Identifies with the feelings of others; shows concern for others; helps his peers with their work...

•Completes tasks assigned... | X | •Acts independently; makes his own decisions;

•Will take directions from authority figure; relates home and family experiences often. | X | •Sees relationships among things, events and qualities; likes examples in doing educational tasks; sees similarities...

•Makes statements of fact; classifies objects... |

FIGURE 3.5   Bilingual student Number Two. (*Adapted from Baecher, 1973, p. 173.*)

part of the bilingual student. Since the educational cognitive style of the individual is not fixed, the teacher can take advantage of the strengths manifested by the pupil's style and can begin to prescribe activities that will augment or improve performance in areas of probable weakness. A cognitive style map represents a relative concept and depends on: (1) the specific level of educational development of the student; (2) the cultural background of the student; and (3) the symbolic conditions of the educational task to be presented to the pupil.

Each map, then, like each bilingual individual, is different, and therefore suggests a personalized educational program. Each map indicates "strengths" that can be augmented. Missing strengths can be built on a student's existing ones. In other words, the map is a starting point for the teacher. From it the teacher can formulate an educational "prescription," i.e., develop a personalized educational program to fit the bilingual student's cognitive style.

3. Bilingual children and educational cognitive style analysis

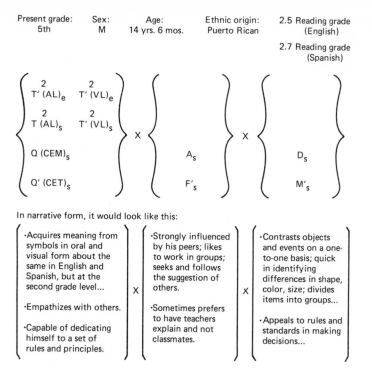

Present grade: Sex: Age: Ethnic origin: 2.5 Reading grade
5th   M   14 yrs. 6 mos. Puerto Rican   (English)

2.7 Reading grade
(Spanish)

$$\left\{\begin{array}{ll} \overset{2}{T'\,(AL)_e} & \overset{2}{T'\,(VL)_e} \\ \overset{2}{T\,(AL)_s} & \overset{2}{T'\,(VL)_s} \\ Q\,(CEM)_s \\ Q'\,(CET)_s \end{array}\right\} \times \left\{\begin{array}{l} \\ A_s \\ \\ F'_s \end{array}\right\} \times \left\{\begin{array}{l} \\ D_s \\ \\ M'_s \end{array}\right\}$$

In narrative form, it would look like this:

$$\left\{\begin{array}{l} \text{•Acquires meaning from} \\ \text{symbols in oral and} \\ \text{visual form about the} \\ \text{same in English and} \\ \text{Spanish, but at the} \\ \text{second grade level...} \\ \\ \text{•Empathizes with others.} \\ \\ \text{•Capable of dedicating} \\ \text{himself to a set of} \\ \text{rules and principles.} \end{array}\right\} \times \left\{\begin{array}{l} \text{•Strongly influenced} \\ \text{by his peers; likes} \\ \text{to work in groups;} \\ \text{seeks and follows} \\ \text{the suggestion of} \\ \text{others.} \\ \\ \text{•Sometimes prefers} \\ \text{to have teachers} \\ \text{explain and not} \\ \text{classmates.} \end{array}\right\} \times \left\{\begin{array}{l} \text{•Contrasts objects} \\ \text{and events on a one-} \\ \text{to-one basis; quick} \\ \text{in identifying} \\ \text{differences in shape,} \\ \text{color, size; divides} \\ \text{items into groups...} \\ \\ \text{•Appeals to rules and} \\ \text{standards in making} \\ \text{decisions...} \end{array}\right\}$$

FIGURE 3.6 Bilingual student Number Three. (*Adapted from Baecher, 1973, p. 190.*)

Educational prescriptions for bilingual pupils

According to Radike (1973, p. 62), prescription writing within an educational context refers to the process whereby the teacher seeks to match the pupil's "map" strengths with available classroom resources (persons and materials) to ensure a high probability of success for the pupil in his or her educational efforts.

To illustrate certain steps that a teacher of bilingual student Number Two (Figure 3.5) might take in formulating an educational prescription, the following example is provided.

Example: The teacher has mapped a bilingual student who shows these map elements:

1. Major $T\,(AL)$ in English
   at the fifth level of educational development
2. Minor $T'\,(AL)$ in Spanish
   at the third level of educational development

3. Minor T' (VL) in English
   at the fifth level of educational development
4. Minor T' (VL) in Spanish
   at the third level of educational development
5. Major Q (CEM)
6. Minor Q (CET)
7. Major (I) and (F)
8. Major (R), minor (M)

Suppose that the teacher needs to write a prescription to develop this pupil's receptive communication abilities in Spanish—in this case, reading in Spanish. Since this pupil's ability to listen and read in English is highly developed, every indication is present that his capacity to understand spoken and written Spanish can be enhanced. In this individual's case, the teacher needs to enhance or augment these elements by developing the pupil's vocabulary and concepts in Spanish.

The teacher has culturally relevant materials on cassette tapes and records expressed in Spanish at the third-grade level, and written materials along with pictures in Spanish at the third-grade level, in order to develop concepts and vocabulary. These materials correspond with the $T'^{\,3}$ (AL_s) and $T'^{\,3}$ (VL_s) elements of the map.

This student works under the close supervision and guidance of the teacher and the educational assistant. This approach fits the (F) major in the map. Another approach might have the pupil work at reading assignments by himself. This second approach would fit the (I) and Q (CET) elements of the map.

The materials provided the student will be in Spanish and at the third-grade reading level. These materials should include numerous examples from which the student can synthesize word meanings and concepts. This procedure will match the (R) element in the map.

In addition, the teacher may provide a few short, definite activities that require step-by-step compliance. Also, as the student acquires new concepts, the teacher will work with the student to group these concepts into classes or categories by means of definitions.

The teacher's prescription would look something like this:

T (AL_s)—tapes, pictures, records at third-grade level in Spanish
F—supervised and guided by teacher and educational assistant
I, Q (CEM)—allowed to work independently
R—materials with examples for synthesis
M—brief, step-by-step assignments; group concepts into classes by definition

This educational prescription provides personalized education for the bilingual child. Similar prescriptions can be drawn up for bilingual students One and Three. It should be added that "collective" cognitive style maps for groups of bilingual children can also be drawn up. Educational prescription writing enables the teacher to match the cognitive style elements identified for the pupil with available classroom resources and with the conditions of the educational task.

Summary

Bilingual–bicultural education can benefit from the common language and conceptual framework of the educational sciences. This framework takes into account the symbolic orientations of the bilingual child, the various cultural influences to which the child is subject, modalities of inference, and, finally, the educational memory context of the bilingual.

Educational cognitive style analysis offers the teacher of bilingual students an effective diagnostic–prescriptive strategy. It can increase the teacher's skill and sensitivity to setting realistic goals for the bilingual classroom, aids the teacher in describing behavioral indicators of the strengths and weaknesses of the student, and facilitates a more exact pinpointing of educational problem areas. Lastly, the educational science of cognitive style provides the alert teacher with cues for treatment or augmentation of style elements.

Educational cognitive style "maps" can be generated for bilingual students. Different mapping instruments and techniques need to be employed for such students, largely dependent on their level of educational development, cultural background, and the context in which the mapping occurs (Baecher, 1975).

Teacher aides, peer tutors, and volunteers, along with materials and media, can be matched with a student's cognitive style. Educational prescriptions can be written to ensure a high probability of success for the student in his or her educational tasks.

The theory presented in the educational science of cognitive style offers many advantages for those carrying out different types of research in bilingual–bicultural education: (1) it makes explicit the factors and conditions to be investigated within an educational context; (2) it aids description and definition; (3) it provides selective and directive functions for systematic research procedures; (4) it points out relationships and analogies; and (5) it generates hypotheses for future research.

References

Baecher, R. *An exploratory study to determine levels of educational development, reading levels, and the cognitive styles of Mexican American and Peurto Rican American students in Michigan.* Unpublished doctoral dissertation, University of Michigan, 1973.

Baecher, R. Focusing on the strengths of bilingual students. In L. Golubchick and B. Persky (Eds.), *Innovations in education*. Dubuque, Iowa: Kendall–Hunt, 1975.

Basco, C. *An exploratory study employing the educational science of cognitive style for students with impaired decoding skills*. Unpublished doctoral dissertation, Wayne State University, 1974.

Bernal, E. M., Jr. Gifted Mexican children: An ethno-scientific perspective. *California Journal of Educational Research*, 1974, *25*, 261–273.

Berry, J., and Sutton, T. *The educational sciences: A bibliography*. Bloomfield Hills, Mich.: American Educational Sciences Association, 1973.

Blosser, J. *A pilot study to explore the relationships between cognitive style, need achievement, and academic achievement motivation*. Unpublished doctoral dissertation, Wayne State University, 1971.

Bowman, B., Burch, B., Hill, J. E., and Nunney, D. *TIP personalized educational programs*. East Lansing, Mich.: East Lansing Public Schools, 1974.

Dewey, J. Qualitative thought [originally published 1898]. In R. J. Bernstein (Ed.), *On experience, nature, and freedom*. New York: Bobbs–Merrill, 1960.

Dworkin, L. *A systems theory approach toward the reconceptualization of curriculum*. Unpublished doctoral dissertation, Michigan State University, 1969.

Eiseman, C. *An exploratory study of conflicts in role expectations in administrative role-sets based upon cognitive and administrative styles*. Unpublished doctoral dissertation, Wayne State University, 1973.

Engle, P. L. *The use of vernacular languages in education: language medium in early school years for minority language groups*. Arlington, Va.: Center for Linguistics, 1975.

Ervin, T. *The human element in the establishment and operation of a PPBS in an educational setting using role-sets based on cognitive and administrative styles*. Unpublished doctoral dissertation, University of Michigan, 1974.

Gagné, R. M., and Briggs, L. J. *Principles of instructional design*. New York: Holt, 1974.

Greyson, M. *A comparison of counseling using the cognitive style map of the educational sciences and the traditional approach in the educational setting*. Unpublished doctoral dissertation, University of Michigan, 1971.

Hill, J. E. *The educational sciences*. Bloomfield Hills, Mich.: Oakland Community College Press, 1972.

Hill, J. E. *How schools can apply systems analysis*. Bloomington, Ind.: The Phi Delta Kappa Educational Foundation, 1972.

Hill, J. E. The educational science of memory: Function X concern X condition. *The Educational Scientist*, 1975, *I* (1), 3–12.

Hollis, J. *A pilot study of a personalized mathematics program for fourth, fifth, and sixth grade students to explore the relationship between cognitive style-performance objectives and achievement*. Unpublished doctoral dissertation, Wayne State University, 1974.

Maunel, H. T. Bilingualism. In C. Harris (Ed.), *Encyclopedia of educational research*. New York: Macmillan, 1960, pp. 146–150.

McAdam, G. *Personalizing instruction through the educational sciences of cognitive style and teaching style*. Unpublished doctoral dissertation, Wayne State University, 1971.

Nine-Curt, C. J. Non-verbal communication in Puerto Rico. Paper presented at TESOL (Teachers of English to Speakers of Other Languages) Convention, Denver, Colorado, March 7, 1974. Mimeo.

Nunney, D. N. Educational cognitive style: A basis for personalizing instruction. *The Educational Scientist*, 1975, *1*, 13–26.

Ort, B. *An examination of relationships between the measurable cognitive characteristics of a French I teacher and the student's success in that course*. Unpublished doctoral dissertation, Michigan State University, 1971.

Palomares, U. Psychological factors teachers must recognize in the bicultural child. In *Proceedings: National conference on bilingual education*. Austin, Texas: Dissemination Center for Bilingual Education, 1972.

Piaget, J. *The language and thought of the child*. New York: Humanities Press, 1959.

Radike, F. (Ed.). *Handbook for teacher improvement utilizing the educational sciences*. Bloomfield Hills, Mich.: American Educational Sciences Association, 1973.

Ramirez, M., III, Herold, P. L., and Castañeda, A. *New approaches to bilingual, bicultural education. Developing cognitive flexibility*, No. 6. Austin, Texas: The Dissemination Center for Bilingual Bicultural Education, 1974.

Rivera, L. *A proposed approach to implement bilingual programs, research and synthesis of philosophical, theoretical and practical implications*. New York: National Puerto Rican Development and Training Institute, 1973.

Saville-Troike, M. *Bilingual children: A resource document*. Arlington, Va.: Center for Applied Linguistics, 1973.

Schroeder, A. *A study of the relationship between student and teacher cognitive styles and student derived teacher evaluations*. Unpublished doctoral dissertation, Wayne State University, 1970.

Sigren, V. *An exploratory study employing the educational science of cognitive style as a predictor of group leadership within an orientation program*. Unpublished doctoral dissertation, Michigan State University, 1973.

Smithers, J. *An investigation into the effect of culture and acculturations on the formation of cognitive style*. Unpublished doctoral dissertation, Wayne State University, 1974.

Steinberg, L. *Report on bilingual education: A study of programs for pupils with English language difficulty in New York City Public Schools*. New York, N.Y.: Department of Public Affairs, Community Service Society of New York, 1974.

Sueiro-Ross, C. Cultural characteristics in bilingual learners. *System*, 1974, *2*, 39–48.

Swanson, M. M. Bilingual education: The national perspective. In G. A. Jarvis (Ed.), *Responding to new realities* (Vol. 5). Skokie, Ill.: National Textbook, 1973.

Vasquez, J. Bilingual education for New York State: The pursuit of the ideal. Paper presented at the Fifth Annual Conference of New York Administrators in Compensatory Education, Niagara Falls, New York, October 27–29, 1974. Mimeo.

Wasser, L. *An investigation into cognitive style as a facet of teachers' systems of student appraisal*. Unpublished doctoral dissertation, University of Michigan, 1969.

Wasser, L. *The educational science of cognitive style*. Bloomfield Hills, Mich.: Oakland Community College Press, 1971.

Willink, E. W. Bilingual education for Navajo children. In P. R. Turner (Ed.), *Bilingualism in the Southwest*. Tucson, Ariz.: University of Arizona Press, 1973.

Wyett, J. *A pilot study to analyze cognitive style and teaching style with reference to selected strata of the defined educational sciences*. Unpublished doctoral dissertation, Wayne State University, 1967.

Part II

PROGRAMS IN BILINGUAL–BICULTURAL
EDUCATION: AN ANALYSIS OF TOTAL
OR PARTIAL IMMERSION PROGRAMS

The Case for Partial or Total Immersion Education[1]

ANDREW D. COHEN, Hebrew University of Jerusalem

Introduction

The last decade has seen the advent of an innovative approach to producing bilinguals, that of carefully controlled immersion education. This approach is not to be confused with what is commonly referred to as the "sink-or-swim" form of language immersion. This chapter will first discuss immersion education within the general framework of teaching second languages. Then, research results from immersion programs in Canada and the United States will be reported and some areas for further investigation will be identified. Finally, possible applications for immersion education among different target populations will be discussed.

A time such as the present, when the North American continent is alive with activity related to bilingual education, is a perfect time to consider innovative means of achieving functional bilingualism, not only for the minority group child, but for the majority group child as well. Although the thrust of the bilingual–bicultural movement has been primarily aimed at efficiently producing competent English speakers from among the non-English speaking, many observers have commented that the ultimate future of the movement will depend on "what's in it for the majority child." And, in fact, there can be some exciting things in bilingual education for these children.

Second-language teaching in the elementary grades

TRADITIONAL METHODS

In a book about foreign languages in the elementary school (a topic hereafter referred to as FLES) appearing almost two decades ago, Andersson (1953) stated that beginning foreign-language instruction in

---

[1] Portions of this chapter also appear in A. D. Cohen & M. Swain (1976).

the early grades, when children are of an age to learn easily and well would produce more efficient results than beginning such instruction later. In a more recent book on the same topic, however, Andersson admitted that the expected results had not been achieved after the implementation of such programs. He lamented that "the advent of efficiency, which is essential to success, continues to elude us because of an all-pervading mediocrity, not only within the ranks of foreign language teachers but throughout the educational system" (Andersson 1969, preface). However, Andersson still noted that "children in elementary-school language classes usually excel high-school students in acquiring basic language skills—though not in learning formal grammar. . . ." (1969, p. xvii). He cited the conclusions of a 1961 Modern Language Associaion evaluation of FLES to the effect that FLES was seen merely as a preview or prelude to "real" language learning in high school, and that language instruction in elementary programs meant teaching lists of words rather than conversation (1969, pp. 102–103).

Andersson was referring specifically to *foreign* language learning in that the students in the programs being evaluated were all native speakers of English learning other languages that were not spoken by the majority group in the society—such as German, French, and Spanish. But for the purposes of this discussion, we will broaden the term to *second-language* learning, to include the learning of a language that is spoken by the majority group in the society, such as the learning of English by Mexican-Americans.

Whereas Andersson would attribute much of the failure of FLES programs to inadequate teacher training, it may be also that features inherent in the instructional methods and materials endorsed by the school districts account for the discouraging results. A recent article by Krashen and Seliger (1975) lists eight features of formal instruction in adult second-language education. The authors suggest that formal instruction is useful to the adult and nonessential for the child language learner since "the prepubescent child has an impressive ability to learn second languages in informal environments. . . ." (p. 174). More will be said about child second-language learning below, but for the present, the interesting point is that at least three of the eight categories that the authors list have particular relevance to FLES programs, as well as to programs for adults. These features are sequencing of materials, performance channel, and exercise type ("focus-on" type versus "focus-away" type).

First, FLES materials have often been based on adult notions of grammatical complexity and supposed utility and frequency of forms for the child *without* empirical data as to the "natural sequence" of acquisition for learners. What would really be meant here is the "natural sequence" for the *second-language* learner, since as Krashen and Seliger point out, the second-language learner's natural sequence of acquisition is probably not the same as that of the native learner.

Second, FLES programs in many instances have encouraged early emphasis on the productive channel, namely speaking, either in choral repetition or individually, while Andersson and others recommend that pupils have ample opportunity to hear and understand the foreign language before expressing themselves in it (Andersson, 1969, p. 165) and that expression in the foreign language should come only after the child feels ready (p. 140). Third, exercise patterns may well have been largely of the "focus-on" variety, directly concentrating on patterns, rather than of the "focus-away" type, in which patterns are learned through informal communication.

Since, as Andersson points out, few of the present FLES programs have had adequate provision for evaluation, it is impossible to make definitive statements about "the most efficient" means of producing second-language speakers (Andersson, 1969, p. 145). But there seems to be some consensus that FLES generally has not produced American children comfortably fluent in the second language. It may be that an efficient type of FLES still has not had a chance to be tried out. A study by Allen (1966) found that FLES generally was not initiated until Grade 3 and that at this level, students received on the average no more than 20 minutes of instruction, three times a week. Andersson (1969) recommends that such a FLES program be started at nursey school or at the latest kindergarten, and that there be at least one lesson per day.

The case of the non-English-speaking minority in the United States has been somewhat different from that of the English speaker learning another language. In many instances, the non-English speakers have simply been submersed in the English-medium elementary schools. The specifics of what this submersion entailed will be discussed later. Generally, however, it implied that the students received no special second-language instruction. And in fact, only a few of these students received formal English-as-a-second-language (hereafter, ESL) lessons. More recently, these lessons included some subject matter, but still basically emphasized language learning itself rather than making the task of the language learning incidental to the task of communicating with others about subject matter (Saville-Troike, 1974).

PSYCHOLINGUISTIC INSIGHTS INTO LANGUAGE DEVELOPMENT

Findings from the study of child first-language acquisition over the last decade (Slobin, 1971; Cazden, 1972; Brown, 1973) have prompted a reconsideration of theories of second-language acquisition. Just as

native-language acquisition was now seen as an active, though uncon-
scious, discovery of the rule system underlying the language, so second-
language learning was now seen to share some of these same developmental patterns (Tucker & d'Anglejan, 1975). First-language acquisition
was seen to extend far beyond the learner's imitation of adult speech
and adult reinforcement of correct patterns. Instead, children were actually seen to be systematically developing interim grammars on the
way to adult grammar.

Research on young second-language learners has shown that their
language acquisition patterns in natural situations are similar in many
ways to those of first-language learners (Hatch & Wagner-Gough, 1975).
For example, Hansen-Bede (1975) found that a 3-year, 9-month-old
English speaker in Pakistan went through most of the same strategies
in learning Urdu as do native speakers. The child had little apparent
interference from English, even in word order. The only area of difficulty
was in negation, where the child used those early negation rules that
native English speakers use. Even research on primary-school-age second-language learners has shown that interference is not as significant
a source of errors in second-language learning as is the developmental
process that native speakers of the language also go through (Dulay &
Burt, 1974; Cohen, 1975d, chap. 8).

In a study of 4- to 9-year-old English speakers in Geneva, Ervin-Tripp
(1974) found that the children overgeneralized and simplified French,
their second language, in much the same way as children overgeneralize
and simplify in the learning of the first language. Notwithstanding the
research on similarities between first- and second-language learning,
there are basic differences, particularly if the learning of the second
language is delayed until the point of school entry (age 5). At this
time, the child already has the rudiments of one language, some cognitive development, greater capacity for organization than at the onset
of the first language, a wider range of semantic concepts, and a longer
memory span. Wagner-Gough (1975), for example, contrasted the
acquisition of the progressive tense by native speakers of English
(Brown, 1973) with that of a 6-year-old non-native. The first-language
learners were restricted by their level of cognitive development to one
temporal mode, the process-state (e.g., in the process of doing something), whereas the second-language learner produced forms with
reference to at least four temporal modes. However, Wagner-Gough
(1975) also noted that her subject's ability to recognize and produce
the progressive was more advanced than his perception of relationships
between form and function. Thus, although he was using the progressive
with reference to four temporal modes, he was not clearly perceiving

the function of each mode. Wagner-Gough goes on to point out that researchers studying second-language acquisition have not, however, paid much attention to the distinction between acquiring a form and acquiring its correct function(s).

Thus, given that there are similarities between first- and second-language learning at different age levels, are there real advantages to learning a second language early? Lenneberg (1967) introduced the notion of a critical period in language learning between the ages of 2 and 10. Rosansky (1975) points out, however, that neurophysiological evidence about a critical period for language acquisition (ending around puberty) is still inconclusive. She stresses the importance of affective and cognitive factors and notes that the child's passage through the Piagetian stages of Pre-Operation (before age 7), Concrete Operations (ages 7–12), and Formal Operations (age 15 and after) will have an influence on the child's second-language learning patterns. She points out that the child initially is highly "centered," focusing on one dimension at a time. She notes that "centration . . . implies very little meta-awareness, an ability most adults have and use" (Rosansky, 1975, p. 97). Whereas the child only intuits transformational rules through the Concrete Operations period, once he reaches the stage of Formal Operations, he superimposes propositional logic on the classes and relationships he developed earlier and pays more attention to differences. Rosansky stops short of suggesting that learners of a second language will experience greater success if they are at one Piagetian stage of development rather than at another, although she suggests that centration and the lack of meta-awareness may actually be advantageous in the language acquisition process.

Experts in the field of language teaching vary in their recommendations about program implementation. Andersson (1974) recommends that bilingual education start several years before school entry. He bases his conclusions on an extensive review of research relating to early childhood development. He notes an agreement among early childhood specialists that children between birth and age 5 have an extraordinary learning potential. Ervin-Tripp (1974), however, concluded from research on 4- to 9-year-olds learning French as a second language that the older learners learned faster because they had "more efficient memory heuristics" (p. 122). Concurrently, Saville-Troike (1973) suggests "there is some reason to believe that a child will experience more interference between language systems if the second is added before the first is completely developed (at about age ten)" (pp. 29–30). On the basis of preliminary findings from research on 3-year-old through adult non-native learners of Dutch, Snow (1975) went even further. She concluded that "youth gives no special advantage in language learning.

Older children and adults do better at all aspects of language acquisition than the younger children. . . ." (pp. 14–15). She also concluded that the strategies and stages of acquisition seemed very similar for all age groups.

Thus, evidence appears to suggest that younger learners are not as efficient at second-language learning as are teen-agers and adults. So perhaps the meta-awareness that Rosansky speaks of above may work to the advantage of the older learners. However, there are other considerations that could, in fact, weigh more heavily in the long run and that have implications for school programs.

First, Snow (1975) points out that there is more free choice in learning a second language than in learning the first language. Therefore second-language learning is more affected by motivation, desire to be able to communicate with the native speakers, interest in and admiration of the culture to which the language gives access, and willingness to endanger one's own personality by using a different, less effective idiom. Intuition and observation have repeatedly confirmed that the younger the learner, the less he is likely to question his own motives for learning a second language, the more uninhibited he is in his willingness to communicate, the more open he is to other cultures (the negative stereotypes are not as ingrained), and the more willing he is to make mistakes. At the teen-age and adult levels, individual differences become so overriding that researchers currently are trying to sort out just what learner characteristics make for good language learning (see Rubin, 1975; Stern, 1975; Cohen & Robbins, 1976, in press).

Thus, the younger learner may not be as efficient a learner, but he may be less resistent to the learning process. Furthermore, as Krashen and Seliger (1975) point out, he may be more receptive to the most natural or "quasinatural" approach to language learning that can be implemented in a classroom. Such an approach would, by implication, avoid tedious drilling. Angel (1975) goes so far as to suggest that gross damage can be done to the child in the early grades of the elementary school by the imposition of adult language structures on him, especially if the approach is formal rather than experiential. And without careful study of how a child learns first and second languages, structured curriculum merely reflects adult intuitions about the language a child "should" learn. A formal curriculum is arduous to prepare and possibly even of dubious validity in terms of the selection and sequencing of structures, given what is beginning to be learned about first-language acquisition patterns in totally natural environments (exposure to second language through nonclassroom experiences exclusively). Interestingly enough, some research evidence shows that even in so-called natural situations between adults and young first- and second-language learners, the adults filter their language, i.e., they use simple language patterns and are forgiving of errors. Apparently, adults tend to be more "natural" with adolescent second-language learners and consequently use more complex language—embedded clauses, idioms, and a wider range of vocabulary (Wagner-Gough, 1975).

Now that a case, albeit tentative, has been made for early exposure to a second language through a process that is intended to mirror as much as possible the learning of a first language, we will now consider an approach to simulating the natural situation in the classroom, namely that of immersion education.

AN INNOVATIVE METHOD: IMMERSION EDUCATION

There has appeared a form of school language experience that attempts to duplicate, as much as is possible in a classroom, the natural context in which a child would learn a first language. In the following list of basic characteristics of this form of immersion education, "L1" refers to the student's native language and "L2" to his second language.

1. All instruction initially (i.e., in kindergarten and Grade 1) is in L2.[2]
2. In second, third, or fourth grade, L1 language arts (reading, writing, and so on) are introduced in L1.
3. By fifth grade, content subjects such as geography or history may be taught in L1.
4. All kindergarten pupils are unilingual in L1. In essence, the successful program starts as a *segregated* one linguistically. This segregation eliminates the kinds of ridicule that students exert on less proficient performers. In immersion education, all learners start off linguistically "in the same boat." In later grades, other children with more advanced L2 abilities can be brought into the class, with positive effects.
5. In first grade, native speakers of L2 may be introduced into the classroom to provide native peer models of L2 and to foster interethnic interaction and friendship. For the native speakers of L2, instruction is actually in their *L1* until the introduction of language arts in *their L2* during second grade or later (see point 2 above).

[2] The form of immersion education described has been referred to as early total immersion. Late immersion programs, consisting of total immersion at the fourth-, fifth-, seventh-, or eighth-grade level, have also been initiated. In these instances, the students had been receiving second-language instruction (French) for at least one year prior to the program. Following the one year of total immersion, at least one content subject is taught via that language in subsequent years (see Barik & Swain, 1976, in press).

6. The learners are selected without special attention to social class, intelligence, personality factors (such as shyness) or any language disabilities they may have.[3]

7. The teachers are bilingual, although they only speak L2 in the classroom. They need not be native speakers of L2, but must be perfectly fluent in it and should possess the appropriate adult-speaking-to-child register. (If the students are intended to get the message that it is desirable for everyone to be bilingual, it may be advantageous to have a blond-haired, blue-eyed teacher as a Spanish-speaking model in, for example, a California Spanish immersion or bilingual education program.)

8. The students rarely hear the teachers speaking L1 to each other. If L1-speaking visitors wish to address the teachers in the classroom, the teachers use students to interpret for them. At the kindergarten level—before the children can perform this task well—the teacher may step outside with the visitor. Outside the classroom, the teacher is also careful to use L2 whenever the students are around. Although this procedure may appear to be excessive, it *does* emphasize to the students that L2 is a language the teachers use—not just when they "have to" in the classroom.

9. In kindergarten, the children are permitted to speak in L1 until they are ready to speak in L2. The teacher makes it clear that she understands L1 by responding appropriately. The teacher will often repeat the children's remarks or comment on them in L2. (For a description of teaching strategies used in response to the use of L1 by the students, see Stern & Swain, 1973).

10. In first grade and beyond, the teacher requests that only L2 be spoken in class, except during L1-medium classes (see items 2 and 3 in this list). Ideally, a teacher other than the immersion teacher teaches L1-medium classes, so as to keep the languages separated by person, at least at the early grade levels.

11. The program follows the regular school curriculum. Sometimes this goal is difficult to achieve if L2 materials are not available in the same series that the school is using for L1 instruction. Careful curriculum planning and development are essential.

12. In the early grades, there are no structured L2 lessons (pattern practice drills, and so on) in class. This approach avoids the selection and sequencing of structures in a way that is inconsistent with how children actually learn language. L2 is the medium of instruction rather than a separate subject. Formal discussion of persistent problem areas

[3] Research results from a French immersion program for working class students indicated initial success (see Bruck, Tucker, & Jakimik, 1973), although the research had to be discontinued because of severe student attrition.

in pronunciation (e.g., aspiration of voiceless stops) and grammar (e.g., gender agreement) may be introduced in later grades.

13. The teacher has the expectation that the children will learn L2 and content material through immersion.

14. When attrition occurs, new unilingual L1-speaking children may or may not be permitted to enter. Programs allowing replacements have varied in the procedures they adopt, some only allowing new entries at the kindergarten level and some allowing new entries at various points up through the grades.

15. The program is optional. Students participate in the program voluntarily and only with the consent of the parents.

16. In many cases, the program has been initiated because of parental pressure. Support of both the community and the educational administration is essential.

17. Some programs elicit and receive parent volunteer support in the classroom.

IMMERSION VERSUS SUBMERSION

Because the term *immersion* as used to describe this new form of immersion education has also been applied to the experience of non-English speakers in English-medium schools, it is important to indicate how immersion for minority students has been a *different* experience. Perhaps a term like *submersion* better reflects the sink-or-swim nature of the school experience for minority groups that do not receive any form of bilingual education. Such submersion has tended to include the following characteristics.

1. The students were grouped indiscriminately with native English speakers for all or most of the school day. Whereas heterogeneous language grouping is valuable at the right time and place, such grouping may be counterproductive at the outset. The child acquiring a second language has initial difficulties in communication and consequently may have a sense of insecurity or even one of failure in the presence of native speakers of that language. Sometimes native English speakers— even from the same ethnic background (e.g., third-generation Chicano) —may tease the non-native speaker because of his imperfect English.

2. If English was offered as a second language, the programs were of a pull-out nature, that is, the students were segregated for ESL instruction. Pulling students out for ESL classes has often resulted in stigmatizing the students as possessing a "language handicap" or a "cognitive deficit," labels that are damaging to student self-esteem.

3. The ESL lessons were of a formal, structured nature, generally from kindergarten or from first grade on. The value of explicit teaching

of ESL syntax at such an early age has been questioned (Dulay & Burt, 1974). Furthermore, such classes have often produced only mixed results in English acquisition,[4] at the expense of progress in the content subjects.

4. The teachers of both the ESL classes and of the regular academic program were unilingual English speakers. Thus even the simplest of requests from a student in his native language were misunderstood or ignored.

5. The students were not permitted to speak their native language in school. The United States Commission on Civil Rights (1972) has documented beyond reasonable doubt that such practices existed.

6. The teachers had low expectations for the success of the students, particularly those from certain ethnic groups. For example, two separate studies (Carter, 1970; United States Commission on Civil Rights, 1973) found that Mexican-American teachers had lower expectations for the academic success of Mexican-American pupils than for Anglos. It is quite possible that these low teacher expectations for minority student success academically—partly a reaction to their imperfect English—have been passed on to the students such that they performed accordingly (the self-fulfilling prophecy syndrome).

7. There was little effort to provide reading or subject matter instruction in the student's native language. The lack of instruction in and through the native language may have heightened minority student feelings of linguistic insecurity already present in a majority society where English is the dominant and more prestigious language.

8. Parental involvement in the school program was limited. The lack of parental involvement in the school program has worked to the detriment of the students. Recent experiences in bilingual education have demonstrated that such parental involvement, even from low-income homes, can be engendered.[5]

Research results from immersion programs

Immersion education as described above has generally encompassed only children whose L1—English—is the majority or dominant language in North America. In Canada, many French immersion programs have been initiated in recent years. Total immersion programs exist in almost all the provinces of Canada, including New Brunswick (Fredericton,

---

[4] Few rigorous evaluations of such ESL programs have been conducted.

[5] The author evaluated a bilingual program (Rosemead, California, 1974–1975) that attracted a number of Spanish-speaking parent volunteers from low-income homes. A community liaison person contacted parents by phone or in person, and arranged some English instruction for volunteer aides. One kindergarten classroom had at least five regular volunteers.

Moncton), Nova Scotia (Dartmouth), Quebec (Montreal), Ontario (Toronto, Ottawa, Cochrane, Brampton), Manitoba (Winnipeg), and British Columbia (Vancouver, Victoria, Coquitlam).

Immersion education for majority group English speakers in the United States is still much more limited. There is the Spanish Immersion Program at El Marino School in Culver City, California (Cohen, 1975c), which began in 1971 with one kindergarten group and has added one grade level each year (K–4 as of the 1975–1976 school year). The Culver City program has had several features distinguishing it from other immersion programs. First, native target-language (Spanish) speakers were introduced into the program in first grade and have comprised anywhere from 10 to 25% of a given class. Also, as of the fourth year of the program, native English-speaking first graders who had already had one year of immersion in Spanish were placed in the same classroom as the new kindergarten pupils. This approach seemed to stimulate the kindergarten pupils to produce more Spanish sooner than had been the case with those kindergarteners grouped separately in previous years (Personal communication with Irma Wright, the K–1 teacher, September, 1974).

There is also a French immersion program going into its second year at the Four Corners Elementary School in Silver Spring, Maryland. The Silver Spring program began in 1974 on a multigraded basis, Grades 1–3.

THE CANADIAN EXPERIENCE

The St. Lambert French Immersion Program for English-Canadian students began in Montreal in 1965 with two kindergarten classrooms, comprising a pilot group. The following year a follow-up kindergarten group was added. This immersion experience was carefully planned and followed closely by researchers over the years. Findings for the pilot and follow-up groups through Grades 4 and 3, respectively, indicated considerable success in that the students involved had acquired a high level of competency in a second language, French, while keeping pace with peers (schooled in the native language) in native-language development (Lambert & Tucker, 1972). They also made normal progress in the content subjects although these were taught primarily, or exclusively, in the second language. Their cognitive or intellectual development showed no signs of a deficit. The students developed a healthy attitude toward the second language and toward their own language and culture (Lambert & Tucker, 1972). As of Grade 5, French immersion students rejected the idea of transfering to a conventional English program, while the English-Canadian controls felt that even their standard

French-as-a-second-language program had given them too much French (Lambert, Tucker, & d'Anglejan, 1973).

Although Grade 5 marked a slowing down in the development of conceptual vocabulary in French and in French grammar (especially gender) compared to a native French control group, by Grade 6, the French immersion group were making no more errors of grammar than the French control group, although the content of compositions written by the immersion students was less rich (Bruck, Lambert, & Tucker, in press). The authors speculated that the French immersion students were purposely simplifying their constructions and avoiding vocabulary embellishments when writing in French. A related piece of research by Hamayan, Markman, Pelletier, and Tucker (1975) found that sixth-grade French immersion students were more prone to certain grammatical errors (e.g., changing the verb from subjunctive to present indicative in an elicited imitation task) than were fourth graders. Whether such performance indicates simplification of a developmental nature or rather a regression in grammatical control warrants further study (see "Research Areas for Investigation" later in this chapter). Furthermore, the immersion students were using the same speech register to tell stories to French children *and* to adults, whereas French controls told different types of stories to the two groups. The authors commented, "The interesting possibility . . . arises that [the students] have developed a type of 'interlanguage' that is compatible with their training and their communicational needs" (Bruck, Lambert, & Tucker, in press).

Results by Grade 7 were most encouraging with respect to content subjects like math, showing that experimental students were coping as well as peers educated in their mother tongue when the curriculum demands became greater (Bruck, Lambert, & Tucker, 1974). At this point, the seventh graders were put in a naturalistic situation where there would be a need to communicate in French: a debate between eight French Immersion students and eight sixth-grade native French students. The students selected the topic, capital punishment. The performance of the non-natives was not only rated favorably by the researchers but by the native French speakers as well, as being both easy to understand and pleasant to listen to.

The findings through grade 8 were not as impressive as in previous years, the slow-down being in part attributed to the fact that French instruction only comprised 30% of the school day at this point. The authors speculated that since French had been reduced to a course subject for the follow-up seventh graders, their French may have been subject to pidginization caused by limited use (Bruck, Lambert, & Tucker, 1975). However, it is still noteworthy that French raters thought that 15 to 20%

of the French immersion students were native French from the way that they filled out an application for a summer job.

A report by Barik and Swain (1975) on a number of French immersion classes (K–2) spread throughout the Ottawa School District confirmed on a large scale the findings of the St. Lambert study. By second grade, immersion students generally performed as well on tests of English language skills as children in conventional schooling. As was the case with the St. Lambert study (Lambert & Tucker, 1972), the Grade 1 immersion pupils lagged somewhat behind their English-speaking peers in English language skills, especially in reading. In both instances, this lag disappeared after formal instruction in English language arts was introduced. The French immersion students in Ottawa were also doing as well in math, and suffered no retardation in cognitive development. Furthermore, their proficiency in French was far superior to English-speaking peers receiving lessons in French as a second language (FSL).

There are other research reports from Montreal, Ottawa, Toronto, and elsewhere on both early and late total immersion progams for English-speaking students (Swain, 1974). The late immersion programs were introduced either in an upper elementary grade or in junior high school. The pattern involved FSL instruction for at least a year before the immersion. Subsequent to the total immersion year, the students continued to receive one or more subjects in French, as well as an "enriched" FSL course.

Results are also available comparing total immersion to partial immersion, as practiced in St. Thomas, Ontario. In the partial immersion programs, students receive instruction through the medium of French in the morning and through the medium of English in the afternoon. English reading is introduced in Grade 1, French reading in Grade 2.

Generally, both early and late immersion programs have produced the desired outcomes, while the partial immersion experience has not proved as successful. With respect to French skills, pupils from early and later immersion programs performed better that FSL students (Swain, 1974), although the immersion students were not approaching native proficiency in their French skills. For example, Swain (1975b) found the French writing of Grade 2 and 3 students to be somewhat lacking with respect to grammar, spelling, and creativity in comparison to their English compositions. Also, the students were developing and reinforcing their own dialect of spoken French. Swain explained that the emphasis was on expressing thoughts, and that the errors developed or persisted because other students used them and because the teachers ignored them. In one study on pronominal usage, Swain (1975a) noted that whereas errors of person decreased over time, gender errors were constant. Tarone,

Frauenfelder, and Selinker (1976) provide a theoretical basis for interpreting the patterns of stability and instability among second-language learners, drawing examples from longitudinal data on French immersion children (Grades 1–2) in Toronto.

With respect to the development of English language skills, findings in Canada generally are positive, even in instances where formal English instruction has been delayed past the second grade. For instance, even where the students did not receive formal instruction in English until Grade 4, as at the Roslyn School in Montreal, the students ultimately developed satisfactory English skills. Curiously, learners in partial French immersion did not keep pace with their peers in English development nor did they develop French skills comparable to those of English-Canadian students in total French immersion programs (Swain, 1974). Since this approach is more like the kind of bilingual program being put into effect in some United States settings, the lack of success may be noteworthy. Swain (1974), speculating on the sequencing of languages for reading, suggested that it may be easier for English speakers to learn to read in French and then to start English reading a year or more later, instead of the reverse. The lesser development of French skills in partial immersion could perhaps be attributed primarily to the lesser exposure to French altogether.

With respect to content subject acquisition, the Canadian results showed that not only students in *early* total immersion but also those in *late* immersion were able to maintain satisfactory achievement in content subjects taught entirely in French. In one late immersion program, English-speaking eighth graders were immersed in French for mathematics, history, geography, science and art (70% of the day) after having had 20 minutes of FSL per day in Grade 7. In Grade 9, the students still received history and geography in French. Whereas the students suffered a slight subject matter loss in science and literature in Grade 8, this loss did not persist through Grade 9 (Barik & Swain, 1976, in press).

Research is also beginning to appear on a new double-immersion, or trilingual, program, in which two non-native languages, French and Hebrew, are being used as media of instruction. Results for children in kindergarten through second grade indicate that students in the immersion schools have developed French and Hebrew language skills that surpass those of pupils following more traditional French and Hebrew language courses. At the same time, native English-language skills are developed as well as those of nonimmersion pupils (Genesee, Sheiner, Tucker, & Lambert, in press). The authors point out that in Canada a double-immersion program allows naturalized English- or French-speaking Canadians to acquire skill in Canada's second official language while maintaining their particular cultural heritage by using their mother tongue as a second school language.

THE EXPERIENCE IN THE UNITED STATES

In the United States, only the Culver City program in California has so far been studied systematically by researchers. The pilot group was not found to have a deficit in speaking or in reading English, at the end of Grade 1 (Cohen, 1974a), at the end of Grade 2 (Lebach, 1974), or at the end of Grade 3 (Jashni, 1975). The follow-up group did experience a slight lag in English reading in Grade 1 in comparison to their monolingually schooled peers (Lebach, 1974), similar to the initial lag noted previously in the Canadian research findings. By Grade 2, however, there were no significant differences (Jashni, 1975). With respect to Spanish language skills, the pilot group was reading at a level comparable to native Spanish speakers in Ecuador at the end of Grade 1 (Cohen, 1974a). The following year, neither the pilot group (Grade 2) nor the follow-up group (Grade 1) were reading at the same level as native Spanish-speaking peers in Ecuador, but their reading proficiency compared quite satisfactorily with native Spanish-speaking students in California (at the 90th percentile). The pilot students also performed slightly better in Spanish reading than native Spanish speaking in the immersion program (Lebach, 1974). The pilot group at Grade 3 and the follow-up group at Grade 2 performed as well in Spanish reading as comparison groups in Tijuana, Mexico (Jashni, 1975).

As part of an ongoing analysis of Spanish language acquisition among the immersion students, Boyd (1974, 1975) studied the Spanish of the 12 Anglo pilot children in second grade. She investigated the hypothesis that second-language learning in children is similar to first-language learning (see section entitled "Psycholinguistic Insights into Language Development" earlier in this chapter). Two Spanish morphology tests, the Bilingual Syntax Measure (Harcourt Brace Jovanovich), an oral storytelling measure, a repetition task, and a reflexive elicitation task were used to elicit speech. Spontaneous speech was also recorded, and 5 hours of teacher language in the classroom were taped. A detailed error analysis was performed on the elicited natural speech data.

Results indicated that subject–verb number and person agreement, adjective–noun gender, and article–noun gender were tenacious morphological problems. Object pronoun omission and misuse and the expression of tense were two other problem areas. The low frequency of object pronouns and tenses other than present in the teacher input data was suggested as a reason for the children's problems in those areas.

Overall, the study found a number of similarities between first- and second-language development data, but also found a number of interesting differences (Boyd, 1974, 1975).

A follow-up study at the end of the third grade (Cohen, 1976, in press) revealed that whereas the appropriate use of the masculine definite article was being mastered, it was also being overgeneralized to contexts in which the feminine article was obligatory. The analysis also pointed out signs of improvement in the present indicative, whereas no such improvement was noted with respect to the preterit. The immersion students' responses to the Bilingual Syntax Measure were compared with those of native Spanish-speaking second graders in Ecuador in order to determine how closely the Spanish immersion group approximated native proficiency in their speech.

Given that the students' primary exposure to Spanish was in the classroom, an assessment of Spanish loss among pilot students over recess between Grades 1 and 2 also was conducted. As might be expected, after the summer, the students said less with more errors (Cohen, 1974b). They also demonstrated certain characterizable effects of forgetting (Cohen, 1975b).

Regarding achievement in content subjects, the pilot group performed significantly better than their English comparison group in mathematics at the end of Grade 2 (Lebach, 1974) and just as well as the comparison group at the end of Grade 3 (Jashni, 1975). The follow-up group also performed as well as the comparison group in mathematics, both at the end of Grade 1 (Lebach, 1974) and at the end of Grade 2 (Jashni, 1975). The pilot third graders and follow-up second graders likewise performed as well on tests of science and social studies as comparison students (Jashni, 1975), suggesting no detriment to subject matter acquisition, even though all the content subjects were taught in Spanish.

The attitudes of participating students, teachers, and parents toward the Spanish Immersion Program have also been assessed. Cohen and Lebach (1974) found that the students had developed positive attitudes toward the Spanish language and culture and toward foreign language learning in general. Both the immersion teachers and the parents strongly supported the program and advocated its continuation (see the transcript of a symposium on the Spanish Immersion Program at the 9th Annual TESOL Meeting, in the appendix to Cohen, 1975c).

Waldman (1975) did a study comparing cross-cultural attitudes of Anglos in the Spanish Immersion Program to Anglos in three other school environments: (1) Anglos in a bilingual education program with Spanish speakers; (2) Anglos in a conventional school classroom that had Spanish speakers in it; and (3) Anglos in a school without Spanish-speaking students. She used the Cross-Cultural Attitude Inventory

(Learning Concepts, Inc.) and a form of matched-guise technique, whereby the students are to rate tapes of various speakers on a series of polar adjectives (e.g., friendly–mean, smart–dumb, rich–poor, and so on) according to how the students react to the varieties of Spanish and English that the speakers use. The former instrument was intended to measure feelings about Mexican-American and Anglo culture, while the latter was aimed at tapping reactions, however stereotypic, toward the speakers of certain language varieties.

Results generally showed that the Spanish Immersion students were more positive toward Mexican-American culture and Spanish speakers than children in other types of school programs. The results also showed that Anglos homogeneously grouped in English-only classrooms without Spanish speakers were more positive toward Mexican-American culture and speakers in their Spanish guise than were Anglos in both the bilingual program and in English-only classrooms that had Spanish speakers. Of the English-only homogeneously grouped students, 39% favored the Spanish guise over the English guise, as did 33% of the Spanish Immersion group. On the other hand, only 19% of the bilingual-program Anglos and 8% of the English-only Anglos in mixed classes favored the Spanish guise over the English. Such results might suggest that mixed schooling without a bilingual program may reinforce the negative stereotypes that Anglos have of Spanish speakers. Even schools with bilingual programs may produce only mixed reactions to Spanish speakers, depending on the nature of the program. For example, if Spanish is used sparingly and not for the "important" tasks, Spanish may become "marked" as inferior in the minds of the students (Shultz, 1975).

Research areas for investigation

This discussion of research findings indicates some of the research issues that have been investigated. A number still remain to be investigated or investigated more thoroughly. The research question of perhaps greatest magnitude concerns the nature of second-language development through an immersion program over time, particularly in contexts where all or most of the second-language learning goes on in the classroom: Do some or many learners reach a fossilized plateau in their second-language development—a form of pidgin—after which their proficiency levels off, shows regression to earlier forms, or simply deteriorates (e.g., some students deliberately develop an exaggerated American accent in Spanish, whereas they never had one before)?

Working with data from French immersion students in Toronto, Tarone, Frauenfelder, and Selinker (1976) have developed a system for rigorously identifying patterns of stability and instability in the learners' interlanguage over time. They identify Type I individuals, who have fossilized competence characterized by stability, and Type II individuals, who are continuing to learn and thus have an interlanguage system characterized by instability. After careful analysis of syntactic forms in the learners' speech, the authors conclude that the data they found in interlanguage speech are not accounted for by any syntactic theory known to them. They prefer to reserve the term *rule* in referring only to those systematic grammatical structures that are "surfacy" in that they can be safely inferred from surface-structure data (e.g., word order, inflection, and function words). A recent grammatical analysis of Culver City Spanish data has led to refinements in Tarone *et al.*'s system (see Cohen, 1976, in press).

Perhaps the kinds of research suggested by Tarone *et al.*, can help provide the data to answer the more pedagogical questions such as: Should teachers introduce formal, if limited, drills or other forms of language instruction aimed at eradicating fossilized forms and developmental forms? If so, at what grade level? What will be the effects of different approaches to remediation? To answer such questions, it would be necessary not only to look rigorously at interlanguage development among students, but also to research different approaches to teacher intervention (Cohen, 1975a).

Research questions are also raised by the Culver City model—whereby native speakers of the target language are in the same classroom as the second-language learners, beginning with Grade 1.

1. Is there a pecking order of social interaction among the students? Are there "integrated" and/or ethnic cliques? Who speaks what language to whom, when, and for what purpose? (For example, do students tend to speak English to each other and Spanish to teachers?)

2. Do the Anglo children use different communication styles or registers when speaking Spanish to teachers, to Spanish-speaking peers, or to Anglo peers? Are the Culver City students exposed to sufficient variety in social situations to make real register shifts probable? Can we even distinguish Anglo talk with peers from talk with adults in Spanish?

3. What happens to the Spanish or native speakers in such a program? Are their Spanish pronunciation and grammar adversely affected by imperfect, but prestigious, Anglo models? [6]

4. Do the Anglo students use the native Spanish speakers as models

---

[6] In Culver City, the native Spanish speakers also receive an entirely Spanish program upon entry in Grade 1. In Grade 2, they receive English reading instruction just as the Anglos do. The native Spanish speakers have not constituted a large enough group to make anything but anecdotal statements about their progress feasible.

of Spanish? How much do the Spanish speakers correct the Spanish of the Anglos? How often do the Anglos correct the Spanish of the native Spanish speakers (especially in reading and writing)?

Clearly there are many questions that could be asked and for which answers should be provided before too much effort is made to initiate immersion programs in new settings. Perhaps a reservation that could be held about United States federal bilingual programs, for example, is that certain teaching methodologies have been advocated and implemented *without* a sufficient research base to attest to their linguistic and cross-cultural effectiveness. Cohen and Laosa (1976, in press) caution that project results are a product of the educational treatments employed, the characteristics of the students, the contexts in which the program takes place, the research design employed, and subtle interactions among all operating factors. Probably there is no end to the number of, say, treatment variables that could be investigated, particularly as concerns the method. All the same, it is important to investigate possible positive *and* negative effects of specific types of immersion education programs. It might be that such programs should only be used with certain students in certain school contexts.

There are also administrative issues to be considered in program implementation—issues that have been raised by administrators of immersion programs in Canada. They include criteria for selection of students into immersion programs (Sanley, 1974; Sweet, 1974), class size and problems of student attrition (Stanley, 1974; Hildebrand, 1974), total development of the children in the program (Sweet, 1974), and the threats to teacher job security (Stanley, 1974).

The next section will address itself in greater detail to possible applications for immersion education.

The immersion model for bilingual programs

It must be remembered that the immersion model is intended as an initial phase in what ultimately becomes bilingual schooling by United States Office of Education standards—i.e., a program in which two languages are used to teach one or more content subjects (therefore excluding language arts itself). Immersion programs usually fall into this category, then, around Grade 4 or 5, when a content subject is introduced in the native language of the students.

If total immersion is not appropriate for a given model, then perhaps the partial immersion approach might be. As stated earlier, in partial immersion students receive instruction for one half of their day entirely in the second language (see Barik & Swain, 1974).

Immersion education has been directed primarily at majority group children, particularly in Canada. Paulston (1975b) suggests that there are not adequate socio-structural incentives for United States parents to want their children to become bilingual. She feels that the success in Culver City can be attributed largely to the idealism and dedication of the parents. Tucker and d'Anglejan (1975) also see little incentive in the United States for the middle class to enroll their children in bilingual instruction. There is no doubt that the language policy at both the federal and provincial levels of Canadian government is helping to provide incentive for English-Canadian parents to enroll their children in French immersion programs (see Lambert, 1974, for example). In the United States, the majority group English speakers have not been the target group of federal and state bilingual programs, and this approach both has limited the majority group's participation[7] and has generated only a moderate concern for becoming fluent in a minority language. Perhaps as English-speaking parents begin to appreciate the benefits of having their children comfortably fluent in a minority language such as Spanish and likewise comfortable interacting with native Spanish speakers in that language, the number of United States immersion programs for the majority-language child may increase.

But what about immersion education as described earlier for the minority group child? It may not be possible to create a comfortable English immersion environment for the minority non-English speaker, nor may it be socially or politically feasible, given the prevailing educational climate, which favors vernacular language as the initial medium of instruction. For immersion to be successful in the case of the non-English-speaking minority student, it would be necessary to provide most or all of the positive factors lacking in what was earlier described as submersion education.

For the minority group child who has already learned English—perhaps as an L1—immersion education might be an appropriate model. For example, Spanish immersion education might be an appropriate model for English-speaking Chicanos, just as French immersion education might be an appropriate model for English-speaking Francophone minority groups. For those Chicanos with some or even substantial skills in Spanish already, but skills that have been passive or dormant, Noonan (1975) suggests that a concurrent approach[8] to bilingual schooling would be most appropriate.

[7] Either because of the ethnic composition of the school or because of the bilingual schooling model employed (e.g., one-way bilingual education), majority-group English speakers have been excluded from a number of programs.

[8] Sometimes referred to as "simultaneous translation," in the concurrent method the teacher uses both Spanish and English interchangably in the same lesson, alternating languages for words, sentences, or sections of the lesson. This approach is intended to remind the student of the Spanish at the same time that he is hearing the content in English.

It is important to note that total immersion for minority groups would have as the intended outcome functional literacy in both languages. What the total immersion model does is reverse the usual *order* in many bilingual education programs from L1 first/L2 second to L2 first/L1 second as far as the medium of instruction and the introduction of reading are concerned.

To date, there is little conclusive evidence that one order is inherently superior to any other (Engle, 1975; Paulston, 1975a; Cohen & Laosa, 1976, in press). Proponents of United States bilingual education may take issue with such a language reversal, but advocates of the English-first/ minority-language-second approach include experienced minority educators (see, for example, Valdés-Fallis, 1972). Ironically, many programs that have supposedly been providing primarily Spanish schooling in the early grades have actually been hurrying the introduction of English to the point where English reading is introduced simultaneously in English and the minority language anyway (in about 52% of the United States Federal Title VII projects started in 1969 and 1970; see Shore, 1974). Such an approach may be less effective than that of L2 reading first, provided there has been an adequate prereading period in L2 (Barik & Swain, 1974). Furthermore, some projects that indicate in their proposals that teachers use Spanish 80% of the time in kindergarten are in reality employing a model where the teacher uses *English* more than Spanish. Shultz (1975) found English used considerably more than Spanish in a bilingual classroom combining first and second grades. He described Spanish as a "marked" language in that classroom, as noted earlier with reference to the Waldman study in Culver City. Phillips (1975) studied the language-switching behavior of teachers in a bilingual project in California. During designated Spanish-medium lessons, teachers frequently switched to English, primarily for disciplinary–manipulative purposes. Phillips concluded that such behavior was inadvertently attributing more "importance" to communication in English.

Perhaps one of the more important side effects of immersion education is the double standard it points up: People applaud a majority group child when he can say a few words in the minority language (e.g., at the beginning of an immersion program) and yet they impatiently demand more English from the minority group child (e.g., going through conventional schooling). Undoubtedly, both groups merit praise for their accomplishments in L2. Furthermore, the immersion approach appears to have a beneficial message for staff involved with other models of ongoing bilingual education: "Be consistent." For example, the Culver City Spanish Immersion Program has had notable positive spin-off effects on bilingual programs in Southern California. After visiting or viewing videotapes of the immersion approach, teachers in Southern Californian bilingual programs have become more conscious about consistently using Spanish, rather than slipping into English. Some teachers have even abandoned the concurrent method in favor of split-day or alternate-day approaches so that they use only one language at a time.[9] They have also moved away from formal second-language lessons in the early grades in favor of the immersion approach.

These consequences are promising. If nothing else, perhaps the advent of successful immersion education will simply motivate bilingual teachers to reconsider their methodology for creating bilinguals. Undoubtedly, there is a long way to go in the design, execution, and evaluation of innovative language programs. But we are certainly beyond the point where bilingual education can be viewed as a simple entity. There are numerous approaches—of which the immersion model as characterized in this chapter is but one—which should all be given consideration before the selection of any particular one is made in a given context.

References

Allen, E. M. Foreign language below the ninth grade: What are we doing? *Modern Language Journal,* 1966, *50,* 101–104.

Andersson, T. *The teaching of foreign languages in the elementary school.* Boston: Heath, 1953.

Andersson, T. *Foreign languages in the elementary school: A struggle against mediocrity.* Austin, Tex.: University of Texas Press, 1969.

Andersson, T. Bilingual education and early childhood. *Hispania,* 1974, *57,* 77–78.

Angel, F. Three different conceptualizations of bilingual education, their implications and consequences: An exploration and a critique. Manuscript, 1975.

Barik, H. C., and Swain, M. English–French bilingual education in the early grades: The Elgin study. *Modern Language Journal,* 1974, *58,* 392–403.

Barik, H. C., and Swain, M. A Canadian experiment in bilingual education at the grade eight and nine levels: The Peel study. *Foreign Language Annals,* 1976, in press.

Barik, H. C., and Swain, M. Three-year evaluation of a large scale early grade French immersion program: The Ottawa study. *Language Learning,* 1975, *25,* 1–30.

Boyd, P. A. Second-language learning: The grammatical development of Anglo children learning through Spanish. Unpublished Master's thesis, University of California at Los Angeles, 1974.

Boyd, P. A. The development of grammar categories in Spanish by Anglo children learning a second language. *TESOL Quarterly,* 1975, *9,* 125–135.

Brown, R. *A first language.* Cambridge, Mass.: Harvard University Press, 1973.

Bruck, M., Lambert, W. E., and Tucker, G. R. Cognitive and attitudinal consequences of bilingual schooling: The St. Lambert project through grade six. *International Journal of Psycholinguistics,* in press.

Bruck, M., Lambert, W. E., and Tucker, G. R. Bilingual schooling through the ele-

[9] The teacher may stick to one language if an aide is available to use only the other language. For example, in the program in Rosemead, California, the kindergarten teacher, an Anglophone, used only Spanish for the entire year while the aide, a male Chicano, used only English (see footnote 5, p. 74).

mentary grades: The St. Lambert project at grade 7. *Language Learning*, 1974, *24*, 183–204.

Bruck, M., Lambert, W. E., and Tucker, G. R. Assessing functional bilingualism within a bilingual program: The St. Lambert project at grade eight. Unpublished manuscript, Psychology Department, McGill University, 1975.

Bruck, M., Tucker, G. R., and Jakimik, J. Are French immersion programs suitable for working class children? A follow-up investigation. Unpublished manuscript, Psychology Department, McGill University, 1973.

Carter, T. P. *Mexican Americans in school: A history of educational neglect.* New York: College Entrance Examination Board, 1970.

Cazden, C. B. *Child language and education.* New York: Holt, 1972.

Cohen, A. D. The Culver City Spanish immersion program: The first two years. *Modern Language Journal*, 1974, *58*, 95–103. (a)

Cohen, A. D. The Culver City Spanish immersion program: How does summer recess affect Spanish speaking ability? *Language Learning*, 1974, *24*, 55–68. (b)

Cohen, A. D. Error correction and the training of language teachers. *Modern Language Journal*, 1975, *59*, 414–422. (a)

Cohen, A. D. Forgetting a second language. *Language Learning*, 1975, *25*, 127–138. (b)

Cohen, A. D. Progress report on the Culver City Spanish immersion program: The third and fourth years. *Working Papers in Teaching English as a Second Language*, 1975, *9*, 47–65. (c)

Cohen, A. D. *A sociolinguistic approach to bilingual education: Experiments in the American Southwest.* Rowley, Mass.: Newbury House, 1975. (d)

Cohen, A. D. The acquisition of Spanish grammar through immersion: Some findings after four years. *Canadian Modern Language Review*, 1976, *33*, in press.

Cohen, A. D., and Lebach, S. M. A language experiment in California: Student, teacher, parent, and community reactions after three years. *Working Papers in Teaching English as a Second Language*, 1974, *8*, 33–46.

Cohen, A. D., and Laosa, L. M. Second language instruction: Some research considerations. *Journal of Curriculum Studies*, November 1976, in press.

Cohen, A. D., and Swain, M. Bilingual education: The "immersion" model in the North American context. *TESOL Quarterly*, 1976, *10*, 45–53.

Cohen, A. D., and Robbins, M. Toward assessing interlanguage performance: The relationship between selected errors, learners' characteristics, and learners' explanations. *Language Learning*, 1976, *26* (1), in press.

Dulay, H. C., and Burt, M. K. Errors and strategies in child second language acquisition. *TESOL Quarterly*, 1974, *8*, 129–136.

Engle, P. L. *The use of vernacular languages in education. Papers in Applied Linguistics, Bilingual Education Series: 3.* Arlington, Va.: Center for Applied Linguistics, 1975.

Ervin-Tripp, S. M. Is second language learning like the first? *TESOL Quarterly*, 1974, *8*, 111–127.

Genesee, F., Sheiner, E., Tucker, G. R., and Lambert, W. E. An experiment in trilingual education. *Canadian Modern Language Review*, in press.

Hamayan, E., Markman, B. R., Pelletier, S., and Tucker, G. R. Difference in performance in elicited imitation between French monolingual and English-speaking bilingual children. *Working Papers on Bilingualism*, 1975, *8*, 30–58.

Hansen-Bede, L. A child's creation of a second language. *Working Papers on Bilingualism*, 1975, *6*, 103–126.

Hatch, E., and Wagner-Gough, J. D. Second language acquisition. In M. Celce-Murcia and L. McIntosh (Eds.), *An introduction to the teaching of English as a second language* (2nd prepublication ed.). Los Angeles: University of California, 1975.

Hildebrand, J. F. T. French immersion pilot program in Fredericton. *Canadian Modern Language Review*, 1974, *31*, 181–191.

Jashni, V. M. The effects of the Spanish immersion program on the kindergarten–primary students in the affective and cognitive domains. Unpublished doctoral dissertation, Brigham Young University, Provo, Utah, 1975.

Krashen, S. D., and Seliger, H. W. The essential contributions of formal instruction in adult second language learning. *TESOL Quarterly*, 1975, *9*, 172–183.

Lambert, W. E. A Canadian experiment in the development of bilingual competence. *Canadian Modern Language Review*, 1974, *31*, 108–116.

Lambert, W. E., and Tucker, G. R. *Bilingual education of children: The St. Lambert experiment*. Rowley, Mass.: Newbury House, 1972.

Lambert, W. E., Tucker, G. R., and d'Anglejan, A. Cognitive and attitudinal consequences of bilingual schooling: The St. Lambert project through grade five. *Journal of Educational Psychology*, 1973, *65*, 141–159.

Lebach, S. M. A report on the Culver City Spanish immersion program in its third year: Its implications for language and subject matter acquisition, language use, and attitudes. Unpublished Master's thesis, University of California at Los Angeles, 1974.

Lenneberg, E. *Biological foundations of language*. New York: Wiley, 1967.

Noonan, K. The 'Chicano' and bilingual education—a matter of exclusion. Paper presented at the Fourth Annual International Bilingual Bicultural Education Conference, Chicago, Illinois, May 22–24, 1975.

Paulston, C. B. Ethnic relations and bilingual education: Accounting for contradictory data. *Working Papers on Bilingualism*, 1975, *6*, 1–44. (a)

Paulston, C. B. *Questions concerning bilingual education. Papers in Applied Linguistics, Bilingual Education Series: 1*. Arlington, Va.: Center for Applied Linguistics, 1975. (b)

Phillips, J. M. Code-switching in bilingual classrooms. Unpublished Master's thesis, California State University at Northridge, 1975.

Rosansky, E. J. The critical period for the acquisition of language: Some cognitive developmental considerations. *Working Papers on Bilingualism*, 1975, *6*, 92–102.

Rubin, J. What the 'good language learner' can teach us. *TESOL Quarterly*, 1975, *9*, 41–51.

Saville-Troike, M. *Bilingual children: A resource document. Papers in Applied Linguistics, Bilingual Education Series: 2*. Arlington, Va.: Center for Applied Linguistics, 1973.

Saville-Troike, M. TESOL today: The need for new directions. *TESOL Newsletter*, 1974, *8* (5–6), 1–2, 6.

Shore, M. S. *The content analysis of 125 Title VII bilingual programs funded in 1969 and 1970*. New York: Bilingual Education Applied Research Unit, Project BEST, New York City Bilingual Consortium, Hunter College Division, 1974.

Shultz, J. Language use in bilingual classrooms. Paper presented at the Ninth Annual TESOL Convention, Los Angeles, March 4–9, 1975.

Slobin, D. I. *Psycholinguistics*. Glenview, Ill.: Scott, Foresman, 1971.

Snow, C. E. Semantic primacy in first and second language acquisition. Unpublished manuscript, Institute for General Linguistics, University of Amsterdam, 1975.

Stanley, M. H. French immersion programs: The experience of the Protestant School Board of Greater Montreal. *Canadian Modern Language Review*, 1974, *31*, 152–160.

Stern, H. H. What can we learn from the good language learner? *Canadian Modern Language Review*, 1975, *31*, 304–317.

Stern, H. H., and Swain, M. Notes on language learning in bilingual kindergarten classes. In G. Rondeau (Ed.), *Some aspects of Canadian applied linguistics*. Montreal: Centre Educatif et Culturel Inc., 1973.

Swain, M. French immersion programs across Canada: Research findings. *Canadian Modern Language Review*, 1974, *31*, 116–129.

Swain, M. Changes in errors: Random or systematic. Paper presented at the Fourth International Congress of Applied Linguistics, Stuttgart, August, 1975. (a)

Swain, M. Writing skills of grade three French immersion pupils. *Working Papers on Bilingualism*, 1975, *7*, 1–38. (b)

Sweet, R. J. The pilot immersion program at Allenby Public School, Toronto. *Canadian Modern Language Review*, 1974, *31*, 161–168.

Tarone, E., Frauenfelder, U., and Selinker, L. Systematicity/variability and stability/instability in interlanguage systems: More data from Toronto French immersion. In H. D. Brown (Ed.), *Papers in Second Language Acquisition*. Ann Arbor, Mich.: Language Learning, 1976, 93–134.

Tucker, G. R., and d'Anglejan, A. New directions in second language teaching. In R. C. Troike and N. Modiano (Eds.), *The proceedings of the first inter-American conference on bilingual education*. Arlington, Va.: Center for Applied Linguistics, 1975.

United States Commission on Civil Rights. *The excluded student: Educational practices affecting Mexican Americans in the Southwest*. Mexican American Education Study, Report III. Washington, D.C.: U.S. Government Printing Office, 1972.

United States Commission on Civil Rights. *Teachers and students: Differences in teacher interaction with Mexican American and Anglo students*. Mexican American Education Study, Report V, Washington, D.C.: U.S. Government Printing Office, 1973.

Valdés-Fallis, G. Bilingual education: Early efforts supply cues to meeting current needs. *Accent on ACTFL*, 1972 (November), 28–30.

Wagner-Gough, J. D. Comparative studies in second language learning. Unpublished Master's thesis, University of California at Los Angeles, 1975.

Waldman, E. L. *Cross-ethnic attitudes of Anglo students in Spanish immersion, bilingual, and English schooling*. Unpublished Master's thesis, University of California at Los Angeles, 1975.

Bilingual Education for the English
Canadian: Recent Developments

MERRILL SWAIN AND HENRI C. BARIK,
The Ontario Institute for Studies in Education, Toronto, Canada

In the 1960s, the political rumblings of possible separation of Quebec from the rest of Canada, and the strong movement toward establishing French as the working language of Quebec, acted as stimuli to a group of English-speaking parents in St. Lambert (a suburb of Montreal) concerned about the possible fate of their children in Quebec if they were not skilled in the French language (Melikoff, 1972). Their children were being taught French as a second language for short daily periods using traditional methods. However, the results of the programs were disappointing; students did not graduate as fluent bilinguals. What was needed, they believed, was a radical change. Basing their arguments in part on theory and research that supported the introduction of bilingualism at an early age (e.g., Peal & Lambert, 1962; Penfield, 1964; Stern, 1963; experience of the Toronto French School established in 1962—see Giles, 1972), they proposed that their children be permitted to attend a kindergarten class in which instruction was provided entirely in French. They were convinced that if French was used as a medium of communication—as a means to an end rather than as an end in itself—second-language learning would be enhanced. The idea was radical and it took the parents a great deal of time to persuade their school board to try it out even on an experimental basis. But they finally succeeded, and in 1965, a kindergarten class attended only by English-speaking children and taught completely in French by a native French speaker was initiated. The following year, again after strong parental pressure was exercised on the school board, these same children entered a Grade 1 class that was also taught entirely in French by a native speaker of French. French reading and writing were introduced at this grade level. It was not until Grade 2, when a period of approximately 60 minutes a day was devoted to English language arts, that English reading and writing were introduced. With each successive year, greater proportions of the curriculum were taught in English, until approximately half the curriculum was taught in English and half in French.

The progress of the students in the St. Lambert program, as well as that of pupils who entered the program in its second year of existence, has been compared each year with that of English-speaking pupils following a conventional English language program as well as with that of French-speaking pupils following a conventional French language program. Very generally, the results of the evaluations of the St. Lambert study have shown that the students in the experimental program maintain their native English language skills at a par with their peers in the regular English program once English language arts are introduced. They also attain a high level of proficiency in French language skills, although they are not at par with corresponding French-speaking pupils. Furthermore, when tested in English on subject material taught to them in French (e.g., mathematics), the bilingually educated pupils do as well as their English-instructed peers. The students also develop a healthy attitude toward French speakers while maintaining positive attitudes toward their own language and culture (see Bruck, Lambert, & Tucker, 1974; Lambert & Macnamara, 1969; Lambert & Tucker, 1972; Lambert, Tucker, & d'Anglejan, 1973).

The Ottawa Study

An emphasis by the Canadian federal government on a policy of bilingualism and biculturalism in Canada, growing dissatisfaction with current traditional programs as a means of attaining these goals, and the effectiveness of the St. Lambert experiment led to the establishment of similar programs across Canada. With the growth of the programs—often referred to as "immersion" or "home–school language switch" programs —concern about the applicability of the St. Lambert findings to other settings has been expressed. Hence, the evaluation of a large-scale immersion program in another city in Canada (Ottawa) was undertaken and is described in detail below.[1] This study, which, generally speaking, replicates the St. Lambert results, responds to the question of the generalizability of the findings, at least for other middle-class populations.

The Ottawa Study involves a total French immersion program. The program, patterned after the one in St. Lambert, was started in Sep-

---

[1] This evaluation has been carried out by the Bilingual Education Project of the Ontario Institute for Studies in Education, which is concerned with a number of innovative programs in bilingual education in Ontario and presently focuses on four areas: total immersion in the early grades in a unilingual English environment (Barik & Swain, 1975a, 1976a), partial immersion in the early grades in a similar environment (Barik & Swain, 1974, 1976b), total immersion in the early grades in a bilingual environment (Ottawa study discussed here; see also Barik & Swain, 1975b), and partial immersion in the late grades in a unilingual environment (Barik & Swain, in press; Barik, Swain, & Gaudino, 1976).

tember 1970 at the kindergarten level in 10 classes from 8 schools under the jurisdiction of the Ottawa Board of Education and the Carleton Board of Education and involved approximately 220 pupils. In this program, classroom instruction is completely in French throughout the (half-day) kindergarten year and Grade 1. During kindergarten and at the start of Grade 1, the pupils are permitted to address the teacher in English (who, however, replies only in French), but they are increasingly encouraged to use French. By about the fourth month of the Grade 1 year, the teacher begins to insist on the use of French by the pupils either when addressing her or among themselves, and French becomes almost exclusively the language of communication in the classroom.

Reading and writing are thus initially taught in French. In Grade 2, instruction in English language arts is introduced, for one hour per day. This is also the case in Grade 3 (the grade level reached in 1973–1974 by the initial stream or cohort of students enrolled in the program, and considered below).

KINDERGARTEN (1970–1971 EVALUATION)

In the spring of 1971, the French immersion classes and appropriate comparison classes from the same or matched schools were administered a battery of tests, aimed at answering two basic questions asked by the school board authorities, and applicable at all grade levels of the program:

1. Does instruction of the prescribed curriculum through the medium of a second language (French) have any harmful effects on native-language (English) skills, on achievement in such basic academic skills as reading and arithmetic, or on the pupil's IQ and general cognitive development?

2. How beneficial is the French program with regard to proficiency in French when compared with the regular school program in which French is taught as a subject and all other instruction is in English?

In the regular kindergarten program at the time, the children received 15 to 20 minutes per day of instruction in French as a second language, and that amount (20 minutes) has been maintained throughout their schooling.

Test Battery

The pupils in both immersion and comparison groups were administered four tests[2]:

1. The *Otis–Lennon Mental Ability Test (Primary I Level)*, a pictorial intelligence or scholastic aptitude test that measures the pupil's facility

[2] A list of the tests employed in the Ottawa Study is to be found in the appendix to this chapter.

in reasoning and in dealing abstractly with verbal, symbolic, and figural materials and that samples a broad range of cognitive abilities.

2. The *Clymer–Barrett Prereading Battery*, a test of prereading skills. Only two sections were administered, one measuring skills in letter recognition (in English), the other discrimination of beginning sounds in (English) words.

3. The *IEA French Listening Test (Population I Level)*. This test achievement test for use in the latter part of kindergarten and beginning of Grade 1. Only parts of two sections were administered, one measuring the children's skills in listening for (English) sounds, the other involving numbers and arithmetic skills.

4. The *French Comprehension Test (1971 edition)*, a test of listening comprehension in French developed by the Bilingual Education Project, since none existed that could apply to the population under consideration. The test consists of pictorial items involving simple words, short phrases and sentences, which the child is to identify by circling the appropriate picture. To check on the conceptual difficulty of the items, an English translation of the test was administered to a random sample of the comparison classes. The instructions for the test are given in English but the items are in French.

TABLE 5.1.　OTTAWA STUDY: DATA FOR GRADES K–3

	Unadjusted $\overline{X}$		Level of significance (p)	
	Immersion group	Comparison group	Unadj. $\overline{X}$	Adj. $\overline{X}$[a]
Kindergarten				
Age (mos., end of year)	70.76	71.35	n.s.	—
Otis–Lennon Deviation IQ	108.68	106.88	n.s.	—
Clymer–Barrett Prereading				
a) Total (max. = 55)	39.04	40.63	n.s.	n.s.
b) Letter recognition (max. = 35)	24.91	26.82	n.s.	.05
c) Beginning sound discrimination (max. = 20)	14.13	13.80	n.s.	n.s.
Metropolitan Achievement Tests				
a) Word skills (max. = 28)	12.34	11.62	n.s.	n.s.
b) Numbers (max. = 20)	10.78	10.61	n.s.	n.s.
French Comprehension Test (1971 ed., max. = 96)	75.88	40.77	.001	.001
Grade 1				
Otis–Lennon Deviation IQ	109.17	107.62	n.s.	—
Metropolitan Achievement Tests (standard scores)[b]				
a) Word knowledge (22–65)	46.37	54.19	.001	.001

(continued)

TABLE 5.1. (continued)

	Unadjusted $\overline{X}$		Level of significance (p)	
	Immersion group	Comparison group	Unadj. $\overline{X}$	Adj. $\overline{X}^a$
b) Word discrimination (21–68)	47.59	55.02	.001	.001
c) Reading (20–70)	44.65	50.53	.001	.001
d) Arithmetic concepts and skills (18–68)	51.13	49.78	n.s.	n.s.
French Comprehension Test (1972 ed., max. = 91)	88.01	50.70	.001	.001
Test de Rendement en Français (max. = 30)				
a) Instructions in French	15.34	—	n.s.	n.s.
b) Instructions in English	15.00	—		
Test de Rendement en Mathématiques (max. = 33)				
a) Test in French	21.71	—	n.s.	n.s.
b) Test in English	23.34	21.94		
Grade 2				
Otis–Lennon Deviation IQ	113.72	111.82	n.s.	—
Metropolitan Achievement Tests (standard scores)[b]				
a) Word knowledge (18–71)	51.80	54.02	n.s.	n.s.
b) Word discrimination (18–66)	55.45	55.40	n.s.	n.s.
c) Reading (18–68)	50.48	52.09	n.s.	n.s.
d) Spelling (28–67)	51.40	54.27	n.s.	n.s.
e) Arithmetic, total (18–74)	51.94	51.11	n.s.	n.s.
i) Concepts and problem solving (15–71)	48.44	49.56	n.s.	n.s.
ii) Computation (23–71)	57.88	53.54	.05	n.s.
Test de Rendement en Français (max. = 30)				
a) Instructions in French	14.04	—	n.s.	n.s.
b) Instructions in English	16.87	—		
Test de Rendement en Mathématiques (max. = 32)				
a) Test in French	24.45	—	n.s.	n.s.
b) Test in English	26.73	24.52		
IEA French Listening Test, Pop. I (max. = 35)	32.70	—	—	—
French Comprehension Test (1973 ed., max. = 65)				
a) Kindergarten level	—	33.15	—	—
b) Grade 1 level	—	22.14	—	—

(continued)

TABLE 5.1. (continued)

	Unadjusted $\overline{X}$		Level of signifi-cance (p)	
	Immersion group	Comparison group	Unadj. $\overline{X}$	Adj. $\overline{X}^a$
Grade 3				
Otis–Lennon Deviation IQ	116.30	113.14	n.s.	—
Metropolitan Achievement Tests (standard scores)[b]				
a) Word knowledge (17–116)	71.14	70.58	n.s.	n.s.
b) Reading (11–118)	70.26	69.04	n.s.	n.s.
c) Total reading (a + b) (3–127)	70.37	69.16	n.s.	n.s.
d) Spelling (39–94)	68.33	70.50	n.s.	.05
e) Language (34–136)	75.50	72.26	n.s.	n.s.
f) Maths. computation (27–106)	70.33	68.66	n.s.	n.s.
g) Maths. concepts (27–106)	74.41	72.86	n.s.	n.s.
h) Maths. problem solving (24–106)	76.72	77.24	n.s.	.05
i) Total maths. (f–h) (9–119)	77.97	77.93	n.s.	n.s.
French Comprehension Test (1974 ed.)				
a) Kindergarten level (max. = 62)	—	31.13	—	—
b) Grade 1 level (max. = 65)	—	24.79	—	—
Test de Rendement en Français (max. = 30)	18.17	—	—	—
Test de Lecture (max. = 28)	20.27	—	—	—
IEA French Listening Test, Pop. II (max. = 40)	29.20	—	—	—

[a] Adjusted for age and IQ.
[b] range of standard score scale for each section is given in parentheses.

Results

The data are shown in Table 5.1. On the basis of analysis of variance, there was no significant difference between the French immersion and comparison (regular English kindergarten) pupils in age or IQ, two factors that can have a bearing on performance in other areas of achievement, and whose effect is systematically taken into consideration through analysis of covariance techniques in the examination of other variables.

There was also no reliable difference between the two groups on the English prereading test. However, the comparison group scored significantly higher ($p < .05$) than the immersion group in the letter recognition section of the test when scores were adjusted for age and IQ.

This result is not surprising, since the immersion pupils have been taught the alphabet in French.

The findings show that the two groups performed similarly on the word skills and number skills sections of the *Metropolitan Achievement Tests,* indicating in the latter case that numerical concepts had been acquired as extensively by immersion pupils via French as by regular pupils via English, and that these concepts could be employed by them in one language context or the other.

On the *French Comprehension Test,* as might well be expected, the French immersion pupils scored significantly higher ($p < .001$) than pupils in the regular program receiving 15 to 20 minutes of French as a second language. Since the test proved to be very adequate conceptually (pupils administered the English translation obtained a near-perfect score), the score on the test can be taken as a measure of proficiency in French comprehension independent of conceptual difficulty.

Thus, at the end of kindergarten, pupils in the immersion program were ahead of their peers in the regular program in French comprehension skills and showed the same level of cognitive development, as measured through IQ tests. The only lag they exhibited was with respect to English prereading skills (letter recognition).

GRADE 1 (1971–1972 EVALUATION)

In the spring of 1972, two groups from the same cohort of students were again tested to determine how pupils in the immersion program stood in relation to pupils enrolled in the regular English program at the end of Grade 1.

Test battery

The following tests were administered at the end of the school year:

1. The *Otis–Lennon Mental Ability Test (Elementary I Level),* the appropriate form for Grade 1 of the intelligence test given in kindergarten.

2. The *Metropolitan Achievement Tests (Primary I Battery).* This test is concerned with reading and arithmetic skills taught in Grade 1. It consists of four sections: *word knowledge,* a test of the child's word recognition ability in English; *word discrimination,* a test of auditory and visual discrimination; *reading,* a test of ability to read silently and comprehend sentences and paragraphs in English; and *arithmetic concepts and skills,* a test of mastery of basic numerical and quantitative concepts, ability to solve verbal problems, and to add and subtract.

3. The *French Comprehension Test (1972 edition),* a revised version of the test administered in kindergarten, which also included new types

of items requiring the pupil to show his understanding of instructions and questions, and of simple short shories in French. Once again, some comparison classes were given an English translation of the test to check on the conceptual adequacy of the items.

4. The *Test de Rendement en Français (Grade 1)*, a test of achievement in French developed for native French-speaking Grade 1 pupils in Montreal by the Commission des Ecoles Catholiques de Montréal and involving the identification of phonetic sounds, word definitions, spelling, vocabulary, and sentence comprehension in French. The test was administered to pupils in the French immersion program only, in order to obtain some measure of comparison with native French speakers. Half the group took the test completely in French while, for the other half, the test instructions read by the examiner were in English and the test items were in French. This division was made in order to determine the degree of difficulty associated with the items themselves independently of the added difficulty introduced by having the directions given in French.

5. The *Test de Rendement en Mathématiques (Grade 1)*, the corresponding test of achievement in mathematics employed with native French-speaking Grade 1 pupils in Montreal. The test was given completely in French to one half of the immersion group while an English translation was given to the remaining immersion pupils and to a sample of regular program pupils.

Results

The data for Grade 1 are shown in Table 5.1. There was again no difference between the two groups with respect to IQ (or, obviously, age). The end of Grade 1 IQ scores, it may be noted, are very similar to those obtained at the end of Kindergarten.

On the *Metropolitan Achievement Tests*, the immersion group scored significantly lower ($p < .001$) than the comparison group on the sections involving word knowledge, word discrimination, and reading in English. This result is to be expected since immersion pupils do not receive any formal instruction in English reading skills in Grade 1. Their scores on the three sections still fall in the 35th to 45th percentile range on the basis of American norms, which result suggests that there is some transfer of reading skills acquired in French to English.[3] (The regular Grade 1 pupils, in comparison, scored from the 60th percentile on the reading section to the 70th to 75th percentile on the word knowledge and word discrimination sections.) There was no significant differ-

---

[3] It is possible that some informal instruction in English reading occurs at home in the case of some pupils enrolled in immersion classes, although such instruction is discouraged by the schools.

ence between the two groups on the arithmetic section of the test. Thus, in Grade 1, immersion pupils continued to acquire mathematical concepts as well via French as pupils in the regular program do via English and could apply them in one language context or the other.

On the *French Comprehension Test*, the immersion pupils again score significantly higher ($p < .001$) than pupils in the regular program receiving 20 minutes of daily instruction in French as a second language. That the test, devised for kindergarten, was too easy for Grade 1 immersion is reflected in the near-perfect score of 88 out of 91. Grade 1 pupils administered an English translation of the test to check on the conceptual adequacy of the items obtained an even higher score; thus the test did not present any difficulties conceptually.

On the *Test de Rendement en Français*, there was no significant difference between the two conditions of administering the test completely in French or with the test instructions in English and the test items in French. Thus performance on the test is not hampered by having the instructions given in French. On the basis of norms for the test, pupils taking the test completely in French scored better than approximately 30% of French-speaking Grade 1 pupils for whom the test was developed; however, they benefited from a 2½ month delay in the administration of the test relative to French pupils.

The results on the *Test de Rendement en Mathématiques* reveal no significant differences among the three groups—immersion pupils given the test in French, immersion pupils given the test in English, and comparison pupils given the test in English. In terms of norms for the test, French immersion pupils taking the test in French score better than approximately 50% of native French-speaking Grade 1 pupils. However, the 2½ month delay in administration again applies to this comparison.

GRADE 2 (1972–1973 EVALUATION)

Test battery

The following tests were administered to the two groups at the end of Grade 2:

1. The *Otis–Lennon Mental Ability Test (Elementary I Level)*, the same test that was administered in Grade 1 and that applies to Grades 1 through 3.

2. The *Metropolitan Achievement Tests (Primary II Battery)*, the appropriate level of the achievement test employed in Grade 1. In addition to the sections corresponding to those of the Grade 1 test, it also has a section on *spelling* in which items are presented orally in a brief context. The *arithmetic* section, moreover, consists of two parts, one on *concepts and problem solving* and one on *computation*.

3. The *IEA French Listening Test (Population I Level)*. This test served as the test of French comprehension for immersion classes only. The test was designed by the International Association for the Evaluation of Educational Achievement (IEA) and is characteristically intended for 10-year-old students currently studying French who have had 1 or 2 years of minimal exposure to French vocabulary and grammatical structure (see Carroll, 1975). The items involve the pictorial identification of short sentences in French.

4. The *French Comprehension Test (Kindergarten and Grade I Levels, 1973 edition)*. Two new forms of this test were developed, one intended primarily for use in kindergarten and the other primarily for use in Grade 1. The test was used as the measure of French comprehension for the comparison group. Half the comparison classes were given the kindergarten level and the other half the Grade 1 level. Their performance could be compared with that of kindergarten and Grade 1 pupils from subsequent cohorts administered the same tests. English equivalent versions of the two forms to check on conceptual adequacy were administered to pupils from the appropriate grade levels.

5. The *Test de Rendement en Français (Grade 2)*, the test of achievement in French employed with French-speaking Grade 2 pupils in Montreal. As with Grade 1, the test was given to immersion classes only, half the classes being administered the test completely in French and the other half the test with instructions in English and test items in French.

6. The *Test de Rendement en Mathématiques (Grade 2)*, the mathematics achievement test for native French speakers. Once again, the test was given completely in French to half the immersion classes, while the remaining immersion classes and some comparison classes were administered an English translation of the test.

Results

The results for Grade 2 are found in Table 5.1. There continued to be no reliable difference between the two groups in IQ when measured at the end of Grade 2, suggesting that the French immersion program as such is having neither a detrimental nor a beneficial effect on the students' mental and cognitive abilities.

The notable findings in the comparison of the two groups occur with respect to performance on the *Metropolitan Achievement Tests*. It is seen that by the end of Grade 2 there was no longer any reliable difference between immersion pupils and pupils in the regular English program on any of the tasks involving English language skills: word knowledge, word discrimination, reading, and spelling, though in the latter instance the difference in favor of the comparison group was very close to statistical significance ($p = .06$) when scores were adjusted for age and IQ.

Thus, after only one year of formal instruction in English language arts for 60 minutes per day, pupils in the French immersion program were performing equivalently to their peers in the English curriculum.[4] On the arithmetic section of the test, there was likewise no reliable difference between the two groups on total score or on the concepts and problem-solving subtest. The immersion group scored significantly higher ($p < .05$) than the comparison group on the computation subtest, though this difference is no longer significant when scores are adjusted for age and IQ. Thus, Grade 2 immersion pupils continued to demonstrate the same level of competence in mathematics as their peers in the regular program and were able to transfer the knowledge acquired via French to an English context.

With respect to performance in French, the immersion and comparison groups cannot be compared directly, since they were administered different tests. The Population I level of the *IEA French Listening Test* proved to be much too easy for the Grade 2 immersion pupils, who obtained an average of 32.7 out of 35. This result is not surprising since the pupils had had much more exposure to French than is demanded by the test. As for the comparison group, the scores they obtained on the "Kindergarten" and "Grade 1" levels of the *French Comprehension Test* were considerably lower than the scores obtained by French immersion pupils of the grade levels for which the tests were intended. Thus, after 3 years of daily periods of second-language instruction in French, pupils in the regular program still did not do as well in French comprehension as children enrolled in a half-day French immersion kindergarten.

On the *Test de Rendement en Français* and *Test de Rendement en Mathématiques*, as in Grade 1, there were again no reliable differences among the various test administration conditions. Comparisons with norms for French-speaking Grade 2 pupils are not appropriate since the Grade 2 tests were administered to native speakers during the frst half of Grade 2 but were given to the immersion and comparison groups toward the end of the year.

GRADE 3 (1973–1974 EVALUATION)

Test battery

The test battery administered in Grade 3 was equivalent to that employed in Grade 2, using appropriate levels of the tests in question. (The

---

[4] It should be stated, however, that the results obtained the following year with a second cohort of students on a different version of the test were not quite as positive (Swain & Barik, 1975). On the basis of unadjusted scores, the only significant difference found, in favor of the comparison group, was on spelling. However, when scores were adjusted for age and IQ, the regular program group scored significantly higher than the immersion group on all English language skills sections except one.

Metropolitan Achievement Tests battery contains an additional English language skills section on *language* involving punctuation, capitalization, and language usage; and there are three mathematics sections—computation, concepts, and problem solving). The French mathematics test was not given, however, and the French achievement test was administered only in French. As for French listening comprehension, a more advanced level of the IEA test (Population II) was employed on an experimental basis with a few immersion classes. That test is intended characteristically for 14-year-old students currently studying French who have had 2 or 3 years of standard French instruction. Thus, the test is not particularly appropriate conceptually for Grade 3 pupils. Items at this level have both pictorial and written answer choices, so that the ability to read French is required. Pupils in the comparison group were given updated (1974) versions of the *French Comprehension Test* ("Kindergarten" and "Grade 1" levels). In addition, immersion pupils were administered a French reading test (*Test de Lecture*) developed by the Bilingual Education Project on the basis of the reading objectives of the French immersion program and consisting of a number of reading passages followed by multiple-choice questions based on their content.[5]

Results

As seen from Table 5.1, the IQ results at the end of Grade 3 agreed with those of previous years, showing no reliable difference between the two groups. There is thus no indication that pupils in the immersion program were negatively affected in their cognitive development during the course of Grade 3.

In English language skills also, as measured by the *Metropolitan Achievement Tests,* no reliable differences were noted between the two groups on any section on the basis of either unadjusted or adjusted scores with the exception of spelling, in which the comparison group still scored significantly higher ($p < .05$) when scores were adjusted for age and IQ. These findings parallel those in Grade 2. On the mathematics sections of the test, there were again no reliable differences between the two groups with respect to either total score or the computation and concepts sections. On the problem-solving section, however, the comparison group scored significantly higher ($p < .05$) than the immersion group on the basis of adjusted scores. In the Grade 3 test, the

---

[5] A sample of pupils from both groups were also asked to write two short stories in English. In addition, the French immersion program pupils in that sample were required to write two short stories in French. The analysis of the writing skills (vocabulary skills, grammatical skills, creativity, and technical skills such as punctuation) are discussed in a separate paper (Swain, 1975a).

problem-solving section consists entirely of written problems that the pupil must read to himself. It thus seems that immersion pupils, who in their formal English reading did not normally encounter mathematical material, were at a slight disadvantage relative to pupils in the regular program on this section of the test.

With respect to French performance, Grade 3 immersion pupils obtained a score of 29.2 out of 40 on the *IEA French Listening Test*. There are no norms relevant for Grade 3 pupils with which to compare this level of performance, which, however, seems quite adequate in view of the fact that the format and content of the test are designed for considerably older pupils. Regular program pupils again scored lower on either level of the *French Comprehension Test* than immersion pupils of lower grades from subsequent cohorts tested at the same time.

On the French reading test, immersion pupils obtained a score of 20.3 out of 28, which, as estimated by consultants to the French immersion program, constitutes a satisfactory level of reading comprehension in French. As for the French achievement test, French immersion pupils obtained a score higher than that of approximately 30% of native French-speaking Grade 3 pupils, but that comparison is again biased in favor of the immersion group, which benefited from a 4-month delay in the administration of the test relative to native French-speakers.

The results of the evaluation of the Ottawa French immersion program from kindergarten through Grade 3 are thus encouraging. They may be summarized as follows:

1. At all grade levels considered, pupils in the immersion program remained on a par with their peers in the regular English program with respect to IQ. The French immersion experience thus did not have a differential effect (either beneficial or harmful) on the cognitive development of the children, relative to regular schooling.

2. Pupils in the immersion program lagged behind their counterparts in the regular program in English language skills involving reading in English up to Grade 1, because of the lack of formal instruction in English language arts. However, once such instruction was introduced into their curriculum in Grade 2 for limited daily periods, they caught up to their regular program peers in all English language skills, with the possible exception of spelling. This equivalence was maintained through Grades 2 (but see Footnote 4) and 3.

3. In mathematical skills, French immersion pupils taught mathematics in French throughout the program exhibited the same level of achievement as pupils taught in English, and showed a capacity for applying concepts learned in one language to another language context. In Grade 3, however, there is some indication that pupils in the French immersion program may have had more difficulty with written mathe-

matical problems in English than pupils in the regular program. This result could be caused by the fact that mathematical material was not normally encountered in their formal English reading.

4. With respect to listening comprehension in French, pupils in the immersion program were much ahead of their peers in the regular program who were receiving short daily periods of instruction in French as a second language. They also performed satisfactorily in other aspects of French language skills, though not on a par with native French speakers.

Other studies and issues

The findings reported here are in large measure equally applicable to the groups of children who enrolled in the immersion program in Ottawa in subsequent years (see Barik & Swain, 1975b; Swain & Barik, 1975), as well as to pupils enrolled in a similar program in a unilingual English setting (Barik & Swain, 1975a; Barik & Swain, 1976a), and correspond closely to those reported by other teams of investigators (e.g., Cameron, Feider, & Gray, 1974; Edwards & Casserly, 1973; Lambert & Tucker, 1972). These programs, it should be noted, have involved largely children from middle-class backgrounds.[6]

The effectiveness of French immersion classes for children from lower socioeconomic levels has been investigated by Bruck, Tucker, and Jakimik (1973) and Tucker, Lambert, and d'Anglejan (1973). They administered a battery of tests to working-class French immersion Grade 1 and 2 students in Montreal and to comparable groups of native English-speaking students an native French-speaking students. The tests were designed to measure native- and second-language development, achievement in mathematics, and overall cognitive development. The investigators concluded that the pattern of results with respect to English language skills conforms to that found for middle-class groups in the St. Lambert study; that the experimental working-class groups are able to use their native language as effectively for oral communication as are their comparison groups; that they are acquiring a sound passive knowledge of French in terms of vocabulary, reading, grammar and comprehension although they are not at par with native French-speaking children; that they learn mathematics as well through French as their English-educated comparison groups; and that they are not being cognitively harmed by their participation in the program. In summary, they suggest "that this educational program is as appropriate for work-

---

[6] Similar programs have also been started in the United States (e.g., Cohen, 1974).

ing class children as it has been found to be for middle class children, and that it is providing the children with the French skills so necessary for education and occupational success in Quebec at no apparent cost to their general cognitive and linguistic development" (Bruck, Tucker, & Jakimik, 1973, p. 43).

Other questions of a more psychological nature have been raised. For example, does participation in an immersion program affect the incidence of learning disabilities? Further, should children with learning disabilities or below-average IQ be permitted to enter a French immersion program? Does participation in the program affect social maturity?

Edwards and Casserly (1973) obtained measures of behavior considered to be closely associated with dyslexia or learning disabilities and social maturity. The findings suggested that exposure during the first several years of elementary school to a French immersion program did not result in a measurable increase in the incidence of learning disabilities. Ratings of social maturity at the Grade 2 level yielded significant differences in favor of the immersion group.

Bruck, Rabinovitch, and Oates (1975) reported on a study they have begun of English-speaking children with diagnosed language difficulties who are enrolled in French immersion kindergarten and Grade 1 classes. They are comparing the progress of these children with children who also have diagnosed language difficulties but who are enrolled in the regular English program; with children who are normal in their language development and are enrolled in the French immersion program; and with children who are normal in their language development and who are enrolled in the regular English program. Their progress is assessed in native-language development, cognitive development, school achievement, and second-language skills.

The children were identified as having language-learning disabilities according to their performance on a screening test battery that consisted of an object-manipulation test, a story-retelling test, a sentence-imitation test, and an echolalia test.

The results are based on a small number of students and must therefore be viewed as preliminary and tentative in nature. However, the general trend is worth noting: The children with language-learning disabilities enrolled in a French immersion class do not fall differentially behind their counterparts enrolled in the English program. In those instances where they do not score as high as their counterparts in the English program, neither do the children with normal language development in the French immersion program relative to their counterparts in the English program.

Swain (1975b) examined the correlations between IQ and achievement measures in English, French, and mathematics of kindergarten, Grade 1, and Grade 2 students. She concluded that:

> the correlational analyses of the IQ and achievement data do not support the notion that IQ plays a more significant role in the immersion program than in the regular English program. Furthermore, learning to understand a second language is of all the skills measured, the least dependent on IQ [p. 15].

In the Protestant School Board of Greater Montreal (PSBGM), where primary French immersion programs had been operating successfully, it was considered unfortunate that senior-level students had missed the opportunity to develop bilingual skills. The result was the initiation, in 1969, of a new type of immersion program—one that started at the Grade 7 level. Students entering the Grade 7 immersion program have had at least 1 year of daily instruction in French as a second language. During the immersion year, most of all of the curriculum is taught in French. As a follow-up to this year, students have the option of taking certain subjects in French; for example, history or geography. In the 1973–1974 academic year, over 30% of the Grade 7 English-speaking students in the PSBGM enrolled in the Grade 7 French immersion program.

The initial 2 years of operation of the Grade 7 immersion program in Montreal were marked by stringent admission standards, especially with respect to the IQ level of the pupils. However, in the third year of the program (1971–1972), these standards were relaxed. The results of the evaluation of the 1971–1972 Grade 7 immersion group (PSBGM, 1973) are discussed here because they provide information on the overall effects of the late immersion course at various ability levels.

Two sections of the *Stanford Achievement Test*, paragraph meaning and language usage, were given to the Grade 7 immersion students and to Grade 7 students in the regular English program to measure achievement in English. The results showed that although performance on both sections was related to IQ, at each IQ level (high 116–130, medium 96–115, low 80–95), students in the immersion program obtained scores equivalent to those of students in the regular English Grade 7 program (PSBGM, 1973).

The evaluation of the Grade 7 immersion students also included a written test of French achievement for native French-speaking Grade 7 pupils (from the *Test de Rendement en Français* battery) and a test of French listening comprehension and speaking. The students' responses in the speaking test were rated according to their grammatical correctness, enunciation, rhythm and intonation, vocabulary, and fluency.

Generally speaking, the results revealed that the Grade 7 immersion students, although not on a par with the Grade 7 native French-speaking students, showed significant gains over the year. In relation to their French speaking skills, they scored highest in the areas of enunciation, rhythm, and intonation, and lowest in the area of grammatical correctness, although all ratings placed them above average on the rating scales. Results on the French achievement test placed the Grade 7 immersion students in the bottom quartile of the norms for native French speakers. Neither IQ nor the sex of the student affected the rate and level of achievement on oral skills. On the other hand, there was a striking and consistent relationship between IQ and performance on the written test of French achievement (PSBGM, 1973).

Partially because of the effectiveness of the Grade 7 immersion program, the concept of a "late" immersion program began to be considered by other school boards. The Peel County Board of Education, for example, started a French immersion program (70% French, 30% English) at the Grade 8 level in Brampton, Ontario, in 1971. Students entering the program in the initial year were a select group: They were of above-average IQ, performed well in French and other academic subjects, expressed a desire to enter the immersion program, and had their parents' permission and encouragement to choose the French immersion option.

The Peel County French immersion program has also been evaluated yearly since its inception (Barik & Swain, in press; Barik, Swain, & Gaudino, 1976). The comparison group was likewise a select group, the students being chosen from several Grade 8 English program classes on the basis of IQ and general academic performance, to match the students in the immersion program.

The last evaluation of the Peel program (Barik, Swain, & Gaudino, 1976) reveals that by the end of Grade 10, students in the bilingual program (40% French, 60% English in Grades 9 and 10) continued to show a level of achievement in French much superior to that of their comparison group. They also performed equivalently in French to students 2 or 3 years ahead of them in the regular program who were considered by their French teachers to be the "best" students in French (taught to them as a subject for short daily periods since Grade 7). The two groups showed the same level of academic achievement in English, mathematics, and science, and each group performed satisfactorily in history and geography, the two subjects (other than French) taught in French to students in the bilingual program.

The advent of immersion programs starting at the later grade levels raises a set of new questions relating to the "optimal" age for second-language learning in the school setting. What differences in ability in the second language exist after a year of total immersion at the Grade 1 level versus at the Grade 8 level? This question seems deceptively simple. One might compare, for example, the effect of a year of early immersion with that of a year of late immersion on such characteristics as pronunciation, rhythm and intonation, enunciation, fluency, and grammatical correctness. However, there are problems inherent in other sorts of comparisons. For example, in the area of vocabulary knowledge, primary and secondary students are being exposed to vocabulary relevant to their respective studies and concerns, which to a large extent do not overlap. In the area of reading, early immersion students are faced with learning to read *and* learning French, whereas late immersion students already know how to read. Is it realistic under such divergent situations to make comparisons of reading ability or vocabulary knowledge in the second language? Even in the area of grammatical development, can we reasonably expect early immersion students to perform as well as late immersion students when the early immersion students may not yet make certain grammatical distinctions in their native language?

Assuming that the two programs lead to differential results with respect to second-language competence, then numerous other questions are raised. Do children and adolescents process and learn a second language in the same way? Dulay and Burt (1973) argue that they do. Rosansky (1975) argues that they do not—the onset of the formal operations stage affects the learner. But other things change, too—for example, the nature of the motivation to learn the second language (Macnamara, 1975), and the nature and extent of peer group pressure. How do these factors affect second-language competence?

Another set of questions is raised concerning the effects on cognitive and social development of early bilingualism versus bilingualism acquired as an adolescent or adult. For example, it has been suggested that early bilingualism may lead to an increase in divergent thinking skills or an increase in cognitive flexibility (Peal & Lambert, 1962; Balkan, 1970), and to an acceleration of cognitive development (Ianco-Worrall, 1972; Liedtke & Nelson, 1968). Are these advantages observed also in individuals acquiring a second language during their adolescent or adult years? Does learning a language early in life tend to increase the use of that language as an adult? Is the early bilingual necessarily more "comfortable" using the second language than the adult learner? Research addressed to these issues is essential.

In the meantime, the demand for French immersion programs is increasing in Canada. But the search for other viable alternatives to the attainment of English–French bilingual skills is continuing. For example, a large grant from the Canadian Federal Government to the four boards of education in the National Capital Region (Ottawa) has made possible not only the expansion of French immersion programs at the primary level, but the possibility of experimenting with other options such as a bilingual high school, an expansion of the traditional 20 minutes a day of French as a second-language program to an enriched 40, 60, or 90 minutes a day program, and the teaching at various grade levels of one subject in French in addition to the traditional French class. All these alternatives are being evaluated by a team of researchers. Preliminary findings, summarized in Stern et al. (1976), have already contributed to our understanding and appreciation of alternate forms of bilingual education within the Canadian context. Future trends in bilingual education for the English Canadian will depend in some measure on these research findings. However, the importance of the continuation of a political climate favorable to a policy of bilingualism cannot be underestimated.

Appendix: List of tests employed in Ottawa Study

Clymer–Barrett Prereading Battery, Form A. Princeton, N.J.: Personnel Press, Inc., 1967.

French Comprehension Test, (Kindergarten Level, Grade 1 Level) Toronto: Bilingual Education Project, The Ontario Institute for Studies in Education, 1971, 1972, 1973, 1974.

IEA French Listening Test (Population I & II Levels). In *French as a Foreign Language, Phase II, Stage 3.* Stockholm: International Association for the Evaluation of Educational Achievement, 1970.

Metropolitan Achievement Tests (Primer, Form F, 1970; Primary I, Form A, 1958; Primary II, Form A, 1958; Elementary, Form F, 1970). New York: Harcourt Brace Jovanovich, Inc.

Otis–Lennon Mental Ability Test (Primary I, Form J; Elementary I, Forms J and K). New York: Harcourt, Brace & World, Inc., 1967.

Test de Lecture (Grade 3). Toronto: Bilingual Education Project, The Ontario Institute for Studies in Education, 1974.

Test de Rendement en Français (Grade 1, 1971–1972 edition; Grade 2, 1972–1973 edition; Grade 3, 1973–1974 edition). Montreal: La Commission des Ecoles Catholiques de Montréal.

Test de Rendement en Mathématiques (Grade 1, 1971–1972 edition; Grade 2, 1972–1973 edition). Montreal: La Commission des Ecoles Catholiques de Montréal.

References

Balkan, L. *Les effets du bilinguisme Français–Anglais sur les aptitudes intellectuelles.* Brussels: AIMAV, 1970.

Barik, H. C., and Swain, M. English–French bilingual education in the early grades: The Elgin study. *The Modern Language Journal*, 1974, 58, 392–403.

Barik, H. C., and Swain, M. Early grade French immersion classes in a unilingual

English–Canadian setting: The Toronto study. *Scientia Paedagogica Experimentalis*, 1975, *12*, 153–177. (a)

Barik, H. C., and Swain, M. Three-year evaluation of a large scale early grade French immersion program: The Ottawa study. *Language Learning*, 1975, *25*, 1–30. (b)

Barik, H. C., and Swain, M. Primary-grade French immersion in a unilingual English–Canadian setting: The Toronto study through grade 2. *Canadian Journal of Education*, 1976, *1*, 39–58. (a)

Barik, H. C., and Swain, M. English–French bilingual education in the early grades: The Elgin study through grade four. *The Modern Language Journal*, 1976, *60*, 3–17. (b)

Barik, H. C., and Swain, M. A Canadian experiment in bilingual education at the grade eight and nine levels: The Peel study. *Foreign Language Annals* (in press).

Barik, H. C., Swain, M., and Gaudino, V. A. A Canadian experiment in bilingual schooling in the senior grades: The Peel study through grade ten. *International Review of Applied Psychology*, 1976 (in press).

Bruck, M., Lambert, W. E., and Tucker, G. R. Bilingual schooling through the elementary grades: The St. Lambert project at grade seven. *Language Learning*, 1974, *24*, 183–204.

Bruck, M., Rabinovitch, M. S., and Oates, M. The effects of French immersion programs on children with language disabilities—A preliminary report. *Working Papers on Bilingualism* (Ontario Institute for Studies in Education), 1975, *5*, 47–86.

Bruck, M., Tucker, G. R., and Jakimik, J. *Are French immersion programs suitable for working class children? A follow-up investigation.* Montreal: McGill University, 1973. Mimeo.

Cameron, A., Feider, H., and Gray, V. *Pilot evaluation of French immersion grade 1 in Fredericton, N.B., spring 1974: Interim report.* Fredericton: University of New Brunswick, 1974. Mimeo.

Carroll, J. B. *French as a foreign language in eight countries.* New York: Wiley, 1975.

Cohen, A. D. The Culver City Spanish immersion program: The first two years. *The Modern Language Journal*, 1974, *58*, 95–103.

Dulay, H. C., and Burt, M. K. Goofing: An indicator of children's second language learning strategies. *Language Learning*, 1973, *22*, 235–252.

Edwards, H. P., and Casserly, M. C. *Evaluation of second language programs in the English schools: Annual report 1972–73.* Ottawa: The Ottawa Roman Catholic Separate School Board, 1973.

Giles, W. H. The Toronto French school, In M. Swain (Ed.), *Bilingual schooling: Some experiences in Canada and the United States.* Toronto: Ontario Institute for Studies in Education, 1972.

Ianco-Worrall, A. D. Bilingualism and cognitive development. *Child Development*, 1972, *43*, 1390–1400.

Lambert, W. E., and Macnamara, J. Some cognitive consequences of following a first-grade curriculum in a second language. *Journal of Educational Psychology*, 1969, *60*, 86–96.

Lambert, W. E., and Tucker, G. R. *Bilingual education of children: The St. Lambert experiment.* Rowley, Mass.: Newbury House, 1972.

Lambert, W. E., Tucker, G. R., and d'Anglejan, A. Cognitive and attitudinal consequences of bilingual schooling: The St. Lambert project through grade five. *Journal of Educational Psychology*, 1973, *65*, 141–159.

Liedtke, W. W., and Nelson, D. Concept formation and bilingualism. *Alberta Journal of Educational Research*, 1968, *14*, 225–232.

Macnamara, J. Comparison between first and second language learning. *Working Papers on Bilingualism* (Ontario Institute for Studies in Education) 1975, *7*, 71–95.

Melikoff, O. Parents as change agents in education: The St. Lambert experiment. Appendix A in W. E. Lambert and G. R. Tucker, *Bilingual education of children: The St. Lambert experiment*. Rowley, Mass.: Newbury House, 1972.

Peal, E., and Lambert, W. E. The relation of bilingualism to intelligence. *Psychological Monographs*, 1962, *76*, No. 27 (Whole No. 546).

Penfield, W. The uncommitted cortex: The child's changing brain. *Atlantic Monthly*, 1964, *214*, 77–81.

Protestant School Board of Greater Montreal. *Report on the evaluation of the grade seven French immersion programme, 1971–72*. Montreal: Authors, Student Personnel Services and Curriculum Departments, 1973. Mimeo.

Rosansky, E. J. The critical period for the acquisition of language: Some cognitive developmental considerations. *Working Papers on Bilingualism* (Ontario Institute for Studies in Education), 1975, *6*, 92–102.

Stern, H. H. *Foreign languages in primary education: The teaching of foreign or second languages to younger children*. Hamburg: UNESCO Institute for Education, 1963.

Stern, H. H., Swain, M., McLean, L. D., Friedman, R. J., Harley, B., and Lapkin, S. *Three approaches to teaching French: Evaluation and overview of studies related to the federally funded extensions of the second language learning (French) programs in the Carleton–Ottawa school boards*. Toronto: Ministry of Education, 1976.

Swain, M. Writing skills of grade three French immersion pupils. *Working Papers on Bilingualism* (Ontario Institute for Studies in Education), 1975, *7*, 1–38. (a)

Swain, M. More about primary French immersion classes. *Orbit*, 1975, *6*, 13–15. (b)

Swain, M., and Barik, H. C. *A large scale study of French immersion: The Ottawa study through grade three*. Toronto: Ontario Institute for Studies in Education, 1975. Mimeo.

Tucker, G. R., Lambert, W. E., and d'Anglejan, A. French immersion programs: A pilot investigation. *Language Sciences*, 1973, *25*, 19–26.

6

Attending a Primary School of the Other Language in Montreal

JOHN MACNAMARA, JOYCE SVARC, AND SHARON HORNER,[1]
McGill University

In a city like Montreal, where two major languages coexist and where most people, at least to some extent, need to know both, which language should parents choose for the education of their children? Should they stay on what seems to be the secure path and send children to a school in which the language is that of their own home? But then the children may never become fluent in the second language and never be at ease with the people who speak it. Or should parents dare more and send them to schools that teach in the second language and where they will meet children who speak it? But then what about their school work? Will they suffer because they do not quite master the new language? Will their ability to read and write their mother tongue be underdeveloped? What is it like for a child to go to a school where he knows not a word of the language that the teacher and the majority of his companions speak? Will the teacher welcome him and help him along, or will the teacher resent his presence as a hinderance to the work of the class? How long will it be before he can take part with some ease in the work of the class? Will the other children welcome him? Or will they pick on him and call him names? If they pick on him, will they do so for long? Will he huddle together with any other children who speak his language? Or will he make friends with the other linguistic group? Are there both certain types of children who can manage all the confusion, academically and socially and certain ones who have special difficulty, such as the less intelligent, or the shy, or the handicapped? These are reasonable questions that any parent of a 5-year-old might ask. The present study was conducted to provide answers.

The problems we are investigating are familiar to all immigrant families in a region where the language is not their own. Countless Italian, Polish, Spanish, and Swedish immigrants to the United States have faced them. Often they scarcely can have asked themselves the

[1] John Macnamara received a grant for this study from The Canada Council, and Sharon Horner received a Postdoctoral Fellowship from the Quebec government.

questions we ask, because there was no choice and no purpose in asking. Others established ethnic schools to safeguard the language and religion of the children. Even when, as often happened, the schools became English, they still provided shelter from the large, and perhaps strange world of the English speakers. In some respects, such schools resemble those Montreal schools for the English-speaking Protestant population that in recent years have taught their English-speaking pupils mainly in French. French is the language of about 82% of the Quebec population. In this chapter, we shall not be directly concerned with such schools, but only with schools that take children from a linguistic group other than that of the school. We studied children from French-speaking homes who had been placed in English schools and children from English-speaking homes who had been placed in French schools.

Our approach was a direct one. We selected five English and four French Montreal primary schools in which children from the other linguistic group were to be found. Of these children, we interviewed a number at each grade level; we also interviewed teachers at each level. We asked questions about how the other-language children settled into the school; how well they spoke the new language; whether their native tongue suffered; how their studies went in general; who they made friends with; and whether they were welcome in the school. We asked each child for the names of the three students he liked best; with their answers we studied the degree of integration among the linguistic groups. We tested the sixth-grade children in English and French with standardized tests. We had hoped to administer arithmetic tests, too, but we found such variations in arithmetic programs that we eventually dropped the idea. It seemed much more difficult to find an arithmetic test than language ones that would be fair to all groups of children.

Strangely, the psychological literature has almost nothing to say about the problems of social and personal development with which we shall be involved. The psychological literature has confined itself to academic attainment. The work that appeared before the middle of the 1960s was reviewed in Macnamara (1966). At that time, there was general, but not quite universal, agreement from scores of studies that children whose home language differed from that of the school obtained lower scores than monolingual children on all manner of written and oral language tests, spelling excepted. It is important to note just what that agreement is about, and this can best be illuminated by means of an example. In the southwestern states of the United States, there are homes where Spanish is the main language. Frequently the children of such homes attended English schools and their knowledge of English came from English classes and their English-speaking companions. Such Spanish-background children were compared with English-background ones, in the knowledge of English. The English-background children were found to be better—for a good example, see Carrow (1957).

Since the middle 1960s, several reports of bilingual schooling have appeared that seem, but only at first glance, to contradict these conclusions. These reports come from the "immersion" programs that have become particularly popular among English-speaking Canadians. These are specially instituted bilingual programs mainly for English-speaking children who are taught, in whole or in part, through the medium of (to them) a new language.

In French immersion programs, for example, two findings have been heavily emphasized. Provided that there have been lessons on English reading, English children do not in such circumstances sacrifice command of English, spoken or written, to their knowledge of the new language. Their knowledge of the new language, though inferior to that of native speakers, is superior to that of students who have merely followed normal language classes in the language. For a well-known example, see Lambert and Tucker (1972), and for overviews of the literature, see Swain (1974) and Paulston (1975).

There has been a change of emphasis mainly because the newer research has been carried on from the viewpoint of English speakers. What is new is the finding that the English-speaking children do not seem to lose out in English reading skills by being taught mainly in another language. This aspect of research on bilingual education was largely ignored in the early research. Since Italian immigrants to the United States, for example, were seen as replacing Italian with English, little heed was paid to their Italian. The new finding is important, and suggests that, apart from developing some low-level skills in reading, schools do little to improve one's ability to read effectively. That ability appears to grow as one's mind develops and as one's general reading and conversation expands.

However, there is strong agreement between the early and new research that children whose school language differs from their home language do not, by the end of primary school (or secondary, though secondary education does not concern us directly), equal native speakers of the new language. The good news that they are better than students in normal language classes seems to have obscured the now very general finding that they do not equal native speakers. The new research provides very little indication of the size of the difference. Here, the older research is more informative.

The setting of the schools

Montreal is a large, cosmopolitan city, frequently described as, after Paris, the largest French-speaking city in the world. As always, the truth is more complicated. Montreal is about two-thirds French-speaking; it contains large groups of Italian, Greek, Spanish, and Portugese speakers;

about a quarter of its inhabitants are English-speaking. Together with these figures, one must bear in mind that, on the one hand, the Province of Quebec as a whole is about 82% French-speaking. On the other hand, French is the native language of only just over a quarter of the Canadian population. And in North America as a whole, French is the language of only a small minority. It is inevitable that, even in Quebec, French speakers are uneasy about the future of their language, while English speakers are not uneasy about theirs. Yet many English speakers in Quebec are also uneasy about language and want to see that their children learn French, a desire that is supported by the fact that French is one of the great languages of European civilization. On the reasons why some Quebec parents chose an other-language school for their children, see Frasure-Smith, Lambert, and Taylor (1975).

Besides the linguistic division of the Montreal population, the religious division is of marked importance. Education at the local level is run by school commissions that are based on religious affiliation. Administratively, there are two religions: Catholic and Protestant, all non-Catholics being treated as Protestant. Each householder pays taxes to one of the school commissions, which payment entitles his or her children to "free" education in a school of that commission. The Protestant commissions' schools are almost exclusively English, whereas the Catholic commissions run English as well as French schools. Although the majority of Montreal's Catholic commissions' schools are French, there is a sizeable number of Catholic English schools. Indeed, Montreal has almost as many Catholic as Protestant English-speaking children. The importance of this fact, from our point of view, is that up to 1976 (when new legislation has changed things) Catholic parents could, without much difficulty, choose either a French or an English school, and a number of parents exercized that right. Our study is based on the children of the parents who did so choose: the French-speaking parents who chose English schools and the English-speaking parents who chose French schools.

Apart from some pilot studies, our work was conducted in nine primary schools: five English and four French ones. Six of the schools could be described as middle class, one as upper middle (a French one), and two (English ones) as working class. Matters were complicated by the fact that in some schools almost all the students spoke either French or English as their native tongues, whereas in one English school 25% and in another 43% spoke some other language (mostly Italian) as theirs. The schools varied in size from about 200 to about 1000. In each school, there were both boys and girls. The ratio of English speakers to French speakers varied within English schools from about 7 to 1 to about 2 to 1; in the French schools, it varied from about 1 to 3 to about 4 to 3. Since the classifications *French* or *English* are a little vague, our figures are approximate. They are based on the children's answers to a language background questionnaire. One other variation is important. In one school, a French one, the English speakers were placed in separate classes from the French ones in Grades 1 and 2, thereafter the two groups were gradually mixed. This procedure, one would predict, would have an important effect on social groupings. In our analysis of the data, we will endeavor to determine which, if any, of these factors have had an effect.

Data gathering

The data for the English schools were gathered in spring and early summer of 1974; those for the French schools were gathered in the second semester of 1975. The study developed as we progressed, so the work of one year does not exactly duplicate the previous year. Nevertheless, we were careful to maintain comparability in essentials. The work of 1975 differs from that of 1974 mainly by being more comprehensive.

The data on social and personal development come from three main sources: interviews with teachers, interviews with children, and questionnaires completed by children. In each school at each of the six grade levels and, where appropriate, at the kindergarten level, one teacher was interviewed and posed a fixed set of questions. The questions were mainly those with which we opened this report. The teacher was chosen by the school principal as being experienced in relevant ways. All teachers so chosen agreed to be interviewed: 33 English teachers and 24 French ones. Interviews were recorded and subsequently analysed. In the English schools, about three French-speaking children at each grade level were interviewed in French. In the French schools, about five French-speaking children at each grade level were interviewed in French and five English-speaking ones in English. The children were chosen at random, unless they happened to be the only representatives of their type, and they were all posed the same set of questions. The questions were mainly about social relations between the French-speaking and English-speaking children and about the way the teachers treated the two groups. As far as possible, equal numbers of boys and girls were interviewed. Finally, in English schools the sixth-grade children and in French schools the fourth-, fifth-, and sixth-grade children of at least one class answered questions about the language(s) they spoke before coming to school, the languages they now spoke, and the grade level at which they came to English school. In addition, each child was asked to pick out the three children in his class whom he liked best. The purpose of this was to determine the degree to which the two major linguistic groups were integrated.

The sixth-grade children in the English schools had all been tested by the school authorities with the *Gates–MacGinitie Reading Test of English*, and we employed the raw scores they were thus assigned for vocabulary and comprehension. We obtained such scores for all the children of one sixth-grade class in each school. To each raw score we assigned a standardized score from the test manual. We administered the test ourselves to the English-speaking children in one sixth-grade class in each French school, and assigned to each a standardized score. To the French-speaking children in the English classes and to all the children in the French classes that we had selected we administered a test of French reading that had been standardized in 1965 for the Province of Quebec: *Test de Lecture Silencieuse* by M.-J. Joly. This test yielded, for each child, percentile scores for speed and comprehension.

For the purposes of analysis, we divided the children in each of the selected classes into three groups: children whose mother tongue was clearly French, children whose mother tongue was clearly English, and children whose mother tongue was some other language or who did not fall readily in one of the other two groups. We will refer to the first group as the French children, to the second as the English children, basing the name on language rather than on nationality. We will not be further concerned with the third group. The division was made on the basis of the children's responses to the language-background questionnaire. The numbers of English and French sixth-grade children are set out in Table 6.1.

TABLE 6.1. NUMBER OF FRENCH AND ENGLISH CHILDREN WHO COMPLETED THE LANGUAGE BACKGROUND QUESTIONNAIRE IN EACH SCHOOL[a]

	Children		
	French	English	Others
Immaculata (E)	7	38	18
St. Malachy (E)	2	34	26
St. Joseph's (E)	5	28	13
Edward Murphy (E)	5	5	16
St. Aloysius (E)	12	4	15
St-Antonin (F)	62	21	15
Nôtre Dame de Grâce (F)	52	24	14
Ste-Catherine (F)	70	62	38
Town of Mt. Royal School (F)	187	54	50

[a] E in parentheses after school name signifies English, F signifies French. The numbers in English schools are for Grade 6; those in French schools are for all the children in Grades 4, 5, and 6.

Learning the other language

By "other language," we mean English for French children in English schools and French for English children in French ones. Presumably the main concern of the parents on whose children we are concentrating was knowledge of the other language, so we discuss the other language first. We shall base ourselves mainly on teachers' judgments and then on the test results; the teachers' judgments are more comprehensive, covering all grades and all language skills. We will not give all the numerical details but content ourselves with the main trends and with particularly insightful remarks.

How well do the children speak the other language? Here a practical difference between the French and English schools forces itself on our attention. In the English schools, French children began English schooling at different levels, some beginning in kindergarten or Grade 1, others as late as Grade 5 or 6. For reasons we do not understand, this variability was not true of the English children in French schools. The number of late starters there was negligible. This difference was reflected in teachers' responses. The English teachers all spontaneously contrasted late starters with early ones, whereas only half of the French teachers did. The French teachers, who had had little experience of this variability, did not think it an important factor, whereas all the English teachers did. The latter were unanimous that the child who arrived in English school after Grade 2 rarely mastered English and was usually disrupted in his studies.

Most English teachers claimed that after 4 years in English school, beginning at Grade 1, most French children spoke English without an accent. French teachers were in broad agreement with this, although more reserved. All teachers agreed that, by Grade 6, all children had acquired a good knowledge of the other language, but that there were always some children who for some unknown reason did not quite master the accent. In the St. Lambert immersion experiment (see Lambert & Tucker, 1972) where the teachers, but not the children, were French, French accent was not nearly so impressive. None of the St. Lambert children in Grade 6 would be mistaken for a native speaker of French, and there was some informal evidence that French accent did not improve much beyond Grade 1. Perhaps the important lesson is that the main teachers of accent are other children; in the schools of our study, there were children whose native language was the other tongue, whereas in the St. Lambert school, there were not. Peer pressure to conform in accent is surely a very powerful influence on children.

We may now ask how long it takes children to acquire sufficient knowledge of the other language to take part in the class work. Almost all the 57 teachers agreed that children who enter Grade 1 in September flounder until Christmas. However, most English teachers and some French ones felt that by Christmas the period of floundering was over. We might remark here that, in all questions related to learning the other language, French teachers were less sanguine than English ones. Can we conclude that English children take longer than French ones to learn the other language and that fewer English children master the accent? It may be that attiudes toward correct speech among French teachers are more exacting than among English ones. But it may be, too, that English children are indeed more resistant to the other language than French children, or less anxious to acquire it. The disregard for French among Montreal's English speakers used to be proverbial, and perhaps the same forces are still at work surreptitiously. Be that as it may, some French teachers were of the opinion that many English children require 2 years in school before they can manage the class work reasonably well. They said that if the parents spoke some French to the children, or if the children had any contact with French children outside school, progress was very much quicker.

Perhaps the main factors that determine whether one can pass as a native speaker of another language are prosody and intonation. We can be reasonably sure that many of the children we studied mastered these aspects and also the phonology of the other language. Beyond these factors, however, lie syntax and vocabulary. A person, by sticking to simple vocabulary and syntax, might with correct phonology and intonation give the impression of being better at a language than he really is. We questioned teachers about this possibility. The responses were quite impressive. All but a few of the 57 teachers felt that almost all the other-language children were weak at levels deeper than accent. On this point, responses did not tend to vary with grade level. The weaknesses singled out were partly in grammar, but mainly in vocabulary. They showed up particularly in writing, but to some extent in reading.

The standardized test results of sixth-grade students bear out the teachers' judgments. Our basic design was analysis of variance. We shall begin with the French scores for reading speed and comprehension, which are set out in Table 6.2. Mean times for reading speed differ significantly: $F(2,171) = 16.3$, $p < .01$. Posttests show that each mean differs significantly from each of the other two. Mean times for comprehension also differ significantly: $F(1,171) = 8.26$, $p < .01$. The posttests showed that the mean obtained by French children in French school differs significantly from each of the other two, but that the other two do not differ significantly from each other.

The findings suggest that in French reading the English children manage as well or better than French children in English schools, but not nearly so well as French children in French schools. We also looked at

6. Attending a primary school of the other language in Montreal

TABLE 6.2. RESULTS OF FRENCH READING TEST BY LINGUISTIC GROUP AND SCHOOL TYPE

	French school		English school
	French	English	French
Speed	65.7	50.3	35.8
Comprehension	72.0	58.9	50.8

the data for French schools by school (four of them) and linguistic group. This review yielded no significant interaction and no significant effect associated with schools in speed or comprehension. However, it yielded highly significant effects for speed and comprehension associated with language group: $F(1,3) = 84.9$, $p < .01$ for speed, and $F(1,3) = 36.9$, $p < .01$ for comprehension. This finding means that the English children in the French schools were surpassed by the French children there by roughly equal amounts in each school.

We turn now to the results of the English test, which are set out in Table 6.3. Here the pattern is relatively clear. One-way analysis of variance of the data in Table 6.3 shows that English children, whether in English or French school, were superior to French children in English schools. For vocablary: $F(2,139) = 33.4$, $p < .01$; for comprehension: $F(2,139) = 46.1$, $p < .01$. On each measure, the posttests showed no significant differences between the two groups of English children, but the French children fell significantly below each of the English groups. We also carried out a school-by-linguistic-group analysis of variance of the data from the English schools. Neither the effect of schools nor the interaction of schools and linguistic group was significant, but the effect of linguistic group was. This finding means that in vocabulary and comprehension the English outstripped the French by about the same amount in each school.

The reader will recall that English teachers made a sharp distinction between French students who began English school early, in kindergarten or Grade 1, and those who began it late, say, in Grade 5 or 6. When we separate the English score of these children, we obtain the

TABLE 6.3. RESULTS OF ENGLISH TEST BY LINQUISTIC GROUP AND SCHOOL TYPE

	English school		French school
	French	English	English
Vocabulary	41.2	53.6	54.9
Comprehension	39.1	51.2	53.7

TABLE 6.4. MEAN ENGLISH SCORES FOR FRENCH CHILDREN BY LEVEL OF ENTRANCE TO ENGLISH SCHOOL

	K or Grade 1	Grade 5 or 6
Vocabulary	48.6	34.2
Comprehension	47.0	34.7
Numbers	21	19

means of Table 6.4. In fact, we found a significant correlation between these children's English scores and their attendance at English school— $r = .86$ for vocabulary and $r = .62$ for comprehension. The longer they had been at English school, the better their marks. The figures of Table 6.4 show that a major factor is length of time in English school—not an unexpected result. The French children who had spent 5 or 6 years in English school were very much better in English than the overall French figures would suggest. Nevertheless, on each test, they fell significantly behind the English children in English schools: for vocabulary $t(68) = 2.36$, $p < .05$ and for comprehension $t(68) = 2.83$, $p < .05$.

To sum up, our findings support the teachers' judgments. Children from the other language group do not catch up with native speakers in ability to read the school language. Though they may learn to communicate very well in it, weaknesses can be discovered. In interpreting Tables 6.2 and 6.3 it is necessary to bear in mind that each component of the English test is standardized to a mean of 50 and a standard deviation of 10. On the other hand, the components of the French tests are in percentiles, which likewise implies a mean of 50, but which implies a standard deviation more than twice as large as that of the English subtests. Note that the mean differences in English between linguistic groups in English school are about 12, and the mean differences in French between linguistic groups in French schools are about 14. In one sense, the differences in English are about twice as large as those in French. However, not too much should be made of this point because there is no evidence that the two language tests use a comparable, let alone similar, metric.

The native language

Although we describe schools as French or English, each type gave classes in the other language. In all of our English schools, French classes began in Grade 1. Such classes are basically foreign language ones intended for non-native speakers. In French schools, the linguistic groups were separated for English class, which in one school began in Grade 3 and in the others in Grade 5. We inquired about our children's competence in their native language. Naturally, parents would be anxious to know if by attending a school of the other language their children's competence in their native language might suffer.

Practically all teachers who felt competent to express an opinion felt that children from the other linguistic group would not lose anything in ability to speak their native language by attending a school of a different language. Teachers felt that in their family and home circles the children had plenty of scope to practice and learn conversational skills. A few teachers (only 5 out of 46) felt that a child's ability to read and write his native tongue would not be adequately developed in such a school.

We have just seen that the sixth-grade test results in English bear out the majority opinion. The English in French schools, if anything, score slightly, though not significantly, higher in English than the English in English schools. It is perhaps worth noting that the class we tested in one French school was the "enriched" class, i.e., a class of specially selected bright students. If we lay aside the English students of this class, the means for English in English school and English in French school are almost exactly equal. Interestingly, there is no evidence in our data that beginning English class in Grade 3 rather than Grade 5 made any difference to the Grade 6 scores. These findings are in basic agreement with those of the immersion studies. Swain (1974) cites a great deal of evidence showing that very little instruction in reading the native language is needed to bring children in immersion programs up to the level of children in schools that work in the child's native language. The conclusion from our studies, too, is that school seems to contribute little to reading one's native language apart from some basic mechanical skills.

However, the test data for French children in English schools are not so unproblematic. We examined the correlation between years of attendance at an English school and scores on the French test. Neither French measure yielded a significant coefficient: for comprehension, $r = -.04$, and t is less than 1; for speed, $r = -.06$, and t is less than 1. There is no need, then, to examine subdivisions of this French group. This finding is in keeping with the findings just cited. Children who came late to English school had come from French schools, so that years in English school is inversely related to years in French school. We find that number of years in English school, and by implication, number of years in French school, is not related to these children's French reading skills. In other words, skill in reading one's native language is not related to the number of years instruction in reading that language.

How do we reconcile this finding with the finding that French children in French schools obtained higher French scores than French children in English schools? In order to explore this question further, we made some separate analyses of the data, this time taking account of school language and of school differences. Only the data for native speakers of French were included. In order to make the number of schools equal, we dropped one English school. It was a working-class school and was the one that had the largest number of children whose native tongue was neither English nor French.

The results for speed and comprehension are equivalent. In neither is language of school associated with a significant effect. School differences are significant, but this result is to be expected in any study such as ours. The important outcome is that we have no evidence from these analyses that attending English rather than French school had detrimental effects on a French child's ability to read French. Thus, by dropping one school with a very large number of immigrant children, we find that the difference previously found between French in English and French in French schools disappears. This result is support (though not fully convincing, because of having to drop one school) for the general finding that schooling in the other language does not detrimentally affect ability to read the native language—at least at the primary school level.

Other subjects

What about subjects other than English and French? Teachers were generally encouraging, and a slight majority felt that children from the other-language group tend to keep up with native speakers of the school language. However, a large minority believed that other-language children experience some difficulty. The general view was that if a child has difficulties they come from reading requirements for a subject rather than from oral presentations. Thus, many teachers singled out as difficult social studies, which demand a lot of reading, as problem subjects. Others mentioned mathematical problems, rather than computations, because problems are presented as written paragraphs. The teachers are supported by the empirical work on arithmetic surveyed in Macnamara (1966). However, the immersion program literature suggests no such deficit—see Swain (1974).

We did not go deeply into the matter and it must be remembered that most teachers felt that the other-language children had no special difficulties in subjects other than English and French. We do not wish to stress unduly minority views that in any event relate to minor, not major, difficulties.

Social development

What are the social effects of attending a school where initially one does not know the language? On this matter we have the opinions of the 57 teachers—about 9 at each grade level. And we have the opinions of

344 children whom we interviewed individually. In the English schools, we interviewed 2 or 3 French children at each grade level in each school, 87 children in all. In each of the French schools, we interviewed about 5 English children and 5 French ones at each grade level, 134 English and 124 French children in all. Often we interviewed all the other-language children in a class. When there were more than the number we wanted, we chose at random. In the French schools, the French children were chosen at random for interview.

Were the other-language children frightened at first about going to a school where they did not know the language; frightened, that is, precisely because they did not know the language? About a quarter of the children answered yes and the others answered no or "only a bit". Most of the children, then, did not recall it as a particularly frightening experience. Those who admitted fear mentioned, sensibly, that they were afraid that they would not understand the teacher and would not be able to do the work. Some mentioned fear of being alone and left out by the other children.

Were children from the other-language group welcomed by teachers and by the rest of the children? Virtually all the teachers and all the children, English and French, said that the teachers welcomed the other-language children and liked them. The children had nothing to fear on that score. However, five teachers and a handful of children noted that other-language children made the teacher's load heavier. Interestingly, in view of the public clamor that has attended the appearance of provincial legislation regulating the admission of other-language children into schools, only two teachers said that they had had comments from parents about the presence of other-language children in the school. At the neighborhood level, there was no evidence of dissatisfaction with admission policies and practices.

On the question of whether the other-language children were welcomed by the rest of the children there was less unanimity. A strong majority of children in all categories said that the other-language children were liked, but the number in each category who said that they were not was not negligible. English children were less likely to be welcome in a French school than French children in an English one. This pattern was supported by other evidence. The reasons given by certain children for why the English were not liked by the French in French school were mainly lists of differences between the groups and the aggression of one group toward the other. However, the English were accused, and accused themselves in effect, of forming cliques and of being arrogant and refusing to speak French. There was also some awareness among the children of adult disputes related to language legislation in Quebec.

When we look at the behavior of the linguistic groups to each other, we see more of the negative tendencies just noted. In the English and

French schools, most other-language children said that they had no problems with the rest of the children. However, about 20% said that the rest of the children picked on them when they first came to school. We asked the French children in French schools if the English had been picked on at first, and surprisingly about half said yes. "Picking on" was mostly calling names and mocking of the English for mistakes in French, but in many cases, if we are to believe the reports, it went as far as physical fights. All groups agreed that "picking on" tended to disappear with time, in some cases after a matter of a month or so. Some children observed that the teacher had taken a hand in suppressing it. A small number of children from both groups in French schools said that the aggression continued much longer and in a few instances actually increased.

The teachers in both types of school were almost unanimous that there was no deep-rooted antagonism between the linguistic groups and that other-language children had no lasting social problems. Our own impression is that the teachers are right; although we are well aware that a class feels very differently from a desk and from the rostrum. Nevertheless, we received enough indications of animosity to advise vigilance on the part of the teachers lest matters should worsen, particularly in the French schools, and lest any individual child should be damaged. But we saw no cause for alarm. There is always a certain amount of aggression between school children and if it is between members of the different linguistic groups, it will, no doubt, be often attributed unfairly to the language differences.

A word on the differing reports on what was supposedly the same behavior by the two groups in French schools. English children were asked "Were you picked on by the French children?" whereas French children were asked "Were the English children picked on?" Conceivably, if all French children had seen even one French child "pick on" one English child, all English children except one could truthfully answer no, and all French ones, yes. Responses were not really comparable. We also received an impression that another factor was at work. The English children may have wished to repress the idea that they had been maltreated by the French, simply because honor would not admit the possibility. On the other hand, a reciprocal honor code may have led the French to boast of superiority exhibited by domineering behavior. But whatever the interpretation, the phenomenon does not appear grave.

This general interpretation is strengthened by the other-language children's responses to the question of whether they would recommend that other children of their linguistic group should go to their school. They almost all said yes. They would scarcely have answered so if school had been made a bad experience for them because of language. The majority of French children, too, would advise other English children to go to French school, but about 20% said they would not advise it. We also asked the French in French schools if they would like to see the number of English children increased to half the class. Only a few said yes. Of the remainder, about one-third said it would make no difference and two-thirds thought it would be bad. This result we take as a sign of ambivalence toward the English.

Sociograms

The other method we employed to look at social processes was the sociogram. The basic idea is familiar, but we employed a slightly complicated method of quantifying the data, so we will begin by explaining our method. In the English schools, each child in the sixth-grade classes with which we worked was asked to write down the names of the three students he liked best. In the French schools, all the children in Grades 4, 5, and 6 were asked to do so. From each child we took only those choices that were either of an English or a French child, as we have defined such children. We omitted choices of immigrants or of children whose linguistic background did not admit of a clear categorization. In this way, we were able to examine whether English children tended to choose English and French children to choose French.

The data were first quantified by attributing a value of −1 to the choice of an English child and 1 to the choice of a French one. If a child chose less than three from the English and French groups, his score was weighted to make it comparable with three such choices. So far, we had not taken account of group size. If there were only one English child in a class, he would have been forced to choose all French children, and his choice would not be equivalent to that of a child who chose three French children when there were ten English ones to choose from. We therefore weighted scores a second time, to what, on the evidence available, they would have been if the numbers of French and English children were equal. We thus hope to have obtained measures that are comparable from school to school and from linguistic group to linguistic group.

With the data thus obtained, we carried out two analyses of variance. The first was of data in French schools in which alone we had scores for three grades. The analysis was by grade, linguistic group of chooser, and school. Grade was not associated with any significant F-value. The interaction of school and linguistic group was significant: $F(3,505) = 9.06$, $p < .01$. We then tested the "simple effect" of linguistic group and found that, in each school, it was highly significant. The means can be seen in Table 6.5. In each school, the effect is in the same direction, but

TALBE 6.5. WEIGHTED MEANS FOR SOCIOGRAM DATA
IN FRENCH SCHOOLS: NUMBER OF CHOSERS IN
PARENTHESES

Schools	Language of chooser	
	English	French
1	− 2.64 (24)	.89 (52)
2	− 1.64 (21)	.46 (62)
3	− 1.51 (62)	1.03 (70)
4	− 4.10 (54)	1.21 (187)

since the interaction was significant, we can conclude that the differences are not equal. The meaning of all this is that there is some degree of segregation between English and French in all our French schools, but in some it is more marked than in others. There is a reasonable explanation for this last finding. In the first three schools as listed in Table 6.5, the English and French children had been in class together since Grade 1. In the fourth school, the groups had been in separate classes in Grades 1 and 2; they were together for mathematics only in Grade 3; in the higher grades, they were much more together but were separate for English lessons. It seems, not unnaturally, that this pattern of grouping had an effect on friendships and made the linguistic segregation more marked. Before commenting on these results, we will look at the second analysis.

We submitted the data for sixth grade in eight schools to analysis of variance: language of school × school × language of chooser. The English school we omitted was the one with the most children who could not be categorized as English or French. The only interaction that was significant was that for language of school and language of chooser: $F(1,6) = 9.28$, $p < .05$. The relevant means are in Table 6.6.

An analysis of the simple effects showed no significant difference between linguistic groups in English school: $t(302) = 1.30$, $p > .05$. There was a significant difference between linguistic groups in the French schools: $t(302) = 13.63$, $p < .01$. The second finding merely

TABLE 6.6. WEIGHTED MEANS FOR SOCIOGRAM DATA IN EN-
GLISH AND FRENCH SCHOOLS: NUMBER OF SIXTH-GRADE
CHOOSERS IN PARENTHESES

Language of school	Language of chooser	
	English	French
English	− .76 (104)	− .11 (26)
French	− 2.27 (44)	.93 (134)

repeats that of the first analysis. The second analysis shows that English and French schools differ in the degree to which the two linguistic groups are integrated. In the English schools, there is no evidence of separation, whereas in French schools there is. Notice that these results are independent of the size of the school or the proportion of other-language children in the school. The results are not, as we saw in the first analysis, independent of whether the school separates the French and English children.

When we stand back from these results, we see that they confirm the remarks of the children whom we interviewed. French children in English school seemed, by their own reports, better integrated than English children in French ones. How deep-rooted, though, is the separation in the French schools? We must not confuse the significance of a statistical result with the importance of the social phenomenon that we are examining. Moreover, a sociogram is an index of friendliness, not of enmity. Our overall impression is that, in French schools, there is a tendency for the linguistic groups to stay apart, and there is some antagonism, perhaps more potential than actual, between them. There is also a good deal of friendliness across groups that our concentration on differences must not obscure. The de facto maximum and minimum scores on sociogram data are about $+9$ and -9. This gives us some idea how to evaluate the means of Tables 6.5 and 6.6. In fact, many children chose at least one child from the other linguistic group. Thus it would really be more just to speak of "segregation" rather than "cleavage" in the French schools.

Are there special cases?

Are there certain types of children whom it would be wise not to send to a school of the other language? This question was put to teachers. There was strong agreement that it was a bad plan to try to solve a child's academic or personal problems by changing him from a school of his own language to a school of the other language. Most teachers felt that the change was likely to aggravate his difficulties. Several teachers thought that an other-language school was not advisable for children who were dull and backward.

Apart from such comments, English teachers had little to say in response to the question. Two of them mentioned that if a French child was particularly shy, English school was not a good idea. One teacher said the same of children who lack confidence.

The French teachers had much more to say, and in the light of all we have seen, most of it can be considered here with profit. Several said that French school was a bad idea if one parent of an English child, and particularly if the child himself, was strongly opposed to French. They said that it was a great help if English parents sometimes tried to talk French to the child. A few said that some children were not capable of adjusting to another social group, that some feared they would become French and lose their identity. At any rate, teachers were opposed to forcing an English child to continue in French school against his will. In their experience, children who were forced did not do well, were inattentive, and tended to become discipline problems.

Conclusion

We will not attempt to summarize the many findings of our inquiry, but rather will content ourselves with observing that in some respects an English child's going to French school is not the same as a French child's going to English school. We do not wish to exaggerate the differences. There were many respects in which the two situations were reflected as similar. The academic results as assessed by teachers' reports and test results are very similar. And most English and French children we studied seemed to be happy and well integrated in schools of the other language. Nevertheless, there were indications of differences. English children seem to take longer to become fluent in the other language, and fewer of them seem to pass as native speakers of it by Grade 6. Moreover, English children seemed to stay more aloof in French schools than French children in English ones. English children tend to make friends more in their own linguistic group. There were more reports of enmities and animosities between the linguistic groups in the French schools, and the conflicts appeared to last longer.

For all that, the division between Montreal's English and French children does not appear to be at all comparable to that which one frequently finds between black and white children in the United States, or between Protestant and Catholic in Northern Ireland. In Montreal, we find nothing deeper than a certain rivalry. It ought, in our view, to be watched, but at present it seems to be comparatively mild.

One other point merits attention. Children in schools of the other language are likely to lag behind native speakers of the language in grammar and particularly in vocabulary. The difference shows up in reading and, we imagine, in writing. It would be wise for parents who can manage it to give extra help in these areas to such children. Perhaps parents might encourage their children to read the other language at home and might explain difficult words to them. Some such support seems indicated on several counts.

The main positive finding, with which we would like to conclude, is that children learn to speak the other language very well indeed in school. By sixth grade, many can pass for native speakers of the language, without any noticeabe loss in their mother language. This achievement must be highly gratifying to those parents and children who have had the courage to try the other-language school.

Acknowledgments

We thank the Commission des Ecoles Catholiques de Montréal and La Commission Scolaire Sante-Croix, not only for permission to carry out the study, but also for co-operation when we needed it. We also thank the headmasters, teachers, and children in the schools who gave so generously of their time. Others who helped in the planning or carrying out of the study were John Edwards, Erica Baker, Marjory Topham, Raymonde Doyle, and Hélène Poitras. We are grateful to all these people and institutions, but we alone are responsible for the views expressed in our report.

References

Carrow, M. A. Linguistic functioning of bilingual and monolingual children. *Journal of Speech and Hearing Disorders*, 1957, *22*, 371–380.

Frasure-Smith, N., Lambert, W. E., and Taylor, D. M. Choosing the language of instruction for one's children: A Quebec Study. *Journal of Cross-Cultural Psychology*, 1975, *6*, 131–155.

Lambert, W. E., and Tucker, G. R. *Bilingual education of children*. Rowley, Mass.: Newbury House, 1972.

Macnamara, J. *Bilingualism and primary education*. Edinburgh: Edinburgh University Press, 1966.

Paulston, C. B. *Ethnic relations and bilingual education: Accounting for contradictory data*. Working papers on Bilingualism, No. 6. Toronto: Ontario Institute for Studies in Education, 1975.

Swain, M. French immersion programs across Canada. *Canadian Modern Language Review*, 1974, *31*, 117–129.

Socioeconomic Implications of Bilingual Education on the Navajo Reservation[1]

JOHN READ, BERNARD SPOLSKY, AND ALICE NEUNDORF,
Navajo Reading Study, University of New Mexico, Albuquerque

In the continuing quest for quality and value-for-money in education in this country, evaluation has a major role. Virtually all educational programs these days are subject to periodic inspection and assessment as a matter of course, and bilingual programs are no exception. In fact, they are more at the mercy of the evaluators than many other programs in that, being of recent origin and having an element of faddism about them, they have no assurance of continued federal or state support. They risk falling victim to the rhetoric of their proponents if the positive effects that were anticipated cannot be demonstrated. The problem created is twofold: choosing what to evaluate and measuring what has been chosen.

Characteristically, evaluation of bilingual education programs has focused on the efficacy of the instructional process as reflected in measures of the students' cognitive and linguistic development. However, since part of the rationale for bilingual education is that minority group children are often penalized by the use of Anglocentric instruments, there is a clear need to develop more appropriate measures. Test development is never a simple process. It is complicated in the bilingual situation by the fact that two languages are involved, one of which may not have been used previously as a medium of instruction. Beyond that is the question of what reference group to use in standardizing such bilingual tests: Should purely local norms be established or should a wider validity be sought?

To follow this line of reasoning, though, is to accept the idea that evaluation of bilingual education should proceed along similar lines to that of monolingual education, with appropriate adaptation. This assumption ignores the fact that very often bilingual education involves more than a new kind of curriculum organization. It may represent a

[1] Originally presented at the Annual Meeting of the American Educational Research Association, Washington, D.C., April, 1975. Preparation of this chapter was made possible by a grant from the Ford Foundation.

whole new approach to education and reflect complex processes of social change to which it contributes in turn. As Spolsky, Green, and Read (1974) have argued, educational results are only one set of outcomes among several that are relevant. At each stage of development, starting from the decision to establish a bilingual program, there are economic, political, sociological, psychological, religious, and cultural factors and effects that need to be taken into account. What happens in the classroom is important, but it is also necessary to study the school in relation to the community it serves.

Since our research interests center on the Navajo Reservation (Spolsky, 1974a), we shall base the rest of our discussion on that situation. Moves to introduce bilingual education there should be seen in the context of broader developments in the Navajo Tribe. Navajo people have been concerned about the schooling of their children for a long time. This concern was given formal expression in the 1930s, when the newly reconstituted Tribal Council appointed its own advisory Education Committee. However, the possibility of controlling the schools that their children attend and implementing an overall Navajo education policy is much more recent. The first community-controlled school was established at Rough Rock, Arizona, in 1966. It was a "demonstration" school, intended to prove to the Navajos themselves and to the educational authorities that such a school was viable and beneficial for the children. Since then, three more communities have taken control of their local schools and others will no doubt follow. This trend reflects changing policies on Indian education at the federal level, as illustrated for example by the setting up of community advisory boards at Bureau of Indian Affairs (BIA) schools and the requirements in the Indian Education Act (Title IV) that applications for funding under the act be developed "in open consultation with parents of Indian children."

At the same time, the Navajo Tribe has taken other important initiatives. The Tribal Council has stated its belief in the value of education in improving the socioeconomic situation on the reservation. The Navajo Division of Education, established in 1971, has reviewed the educational situation as it now exists and published a comprehensive program of planning and development (Navajo Division of Education, 1973) in preparation for the time when the BIA will turn over to the tribe all the bureau's present operations on the reservation, including the schools. Eventually it is intended that all Navajo schools will be community controlled and under the supervision of a Tribal Education Agency, analogous to a state department of education.

Navajo bilingual education, then, is not an independent phenomenon so much as an integral part of the overall development plan. It is tied up with the question of who should control the schools, which is clearly a political matter, part of the Indian struggle for self-determination. The process of transition to community control and its effects on the school are certainly of interest, but fall beyond the scope of this paper. We wish rather to focus on socioeconomic implications of bilingual education in the Navajo case.

If we pursue the logic of bilingual education, it becomes clear that economic effects are inevitable. A primary rationale for bilingual education is the fact that the students come to school not knowing English and, at the very least, something must be done to facilitate their transition to instruction in English. On the Navajo Reservation, sociolinguistic studies (Spolsky, 1970, 1971) have shown that 90% of the first graders speak Navajo and nearly 70% of them either know no English or have insufficient knowledge to do first-grade work in it. So the case for using Navajo in early grades is strong, and made stronger by the fact that the attempt to ban Navajo from the classroom has failed to improve student achievement. This fact means that school staff need to speak Navajo. In 1974, there were nearly 3000 teachers in schools on the Navajo Reservation and it was estimated that no more than 100 of them spoke the language. This situation is the result of the prevailing policy of hiring already certified teachers from off the reservation rather than recruiting and training Navajos. A lot of these teachers now find their jobs at stake, as bilingual education is more and more widely adopted.

It is theoretically possible for large numbers of the present teachers to learn Navajo, but this is unlikely in more than a handful of cases. Not only is Navajo a difficult language to learn, but also there is strong sentiment among Navajos in favor of having their own people teaching in the schools. Another possibility is the compromise situation that is commonly found, not just in Indian schools, where bilingual aides are employed to assist the teacher in communicating with the children and in teaching them about their culture. While the teacher–aide team works well in many cases, resentments do arise. Teachers may feel their position in the classroom is undermined if the aide has a more effective rapport with the children. An aide may resent the fact that she (or he) does the same work as the teacher, yet has a lower salary and inferior status. In fact, many aides have the opportunity to take courses for college credit and receive training that leads to teacher certification. Furthermore, the Navajo Division of Education has established the goal of producing 1000 Navajo teachers in 5 years and serious efforts are being made to achieve this goal, through recruiting Navajo education majors at southwestern universities and through teacher training programs conducted mainly on-site at reservation schools. Another program sponsored by the Navajo Division of Education is providing graduate-level training for Navajo school administrators.

Thus, the number of teaching jobs available to non-Navajos will decline in the next few years, though even if 1000 Navajo teachers are produced, there will still be twice as many non-Navajos in the schools. Nonetheless, it is interesting to speculate what kind of socioeconomic impact the new teachers will have. Two possibilities may be set out as follows:

1. There will be a large number of Navajos going into well-paying jobs previously held almost exclusively by non-Navajos. They will be distributed throughout the reservation, rather than being concentrated in a few relatively urbanized communities in the border areas. Their spending power is likely to have considerable effect on the economies of local communities. Of greater significance will be their relatively high level of education and knowledge of the ways of the outside world, which will enable them to be valuable "culture brokers" for the local community. For example, they will be in a better position to interpret government policy affecting the community and to lobby for basic services, such as roading, electricity, and water.

Many of the potential teachers are older married people who have some experience of the outside world, but who have returned to the reservation and have a commitment to their community as well as some social standing there. These people will have largely been trained in a program based at a reservation school, with the primary concern being to provide training that responds to the needs of Navajo children. They should be able to become respected members of the community and help break down the barriers that have existed between Navajo schools and the communities they serve.

2. A large number of the new teachers will be graduates of colleges of education in the Southwest and will have completed a regular teacher certification program. Their several years of study and life in the non-Navajo college world will undoubtedly have affected them and caused varying degrees of acculturation, so that the prospect of returning to the reservation may not be congenial. Some may prefer to teach off the reservation, but find that jobs are not available because of the prevailing economic conditions and a surplus of teachers. Thus, their return will be motivated by economic necessity, rather than a genuine desire to work there.

Such teachers will not find it easy to relate to an isolated rural community, far from civic amenities. For their part, the local people may not have much respect for them, especially if they do not originally come from that community, so good school–community relations will be difficult to foster. It is not inconceivable that Navajo teachers would adopt the same "compound mentality" as Anglo teachers have characteristically exhibited till now: living on the school campus, having minimal contact with community people, sending their children to an off-reservation school. Like teachers in the society at large, many will want to live in urbanized communities, rather than remote rural areas where basic services are poor and accessibility to the outside world is limited.

Of course, there will be Navajo teachers of both kinds, and others who do not fit either of these patterns. Further, there is an underlying assumption in the outlined patterns that the Navajo teachers should be expected to go beyond their primary role of educating children in the classroom and to play a leading part in community development, an assumption that might be challenged. Another temptation is to idealize "the Navajo community." The Navajos have a tradition of pragmatic adaptation to changing times and today we find communities with different degrees of acculturation to the mainstream society. In addition, there are divisions within many communities, often based on different religious affiliations but having their effect on local affairs generally. It is misleading, then, to conceive of Navajo communities as closely knit groups sharing a consensus on what their social and economic goals should be. The development plans articulated by the Tribal Council and its agencies are not necessarily understood or accepted by people at the grassroots level. A pervasive concern is expressed for an improvement in the economic opportunities available to their children, but there is no agreement as to how this improvement should be achieved.

At a more concrete level, the economic importance of a school to a Navajo community is quite clear. Even if there are no Navajo teachers, many local people can find work there as teacher aides, cooks, dormitory aides, bus drivers, secretaries, and maintenance personnel. The school may be the only major source of employment in the area. For this reason, a transition to community control has considerable economic significance, since an important element of control is the power to hire and fire staff. While a school board may not feel competent to evaluate applicants for teaching and professional positions, it is likely to take very seriously the hiring of cooks, bus drivers, and other service employees drawn from their own community. There will undoubtedly be a concern that as many people as possible should benefit financially from the school, a concern that may tend to override considerations of economics.

We now wish to set out some specific lines of research designed to give a socioeconomic perspective on Navajo bilingual education. Ideally we need detailed community studies that document as many relevant factors as possible so that they may form the baseline for research on the changing situation in later years. Such studies would need to be primarily ethnographic in nature, since many of the socioeconomic measures used elsewhere are inappropriate and misleading when applied to the reservation. A prime example of this is found in the United States Census, which significantly underestimates the population and gives an inaccurate picture of employment patterns among the Navajos.

However, there are measures that may prove useful in understanding the educational situation. For example, Spolsky (1974b) found a significant relationship between the degree of language maintenance in a Navajo community and its accessibility to an off-reservation town. The indication was that the closer a community was to an urban area (and the better the quality of the roads), the greater the likelihood that the children knew English. Road building, then, is a variable that seems to reflect the advance of English and the Anglo culture, but there must be others. It is worth investigating the quality of housing, together with the provision of electricity, running water, and inside plumbing, as a variable cluster that may show the same process at work. There are tribal agencies responsible for developing housing and utilities, so figures are available, at least for new units and services provided since the agencies began operation.

It should be noted, though, that modern amenities have uneven effects on the acculturation process. Let us take motor vehicles for instance. The most common form of transport on the reservation is the pickup truck, a vehicle designed to withstand the rigors of bumpy ungraded roads and, with its large freight capacity, appropriate for an agricultural economy. Automobiles are less suited to the environment and are confined to the more developed areas with better roads. Of course, owning any motor vehicle involves capital outlay and maintenance costs, which require a cash income, but the choice between a pickup and a car seems more significant than the mere fact of having a vehicle. Or we can look at the communications media. Transistor radios are cheap and, with battery power, can be used almost anywhere. In the hinterland of the reservation, there are a dozen radio stations with a combined total of more than 150 hours programming in Navajo each week, so that radio listening and monolingualism in Navajo are quite compatible. By contrast, a television set is expensive and requires an electricity supply. Programs are almost entirely in English, with only a token amount of Navajo per week on one station. One would expect, too, that the visual images of television would have a greater impact than the purely auditory nature of radio. Thus, the incidence of modern conveniences is indicative of social change, but we should not assume that they all have a uniform impact on Navajo culture.

Another kind of research should focus on school budgeting. It would be interesting to compare the allocation of resources in a school before and after the introduction of a bilingual program, to see whether it reflects a new set of priorities. Of particular relevance in this regard are the community-controlled schools, whose school boards have real power to determine how the funds made available by the BIA are to be spent. The introduction of the bilingual program itself is usually based on a separate new grant from ESEA (Elementary and Secondary Education Act) Title VII, not on funds reallocated from other programs in the school. However, our feeling is that the whole school budget will be affected by the change. We would expect an increase in the percentage of the instructional component being spent on teaching about Navajo society and culture, including the employment of members of the community as resource persons. More emphasis is likely on adult education, with literacy classes, aide training, and the teaching of technical skills. Another area of interest is support services, like the cafeteria, health clinic, school buses, maintenance, and repairs, especially to the extent they benefit not just the school but the community too.

Of course, changes will be reflected not only in budgetary categories, but also in the way current resources are used. A nice illustration of this pattern is found in the case of Borrego Pass School, an elementary day school on the edge of the Navajo Reservation that was turned over to community control in 1972, just when the BIA was on the point of closing it. One of the first decisions of the new school board was that the school buses should henceforth drive up to the children's homes, rather than picking them up along the main roads at points that were often some distance from the homes. This procedure immediately boosted the school enrollment, the decline in which had been a major reason that the BIA wanted to close the school.

A further area of study concerns curriculum development and the extent to which it incorporates community input. There is widespread confusion in Navajo schools as to what should be taught, what kind of curriculum should be followed, and what goals education should have for Navajo children. There are no firm guidelines yet to govern what teachers do in the classroom; no comprehensive bilingual program has appeared. To a large extent, this situation reflects the incipient state of transition to community control and tribal coordination of education on the reservation. All kinds of problems are involved here, so let us restrict our attention to socioeconomic concerns. A lot of lip service is paid these days to needs assessment and community input in educational planning. Parents are assumed to have social and economic aspirations, if not for themselves at least for their children. This assumption is commonly expressed as a desire that the school should stress the teaching of English, so that the children will be able to get good jobs when they leave school. So the school makes serious efforts to promote

English, but finds that there is little improvement in the pupils' competence in the language. Nor are they any more successful in obtaining better employment. A conventional evaluation may or may not find fault with the quality of instruction the school offers, but quality may well be insignificant as an explanation, when compared to social factors. In a great many Navajo communities, the universal medium of communication outside the classroom is Navajo and someone using English is teased for trying to be like an Anglo. Similarly the kind of mobility orientation that is characteristic of success in the mainstream society is often either lacking or not reinforced in a Navajo setting.

Thus, for the purposes of curriculum development, the goal of improving English needs to be related to the socioeconomic situation and the role of English in the community. Perhaps it will be necessary for the community to find ways of promoting wider aspirations in the children outside the school, so that the community is perceived as supporting the school's efforts. The way in which the parents and children perceive the Navajo teachers is relevant here, too, to the extent that they function as models of biculturalism able to bridge the gap between the Navajo and Anglo worlds.

The tentativeness of our proposals reflects the complexity of the phenomena we are trying to understand. What we are working toward is the identification of key social factors that can be shown to affect the way a school—or a bilingual program—operates. A more concrete goal is to construct matching typologies: types of communities that give rise to types of sociolinguistic situations leading in turn to types of bilingual programs. Whether this goal can be achieved at a level of generality that is still relevant to the real world remains to be seen. This approach will be in the first instance a descriptive approach, though hopefully it will give insight into mismatches between social factors and aspects of the school program that will prove useful in evaluating bilingual education. Thus, we return to our opening theme: a call to broaden the evaluation process for bilingual programs, so that the social environment is given a much more central place. It is necessary to take account of significant trends in the community that are independent of the program and may be working against it. Only in this way can we approach a full assessment of the effects of a program.

References

Navajo Division of Education. *11 programs for strengthening Navajo education.* Window Rock, Arizona: Author, 1973.

Spolsky, B. Navajo language maintenance: Six-year-olds in 1969. *Language Sciences,* 1970, No. 13, 19–24.

Spolsky, B. Navajo language maintenance II: Six-year-olds in 1970. *Navajo Reading Study Progress Report*, No. 13. Albuquerque: University of New Mexico, 1971.

Spolsky, B. The Navajo reading study: An illustration of the scope and nature of educational linguistics. In J. Qvistgaard, H. Schwarz, and H. Spang–Hanssen (Eds.), *Proceedings of the Association Internationale de Linguistique Appliquee, Third Congress, Copenhagen 1972* (Vol. 3). *Applied linguistics: Problems and solutions*. Heidelberg: Julius Groos, 1974. (a)

Spolsky, B. Speech communities and schools. *TESOL Quarterly*, 1974, *8*, 17–26. (b)

Spolsky, B., Green, J. B., and Read, J. A model for the description, analysis and perhaps evaluation of bilingual education. *Navajo Reading Study Progress Report*, No. 23. Albuquerque: University of New Mexico, 1974.

Part III

TEACHER DIRECTED ISSUES: SOME PRACTICAL SUGGESTIONS FROM THEORETICAL DOMAINS

Some New Trends for Applied Linguistics and Foreign Language Teaching in the United States[1]

KARL C. DILLER, University of New Hampshire

In 1960, when William Moulton wrote his state-of-the-art paper on Linguistics and Language Teaching in preparation for the Ninth International Congress of Linguists (Moulton, 1961), he was able to summarize two decades of increasing consensus among structural linguists that language should be taught through an "audio–lingual" method which consisted of "mimicry, memorization, and pattern drill." The rationale for this method lay in an empiricist–behaviorist learning theory which maintained that language was a set of speech habits learned through a process of conditioning and drill. Language was not seen to be rule-governed. It was said that "the habit is the reality and the rule is a mere summary of the habit" (Twaddell, 1948, pp. 77–78), and that "Whenever a person speaks, he is either mimicking or analogizing" (Hockett, 1958, p. 425). Moulton realized that generative transformational grammar was going to cause some adjustment, but in 1960 it still seemed, as he said, that "transformational grammar is too new to permit predictions" (Moulton, 1961, p. 108). He had no idea how far-reaching that adjustment would turn out to be.

In the mid-1970s, we are in a very different position. There is no longer any consensus on methods of foreign-language teaching. In face of the confusion, many teachers have refused to take sides and have acclaimed an unprincipled "eclectic" method. They proudly quote, out of context, Noam Chomsky's statement that we should be "skeptical about the significance, for teaching languages, of such insights and understanding as have been attained in linguistics and psychology" (Chomsky, 1966, p. 43). Now, Chomsky in all his writings, political as well as linguistic, encourages people to be skeptical of experts, but he certainly

[1] This chapter is a reprint of an article originally published in the *TESOL Quarterly*, 1975, 9, 65–73.

does not go around preaching that there is no truth or no knowledge worth knowing. He asks that we be our own experts, deciding for ourselves what is true and important. In the paper just quoted, it is the theories of structural linguistics and behaviorist psychology that he wants us to be most skeptical about. More than half of Chomsky's paper is devoted to an exposition of four aspects of linguistic theory which he feels should have great importance for the language teacher.[2] Chomsky has a kind of hopeful skepticism and it is in this spirit that we should evaluate the developments which have occurred in linguistics and foreign language teaching since 1960, deciding for ourselves which questions, facts, and ideas are most important for good foreign language teaching in the mid-1970s.

I will not discuss all the developments of this transitional period. Rather, I will choose five ideas or trends I see as most important or hopeful for improving the teaching of foreign languages in the late 1970s.

1. The linguistic theories of Noam Chomsky have challenged or overturned many presuppositions about language learning, and have undermined the theoretical basis for mimicry, memorization, and pattern drills as language teaching methods. New conditions have likewise undermined the pragmatic basis of these methods.

2. A renewed appreciation of the importance of grammar in language learning is following the acceptance of the fact that language is not merely a matter of conditioned habits, but, rather, is characterized by rule-governed creativity. Experimental justification has been found for the usefulness of grammar in language teaching.

3. Error analysis is fulfilling the function of contrastive structural analysis in a more workable and pragmatic way.

4. Meaningful use of both oral and written language is being emphasized in the effort to help students understand and generate new sentences. Several very different new methods have developed which have developed this point in common, e.g., those of Asher (1974), Winitz and Reeds (1973), the Silent Way (Gattegno, 1972), and Community Language Learning (Curran, 1972; LaFarge, 1971; Stevick, 1973).

5. In light of these trends, the temporary phase of eclecticism among confused teachers is giving way to a balanced set of methods and techniques suited to several individual learning strategies, as new criteria for choosing and devising language-teaching methods are being developed.

Let us consider each of these five points in detail.

---

[2] Chomsky's "four main headings" are: (1) the "creative" aspect of language use; (2) the abstractness of linguistic representation; (3) the universality of underlying linguistic structure; and (4) the role of intrinsic organization in cognitive processes.

The waning of Mim-Men and pattern drills

It is clear by now that the rationalist–cognitivist theories of Noam Chomsky have undermined the empiricist–behaviorist basis for mimicry and memorization (mim-mem) and pattern drills as language teaching methods. I have discussed this conflict in detail in my book *Generative Grammar, Structural Linguistics, and Language Teaching* (Diller, 1971), and I will review the matter only briefly in this chapter. Chomsky has shown that a language is characterized by rule-governed creativity. The speaker of a natural language can construct an indefinitely large number of sentences which have never been heard before but which can be understood immediately because they are grammatical. Language acquisition is now seen to involve the active use of the highly structured human brain rather than the passive responses of the organism to outside stimulus and reinforcement schedules.

The one argument that still bothers many language teachers is a pragmatic one. "I can't believe," they say, "that these methods would have been accepted so widely if they didn't have some basis in truth." The "truth" was that these methods were ideally suited to teachers who did not really know the language they were teaching but who were only able, as Freeman Twaddell said, "to pronounce correctly and with proper grammar just those sentences and constructions which the pupils are learning and practicing" (Rehder, Thomas, Twaddell, & O'Connor, 1962; p. *xix*). The textbooks were designed to be teacher-proof scripts for the conduct of classes. This was useful when large numbers of teachers could not speak the language they taught or when they could not teach the language they spoke. The language competence of teachers is much greater, now, however, for two reasons. One is that cheaper travel for both teachers and students has allowed many of them to study language abroad. The other reason is that teachers have improved their competence in the oral language through their teaching with the audio–lingual method. People can learn languages even in suprisingly impoverished environments, and since the audiolingual method provides good examples of the language in use it can be reasonably successful if problems of boredom, motivation, and excessive homework can be solved. Now that teachers are more competent, they are less willing to accept mim-mem and pattern drills. The pragmatic basis for this method is therefore much weaker now in the mid-1970s.

The importance of grammar

Grammar is coming back into its own in language teaching, now that linguists accept the importance of rule-governed creativity in the normal use of language. This trend has been resisted by many because of their bad experiences with the disastrous grammar–translation method—a method whose only redeeming feature is that it does not require a teacher at all, much less a teacher who knows the language. The problem with that method is not the grammar, but the fact that the learner is never given an opportunity to make the grammar become psychologically real: He is never given the opportunity to think directly in the language or to express thoughts directly in the language. A sophisticated alternative long available has been the *direct method,* as practiced in the first half of this century by Emile de Sauzé of Cleveland. All instruction is given in the target language with no translation either in the textbook or in class. The direct method always requires, as for example in the Berlitz schools, a careful grammatical progression from easy constructions to difficult with meaningful exercises that help the learner gain functional control of these rules (cf. Berlitz, 1887). But de Sauzé also insisted on the explicit formulation of certain rules of grammar. As he said, the student's knowledge of the principles of grammar will "multiply his experiences a thousand times" (de Sauzé, 1929, p. 4), a phrase that echoes in a modest way von Humboldt's and Chomsky's "infinite use of finite means" (Chomsky, 1965, p. 8). De Sauzé had his own evidence from his informal experiments "that the practical results, such as reading, writing, speaking, and understanding, were achieved in greater proportion and in less time when the technique involved a maximum amount of conscious reasoning" (de Sauzé, [1929] 1953, p. 5). But accurate quantified evidence has been hard to get. The Scherer–Wertheimer experiment (1964) and the Pennsylvania Project (Smith, 1970) both failed to provide crucial evidence on the importance of grammar because of problems in conceptual design. Mats Oskarsson and Tibor von Elek finally have produced experiments in the teaching of English in Sweden in which all extraneous variables have been controlled, and they have demonstrated that grammatical explanations clearly facilitate the learning of the language (von Elek & Oskarsson, 1972; Oskarsson, 1973). The only caution with grammar is to remember that the goal is for the learner to gain functional control over the rules of grammar; that is, to make the rules psychologically real. The Berlitz direct method achieves this goal without formulating the rules at all but only by demonstrating the rules in action. (For more on the Berlitz method, see Diller, 1971, Chap. 7). Formulation of the rules is not the same as gaining functional control over these rules, but the two processes can be very effectively related.

Error analysis

Error analysis is by no means as popular an undertaking as contrastive structural analysis has been, but it holds the potential of being much more fruitful for language teaching than contrastive analysis. A thought-provoking recent discussion of error analysis is H. V. George's book *Common Errors in Language Learning* (1972). It has been assumed that contrastive analysis of two languages can predict mistakes; wherever there are differences, there will be mistakes. But the situation is much more complex. One factor, as George (1972, p. 14) states it, is that:

> Where the foreign language is more efficient than the mother tongue, the pull of the mother tongue is weak or absent. The German learner does not transfer his mother-tongue noun genders to English or attempt to decline the English definite and indefinite article.

Another factor is that "learners' errors show remarkable uniformity irrespective of mother tongue" (George, 1972, p. 1), presumably because of problems in the language being learned. This factor is seen in the mistakes of children learning their native tongues. My own son, when he was almost four, used the form "bees" in place of *is*, a straightforward regularization. He also used that form "everwho" instead of *whoever*. "Everwho" is presumably a *wh*-transform of *everyone* without inverting the *wh* portion to initial position. Foreign students of all language backgrounds make similar mistakes caused by internal inconsistencies or complications in English. Dulay and Burt (1974) suggest that developmental strategies cause up to 87% of the errors in English as a second language made by children 5 to 8 years old, whereas less than 5% of the errors are caused by interference. Error analysis, then, is much broader than contrastive analysis: It uses contrastive analysis to explain (not to predict) errors caused by interference. But many common errors cannot be explained by contrastive analysis and must be dealt with by other forms of error analysis. These analyses (as, for example, in Burt & Kiparsky, 1972) might well help language teachers in the organization and proper ordering of language-teaching material and in choosing which grammar rules to make explicit.

Meaningful use in a variety of methods

Meaningful practice is the common denominator of several new ways of learning languages that are compatible with rationalist–cognitivist theories of language. With the notable exception of a method called *Community Language Learning* these methods can all be called versions of the *Direct method* in that (1) they avoid use of the mother tongue completely; (2) they are based on step-by-step progression of grammatical material; and (3) they use meaningful exercises instead of those mechanical drills whose sentences have no particular truth value. But there similarities end. For example, in one system, the *Silent Way* (Gattegno, 1972), the teacher is silent 90% of the time, whereas in another system, one developed by Winitz and Reeds (1973), the students are silent and the teacher (or tape recorder) talks 100% of the time.

Let me describe a few of these methods and then consider why meaningful practice is now regarded by many to be the key to effective language teaching.

The Silent Way, devised by Caleb Gattegno, is one of the most intriguing new variations on the direct method.[3] In reading Gattegno's book, I was struck page after page by how similar his attitudes are to de Sauzé's. Besides the standard features of the direct method (meaningful practice, the exclusive use of the foreign language, and the progression of grammatical material from easy to difficult), there is common agreement on the early introduction of writing and of the necessity of leading the student to correct his own mistakes since the student must understand the error in order to avoid making it again. But Gattegno does not start out by talking about pencils, books, and desks, as de Sauzé and Berlitz do. Nor does he start with sentences about such self-evident but faraway things as "København er en by. Danmark er et land. Oslo er en by. Norge er et land. Stockholm er en by. Sverige er et land" (Salling, 1964, p. 7). Instead of making these conventional direct method starts, Gattegno begins the silent way by talking about cuisenaire rods. These rods, or *algebricks*, as they are sometimes called, are small wooden blocks of different colors and lengths. In a 30-minute demonstration, I saw students learn four colors and three numbers in Japanese and be able to say such sentences as "Take a red rod and three blue rods and two yellow rods and give them to me." The remarkable feature is not the rods, or the small charts which quickly get students to read; most interesting is that the teacher says each new word only once. The students in chorus or individually do the rest of the talking in response to gestures of the teacher. Even pronunciation and grammar mistakes are corrected through gestures without verbal repetition of a model. Many of the gestures and strategies are similar to those used in charades: the counting of syllables and use of the fact that one syllable might sound like another. This silence by the teacher and his pronunciation of the model only once is the most effective technique I have seen for concentrating the attention of the student on the language lesson.

At the opposite end of the sound spectrum is Winitz and Reeds' method, described in "Rapid Acquisition of a Foreign Language (German) by the Avoidance of Speaking" (1973). In this version of the direct method, the learner's only overt behavior is his choosing of the one picture in a quadrant of four which corresponds to the meaning of each utterance. Actually, for the first utterance there is only one picture, a pencil, and three blank spaces, as the voice says "Bleistift." But after that,

[3] I wish to thank Carol and Nobuo Akiyama for introducing me to the Silent Way and Community Language Learning and for demonstrating these methods to me. Other good introductions are Stevick, 1973 and 1974.

there is always a contrast. This technique apparently succeeds in teaching vocabulary at a much faster rate than usual—some 50 words an hour. After the basic grammar and vocabulary are learned, the students are allowed to begin speaking. By postponing pronunciation for so long, it is claimed that the result is much more native-like speech. But up to that point, this method is the most beautiful refutation of the behaviorist maxim that a language is a set of speech habits. Here are students learning language without acquiring any speech habits at all.

At a more advanced level, Joan Morley has developed a textbook for *Improving Aural Comprehension* (1972) in English as a second language, using meaningful material. However, unlike Winitz and Reeds, the responses are in writing and require a certain amount of reading. It was the apparent lack of reading that bothered me most about Winitz and Reeds' experiment, for many adults are helped tremendously by the written word. Postovsky has shown, however, that Winitz and Reeds' technique can be used to teach students to read Russian as well as to understand it when spoken (Postovsky, 1975).

James Asher's *Total Physical Response* method is another variation on the direct method that stresses listening comprehension. In the first semester 70% of the student's time is listening, 20% speaking, and 10% reading and writing. The distinctive characteristic of this method is that every utterance by the teacher is a command or is embedded in a command on which the students then act. They start out with "Stand up!" and "Sit down!", but Asher shows how complex these commands can be by giving this example: "Gregory, find the picture of the beautiful woman with green eyes, long black hair and wearing a sun hat that has red stripes. When you find the picture, show it to the class and describe the woman!" (Asher, Kusudo, & de la Torre, 1974, p. 27). Asher's evidence shows that this is a very effective method indeed, requiring fewer class hours and no homework to outstrip the average college language student on standardized tests. It is not clear, though, how it would compare with the other variations of the direct method that I have discussed.

More conventional and well-balanced versions of the direct method, like those of Berlitz and de Sauzé, have been described elsewhere (e.g., Diller, 1971). Under the influence of de Sauzé, new French books have been produced by Lenard (1965, 1969), and by Pucciani and Hamel (1967). There are similar books in Italian, German, and Spanish by Traversa (1967), Pfister (1968), and Barcia (1973), respectively. These books stress a multiple approach, with listening, speaking, reading, and writing all occurring from the start. As with the Silent Way, the students continually generate meaningful nonrepetitive sentences (Lenard calls this the "verbal–active method"), yet there is ample listening comprehension practice from the teacher's utterances. All this learning is reinforced visually through reading and writing. Asher's techniques of physical response can still be used extensively in this method as they are in the "Situational Reinforcement" books (Hall, 1967), which, despite their suspicious name, are still another variation on the direct method, since they have (1) meaningful practice, (2) exclusion of the mother tongue, and (3) grammatical ordering.

All these versions of the direct method can be carried out very well with no homework (unless you consider Winitz and Reeds' tape recorder to involve all homework and no class). The direct method, then, is a method of language *teaching* par excellence

One final new method of language learning requires a teacher whose primary qualification is that he or she is a sympathetic bilingual person: *Community Language Learning* (Curran, 1972; LaFarge, 1971; Stevick, 1973). Students sit in a circle and talk to each other in the foreign language about whatever they wish to communicate. At first, though, they say the sentence in their native language, and the bilingual person tells them how to say it in the foreign language. The learner then repeats the sentence in the foreign language. In spite of all this translation, this method involves meaningful practice. On one level, indeed, the practice is more meaningful than with any other method.

At the beginning, to make this method work best, the conversation should be taped for about 20 minutes. Then the group replays the tape, with the bilingual person writing the sentences on the blackboard and analyzing them. This procedure forces the students to write their own textbook—an excellent aid to motivation. One is reminded here of Sylvia Ashton-Warner's Organic Approach to teaching reading and writing, in which the key vocabulary and topics of discourse are provided by the students (Ashton-Warner, 1972).

Community language learning is one method I might try if no teacher were available who was capable of teaching with a direct method. Even with a direct method, one might find Community Language Learning an excellent activity for an occasional change of pace.

When language is thought to be a set of conditioned habits imposed from the outside, a large amount of mechanical drills is in order. But when language is seen to be a symbol system for use in expressing our thoughts, then meaningful practice is in order, and there is no call for mechanical drill—not even for pronunciation, as we have seen in the Silent Way.

A reasonable alternative to eclecticism

In conclusion I would like to say a word about the so-called "eclectic method" which some people say they have moved to. Christina Paulston's phrase is more to the point: She calls it "The Modified Audio-Lingual or

Eclectic Approach" (Paulston, 1973, p. 136). When these believers in mimicry, memorization, and pattern drill have recognized that their position can no longer be held, they have tried to patch up their old method with elements of the direct method or even of grammar–translation. Calling the result "eclectic," they recognize that they have put together inconsistent elements or that they have no principled basis for choosing a method. This eclecticism is not tenable, and cannot endure for long. Responsible language teachers today can construct for themselves a coherent picture of what language is and can build their own method out of elements which are consistent with each other and with the teacher's understanding of how language is learned.

We can avoid the ad hoc variation of electicism by developing a set of principles that guide our choices of apropriate methods for individual learning styles, teaching styles, or special situations. The principles discussed in this paper have indeed fostered a number of quite different but compatible methods. All the new methods emphasize meaningful practice and exclude mimicry, memorization, and pattern drills. They all have a healthy respect for grammar and grammatical ordering—even with Community Language Learning, the group soon begins to isolate grammatical elements and patterns. And all except Community Language Learning find that the exclusion of the mother tongue is one of the best shortcuts to the goal of getting people to internalize their new rules of grammar and to think in their new language.

References

Asher, J. J., Kusudo, J. A., and de la Torre, R. Learning a second language through commands: The second field test. *Modern Language Journal*, 1974, 58, 1–2, 24–32.

Ashton-Warner, S. *Spearpoint: "Teacher" in America.* New York: Alfred Knopf, 1972.

Barcia, J. B. *Lengua y Cultura.* New York: Holt, 1973.

Berlitz, M. D. *Méthode Berlitz.* New York: Berlitz, 1887.

Burt, M. K., and Kiparsky, C. *The Gooficon: A repair manual for English.* Rowley, Mass.: Newbury House, 1972.

Chomsky, N. *Aspects of the theory of syntax.* Cambridge, Mass.: M.I.T. Press, 1965.

Chomsky, N. Linguistic theory. In Robert C. Mead, Jr. (Ed.), *Reports of the working committees, Northeast Conference on the Teaching of Foreign Languages.* New York: MLA Materials Center, 1966.

Curran, C. A. *Counseling–learning: A whole person model for education.* New York: Grune and Stratton, 1972.

de Sauzé, E. B. *The Cleveland plan for the teaching of modern languages with special reference to French.* Philadelphia; Winston, 1929; rev. ed. 1953.

Diller, K. C. *Generative grammar, structural linguistics, and language teaching.* Rowley, Mass.: Newbury House, 1971.

Dulay, H. C., and Burt, M. K. Errors and strategies in child second language acquisition. *TESOL Quarterly*, 1974, 8 (2), 129–136.

Hall, E. *Orientation in American English.* Washington, D.C.: Institute of Modern Languages, 1967.

Hocket, C. F. *A course in modern linguistics.* New York: Macmillan, 1958.

Gattegno, C. *Teaching foreign languages in schools: The silent way.* New York, Educational Solutions, 1972.

George, H. V. *Common errors in language learning.* Rowley, Mass.: Newbury House, 1972.

LaFarge, P. G. Community language learning: a pilot study. *Language Learning,* 1971, *21* (1), 45–61.

Lenard, Y. *Parole et pensee.* New York: Harper & Row, 1965.

Lenard, Y. *Jeunes voix, jeunes visages.* New York: Harper & Row, 1969.

Morley, J. *Improving aural comprehension.* Ann Arbor, Mich.: University of Michigan Press, 1972.

Moulton, W. Linguistics and language teaching in the United States 1940–1960. In C. Mohrmann, A. Sommerfelt, and J. Whatmough (Eds.), *Trends in European and American linguistics 1930–1960.* Utrecht; Spectrum Publishers, 1961.

Oskarsson, M. Assessing the relative effectiveness of two methods of teaching English to adults. *IRAL,* 1973, *10,* 1/3, 251–261.

Paulston, C. A biased bibliography: Comments on selecting texts for a methods course in TESOL. *Language Learning,* 1973, *23* (1), 129–143.

Pfister, F. J. *Deutsch durch Deutsch.* New York: Harper & Row, 1968.

Postovsky, V. The priority of aural comprehension in the language acquisition process. Paper presented to the Fourth International Congress of Applied Linguistics, Stuttgart, 1975.

Pucciani, O. F., and Hamel, J. *Langue et langage.* New York: Holt, 1967.

Rehder, H., Thomas, U., Twaddell, W. F., and O'Connor, P. *Deutsch: Verstehen und Sprechen.* Teacher's ed. New York: Holt, 1962.

Salling, A. *Laer at tale Dansk.* Copenhagen: Grafisk Forlag, 1964.

Scherer, A. C., and Wertheimer, M. *A psycholinguistic experiment in foreign language teaching.* New York: McGraw-Hill, 1964.

Smith, P. D., Jr. *A comparison of the cognitive and audiolingual approaches to foreign language instruction: The Pennsylvania Foreign Language Project.* Philadelphia, The Center for Curriculum Development, 1970.

Stevick, E. W. A riddle with some hints for its solution. *Peace Corps Program and Training Journal,* October 1973, pp. 3–6.

Stevick, E. W. Review of *Teaching Foreign Languages in the Schools The Silent Way* by Caleb Gattegno. *TESOL Quarterly,* 1974, 8 (3), 305–313.

Traversa, V. *Parola e pensiero.* New York: Harper & Row, 1967.

Twaddell, W. F. Meanings, habits and rules. *Education,* 1948, *49,* 77–78.

von Elek, T., and Oskarsson, M. *Teaching foreign language grammar to adults.* Research Bulletin No. 10. Gothenburg, Sweden: Gothenburg School of Education, 1972.

Winitz, H., and Reeds, J. A. Rapid acquisition of a foreign language (German) by the avoidance of speaking. *IRAL,* 1973, *10,* 1/4, 295–317.

9

Bilingualism and Learning to Read

SALLY KAMINSKY, Richmond College of the City University of New York

Oral language and the reading process

Instruction in reading assumes that the learner has control of his or her spoken language. Reading is a second-order language skill in which the reader must be able to make use of his knowledge of language in order to make decisions about visual symbols. He must then be able to transform these representations into meaning. Carroll (1964, p. 62) describes reading as "the activity of reconstructing (overtly and covertly) a reasonable spoken message from a printed text, and making meaningful responses to the reconstructed message that would be made to the spoken message." In order to learn to read, the young child must possess a basic competence of the grammar of his language; that is, he or she must have an ability to use the phonology, syntax, and semantics of the language in order to relate sound to meaning.

LANGUAGE IN A BILINGUAL COMMUNITY

For the bilingual child, the task of learning to read is complicated by the probability that his spoken language consists of two language systems and that control over either of these two languages may be only partial. Although two languages can be acquired, it appears that this can be most successfuly done in cases in which the two language systems are distinguished from one another, resulting in what is known as *coordinate bilingualism*.

Children growing up in bilingual communities in the United States do not typically acquire two or more independent language systems. The languages spoken are often used concurrently, fitting into a complex life pattern. The young children in a bilingual community grow up experiencing a mixture of two languages within their everyday experiences. By the time they enter school, bilingual children have attained partial knowledge of the grammars of two languages, although they may not be separate competencies.

Two language codes are converged in a bilingual community, each language being used with varying degrees of emphasis. Although one can

155

find systematic and regular rules that govern the choice of which language is spoken in given situations (Fishman, 1972), such rules do not appear to be totally predictable. The assumption that the natural or first language is used in affective and intimate contexts is more than likely true, as is the assumption that the second or dominant culture language is reserved for formal and public interactions with monolinguals. The bilingual speaker, however, who has at least partially merged the two language codes, does not act in accordance with these fixed rules. He calls forth both languages, often within the same sentence, to express himself. Each language contributes to the ideas he wishes to convey. Gumperz and Hernandez-Chavez (1972) point to the breakdown in correlations among bilinguals between language choice on the one hand, and situations or contexts of individual speech events on the other hand. While one language may be associated with a particular set of activities and the second language with another group, language mixing occurs frequently.

Undoubtedly, cultural patterns of relative stability exert constraints on language choice and determine settings that are appropriate for the use of first and second languages. Within these fixed patterns, however, bilingual individuals seem to vary in the extent to which they use the languages at their disposal. It appears that certain topics are somehow handled better or more appropriately in one language than in another.

Cognitive strategies may be an underlying basis for individual variation in language choice. The language that best describes the thought may be selected because the individual has made a cognitive relationship to certain vocabulary words in that language. Although there are many studies on language and thought, little research is available on bilingual language development and cognition. Such research is needed to explain the acquisition process in which the bilingual child is engaged when he or she is learning to read.

The work of Heidi Dulay and Marina Burt (1972, 1973, 1974a, b) is a promising attempt to explain cognitive strategies in the learning of a second language. These authors posit two hypotheses: (1) that errors in the speaking of a second language are related to interference from the first language, or (2) that errors are the result of developmental learning that occurs in the acquisition of both a first and a second language. The first hypothesis suggests that children make use of the first language structures in second-language speech. When two languages are learned separately, learning strategies may be very different from those that occur when two languages are learned concurrently. The second hypothesis is based on the notion that in the asquisition of any language, errors are made as part of the natural acquisition process as the child develops his rule system, which is constantly being revised to accommodate the more and more complex language that he is producing and receiving. Dulay and Burt suggest that the second hypothesis seems to be the more frequent explanation for children's errors in second-language use.

Carroll (1964) suggests that the codability of a concept in a language is highly related to the speaker's ability to perceive and describe the concept. Whether the presence of a code, or more broadly, whether the structure of a language, can help or restrain cognitive processes is not yet known. It does appear, however, that some bilingual speakers may "think" differently in one language than in another. The effect this difference may have on problem-solving activity, or on perceptions of what we call "world view," is not altogether satisfied by contrasting language structures and semantics, but must include an undertsanding of the child's culture. In fact, the similarities among languages in their codification of concepts outweigh their differences.

Affective meanings that become attached to the child's first language, however, may have a great deal to do with the young child's acquisition of competence in a second language. The young child's view of his world, his attachments to those who take care of him and his self-image are connected to the language that is introduced earliest. For most bilingual children in this country, the native language of the parent is the first language. While it may be intermixed with expressions from the dominant culture, it is the native language that provides the basic foundations for meaningful communication.

As in all communities, the bilingual community affords its members a primary language system that communicates shared understandings. The primary system is a language that binds members together and promotes cohesive interaction within the community. For the young child, it is a language that communicates the expectations others hold for him; that is, it is a language that defines the child's present and future roles within the community. While all children are socialized to the mores of their community, bilingual children are frequently socialized to cultural expectations that are markedly different from the dominant culture.

THE LANGUAGE OF THE SCHOOL

The language that the child encounters when he enters school differs in many ways from his home language. It necessarily defines a different set of rules and expectations, and is a language that represents the more formal relationships in which the child will be involved. The bilingual child has a double task before him as he enters this more formal setting. He must, as all children, learn the implicit rules that regulate his behavior as a member of the school community, but he must also learn to respond within the school situation by using the language in which he is not dominant. The child is confronted with the task of deciphering a second language, which is used by the teacher, and, therefore, may encounter difficulties in understanding her expectations. Conflicts between the two language systems and different sets of cultural expectations may arise along an informal–formal continuum, requiring that the child modify his role behavior between family and school settings. Furthermore, the bilingual child is expected to use the formal and dominant language of the school to meet his social and academic requirements in school.

How the variation in language acquisition, and, particularly, how second-language acquisition affects the child's ability to learn to read is not fully understood. The linguist's attention to contrastive features between language codes is a promising contribution toward understanding the potential problems a child confronts when he must transfer his oral-language skills to the written symbols of books. While it is not the purpose of this chapter to elucidate these differences between language systems, it is recognized that these analyses might be of direct use to teachers of bilingual children.

Psycholinguistic view of the reading process

Recent ideas about the reading process (Goodman, 1973) provide further understanding of the ways in which bilingual children learn to read. A psycholinguistic analysis of the process takes into account the relationship between oral and written language. It similarly recognizes the relationship between oral and aural language, and asserts that in their preliterate language experiences children possess the competence to both receive and produce their language. Reading, a secondary symbol system, produces "oral sequences and patterns into graphic sequences and patterns" (Goodman, 1973, p. 16). In the early stages of reading, children may recode graphic sequences into aural input, from which they derive meaning. At a point when he achieves relative fluency in reading, the reader probaby collapses the process, simultaneously supplying the aural input with the recoding of the graphic unit. Compression of these processes takes place at the most efficient level of fluency, where the reader decodes meaning directly from graphic sequences.

According to Smith (1971, p. 221), "the difference between fluent and beginning reading may be epitomized in the manner in which the reader makes use of syntax, the bridge between surface structure and meaning." The fluent reader samples "the visual information to confirm his expectations" relying on his knowledge of the language structure to make reasonable predictions.

Beginning readers require mediating skills that permit them to make words out of symbols. When children first learn to read, they engage in a trial-and-error procedure, using decoding skills to help them to make judgments about what they see. Successful matching between the symbol and the context helps the reader attain meaning from the text. Unsuccessful matching allows for another try at a more accurate strategy. The employment of decoding skills helps the beginning reader to reduce the random nature of his responses; the constraints imposed by the rules of the skill narrows the range of errors he is likely to make.

Evidently, if a child is reading for meaning he employs his own intuitive sense of the language to make some inferences or guesses about the symbols before him. The more he understands the material, the more likely it is that his guesses will be accurate. The more he has control over his language (that is, the more he knows its vocabulary and its structure), the more probable that his predictions will be correct.

While most linguists support the view that oral language is operant in learning to read, its effect is not altogether understood. Observations of deaf children learning to read suggest that some success can be obtained without direct use of oral skills. It is possible that deaf children move from written forms to oral forms rather than the reverse. Weaver and Kingston (1971) note that we lack knowledge of the psychological operations involved in reading. Heavy reliance on oral language production does not imply that oral language and reading language share the same operations. At this time, however, it seems to be an impossible task to construct the psychological processes of the reader.

There is evidence that the more the reader can make use of his language skills in predicting correctly, the less he need rely on the mediating skills that he employed in early reading. It seems probable, as well, that the more the young reader is involved with an attempt to derive meaning from the printed page, the more he will make use of his linguistic knowledge.

The beginning reader appears to have "learned to read," when he leaves behind the early strategies, and proceeds to read fluently. The beginning reading skills serve as resources to be used when the reader must decipher a word for which he has no immediate recognition, or must parse a sentence which does not appear to make sense. Obviously, the difficulty of the material and the experience of the reader have a great deal to do with the number of times these early skills are called on for successful understanding.

According to Smith (1971, p. 226), the "processing of visual information is not instantaneous but takes a significant amount of time, during which losses always occur. Information is very quickly lost in reading. A child who has to read letter by letter, or even word by word, has very little chance of comprehending."

Rate, then, is another variable that has an effect on the way in which reading material is understood. The beginning reader uses devices for learning to read that, if employed too frequently, reduce his opportunities for successful comprehension. Since most beginning readers can integrate decoding skills with sufficient language competence, they bridge the gap from labored to fluent reading in the first few years of instruction. The bilingual child frequently has difficulty making the transition.

Syntax, also, serves to aid the reader in his understanding of the text. Although the child cannot consciously describe the syntax of his language, most children past 6 years of age have mastered some of the basic syntactic structures of the languages that they speak. Carol Chomsky (1969) has discovered that children vary in their rate of acquisition of the more complex structures of the English language.

This sense of the syntax of the language reduces the number of alternatives possible in any given sentence. Speakers of a language construct sentences that manifest the rules of the language structure. It is in this sense that the structure is known. When confronted with printed symbols the knowledge of that structure comes into play in deducing the possible words that these symbols might represent.

It is not suggested that reading materials are simply transliterations of speech, but rather that the basic syntax of a language in its graphic form is the same as its oral form. If a child is allowed to make calculated guesses when he reads, he probably will predict words that conform to the grammar of the language. Furthermore, language makes sense; that is, speakers of language expect it to communicate something understandable. And it is in the very nature of humans' inclination to make sense of the world that the knowledge they have of the structure and semantics of their language is brought to bear on the reading process. Evidently, these nonvisual sources of information play a significant role in transferring symbols and sounds into words and sentences. Such knowledge permits the reader to scan visual patterns in order to confirm his expectations. Incorrect guesses will alter the reader's progress toward comprehension. He will have to reevaluate the sentence or lose the meaning altogether. Correct expectations confirm meaning and facilitate fluent reading.

Before the young child begins to read, he needs to know the purpose of reading, which is to abstract meaning from a text. Perhaps developing this understanding is one of the great values in reading aloud to preschoolers, since they are inducted into the reading process prior to its acquisition.

Teachers are conscious of those children who go through the motions of reading without actually "catching on." They recognize that a child is finally reading, or has made significant connections, when he is actively involved in making statements about the content of the printed material. Children who lack a basic knowledge of the language are clearly at a disadvantage in the beginning years of school, since they exist in a setting where instruction is predicated upon the assumption that they have control of their language.

Since reading is one aspect of language, it seems likely that the skills used by children in language development may also be used in learning to read. There are, of course, no immediate one-to-one correspondences between learning to speak and learning to read. The child learns to speak by formulating internal rules based on the input he receives. His correct verbal behavior is expanded and reinforced by others. As Wardhaugh (1971, pp. 6–177) asserts, there is no "conscious beginning point for the child." Learning to read, however, usually takes place within a formal instructional setting, often with resultant anxiety.

It does seem reasonable to assume, however, that some of the language skills that the child has developed in learning to speak are useful in learning to read. Children have already discerned significant differences among the sounds in their language in order to hear and to speak them. Selecting significant differences in sounds can be used as a basis for selecting differences among the visual representations. Gibson, Shurcliff, and Yonas (1962, 1970) theorize that reading is acquired through developmental stages. The first of these processes develops skills for learning to read, namely, the speech and the graphic act. Competence in hearing and speaking must come first; awareness of graphic features develops next. The authors state that children learn to differentiate sounds, letters, and words by becoming aware of distinctive features. They move from this level of perception to the awareness of the internal structure of words, by inducing letter–sound correspondence from known to unknown words. Lastly, the reader forms rules of unit formation, using structural principles to read in larger and more efficient units. At present there exist several models of the reading process, but not one that fully explains acquisition and competence.

It is agreed, however, that the degree to which children attain competence in oral language influences their control of the language they read. The problem of reading in a language over which this fundamental control is hampered can be readily perceived. The bilingual child's problems are compounded by having two language codes that present alternatives to him. The bilingual child may know much about his two languages, but at beginning school age he probably does not separate these languages. The child is confused because he cannot rely on his intuition for adequate information. This pushes him farther away from comprehending.

Teachers frequently assume that bilingual children require a more atomized reading instruction in order to remediate what they perceive as a language deficiency in the school dominant language. Thus, the instructional process tends to move in a direction that may prove to be counterproductive to the beginning bilingual reader. Instead of a format that allows the child to make errors and guesses, teaching methods break the reading process into minute and sequenced parts, removing the context that allows for the possibility of errors. Gumperz and Hernandez-Chavez (1972), in their analysis of first-grade reading sessions in racially integrated California schools, observe that the "slower readers" (in most cases black or Chicano children) were instructed in the alphabet and spelling, while the "advanced learners" were allowed to read stories, deal with words in context, and participate in conversational activities.

Instructional approaches, which have been developed presumably to accommodate differences in learning styles of slow and advanced learners, may produce long delays in bilingual children's acquisition of fluent reading skills.

Socioeconomic factors, achievement, and language

A discussion concerned with teaching bilingual children to read must include an important variable that affects most bilingual children in this country, namely, the socioeconomic status of their families. Much has been written of the relationship between poverty and low academic achievement. There seems to be little doubt that failure in learning to read adequately is one source of generally poor school success, since so much of the academic requirements are based on reading as a mode of learning.

Educational research has contributed much to a store of statistical data on the low achievement of lower socioeconomic groups. Many theories have developed regarding the possible causes of that failure, among which social class differences in educational and occupational goals, auditory perception dysfunctions, language variance, and the more outrageous notions of differential distribution of intelligence among social classes have been proposed.

Let us examine the development of language of lower socioeconomic status groups and, in particular, the theories regarding language difference and its concomitant effect on standard English usage. The "causes" of academic failure are too complex to be explained in terms of only one variable, such as language, but its elucidation for the purposes of inquiring into the potential conflict arising for young children learning to read seems justified.

Clearly, the bilingual children who are having most difficulty in learning to read are children of lower socioeconomic status who suffer the disjunctions between community and school that most persons of such economic status suffer.

Lawton (1968) refers to the differences between lower- and middle-class families in terms of their family structure, child-rearing practices, language, and cognitive styles. These variables are seen as the major factors in the different achievement patterns of the children of each strata. The tendency for lower-income persons to be restricted in their mobility out of the community increases their need to develop strong networks of community and family relationships. Discipline patterns relate to immediate and structured goals. Studies of social class differences in achievement suggest a strong interrelationship between social control, language, and cognition. Josephine Klein (1965) points to the traditional group (ethnic or social class) that limits its member toward change and distrusts the abstract. She suggests that people are affected by their experiences to some extent by the way they speak or think about them in words, and that the more obscure or abstract the factors are in their experiences, the less their actions will be determined by them. Although it is difficult, perhaps impossible, to determine "what people think," there is little doubt that the ways in which persons of different social classes describe their experiences, and the range of verbal behavior they demonstrate, differ between lower- and middle-income groups.

Several explanations for these differences in linguistic behavior have been attempted. Nisbet (1961) studied the relationship between size of family and verbal development and found that size, while not a crucial factor, may be a contributing one toward the apparent slower development of verbal skills among lower-income children. Lawton (1968, p. 20) reports that McCarthy's review of the literature in 1954 found consistent data that support the hypothesis that socioeconomic status was related to differences in verbal usage among children. Subsequent studies have supported these findings; among the most prominent are the studies of Loban (1963) and Strickland (1962). Frequent explanations for these findings are that lower-income homes present fewer or less adequate speech models to children and that large families with traditional frameworks tend to provide less verbal stimulation.

Vera John's study (1963) of language differences among children relates the language abilities of labeling, relating, and categorizing with the linguistic levels of morphology, syntax, and "internal processes," thus providing an analysis of language differences in cognitive and linguistic terms. She concludes that middle-income children perform better than lower-income children on abstract labeling tasks, and in categorizing objects, persons, and events. They also tend to be more sensitive to language socialization and are generally at an advantage where precise and abstract language is required.

While language and thought are not one and the same thing, the relationship between the two seems to be well documented in the theories of psychology and sociology. Lawton (1968, p. 17) supports McClelland's statement that "language is the best, if not the only, operational way at present of investigating thought patterns" (McClelland, 1953, p. 249). The writings of Vygotsky (1962), Piaget (1959), and Bruner (1964) make similar assumptions.

While there are forms of thought that are nonverbal, without language, thinking is limited. Asserting that there are forms of thought that do not include speech, Vygotsky nonetheless concludes that "the speech structures mastered by the child become the basic structures of his thinking. . . . Thought development is determined by language, i.e., by the linguistic tools of thought and by the sociocultural experience of the child" (Vygotsky, 1962, p. 51).

In Piaget's model, language is increasingly important, particularly by the period of concrete operations (the point at which most children receive formal instruction in reading) and at the period of formal operations, in implementing abstract thought. Although Piaget does not give to language the critical role in thinking that Vygotsky does, he does recognize the strong interrelationship between language and the higher thinking processes (Piaget, 1959).

Basil Bernstein's (1961) elaborate theory of linguistic development and social class examines the social processes that determine cognitive development. He proposes that "forms of spoken language, in the process of their learning, elicit, reinforce, and generalize distinct types of relationships with the environment and create particular dimensions of significance" (Bernstein, 1961, p. 288).

Bernstein also notes that the acquisition of certain linguistic forms reinforces skills that are crucial for educational success and that "these forms of language use are culturally not individually determined" (Bernstein, 1961, p. 289). These linguistic patterns are determined essentially by the different social conditions of middle- and lower-class communities. He suggests that the level of linguistic skill is independent of innate intelligence (Bernstein, 1961, p. 291), and that differences in language use between social strata are related to the different emphases on what is regarded as relevant. Once speakers are limited to a mode of language in which syntax and structure are rigid and restricted, however, they are subsequently restricted in their development of abstract forms of expression and thought. The lower-class speaker who uses what Bernstein calls a "public language" or "restricted code" is restrained in his language usage in various social situations that require a more complex language usage. The speaker of this more formal or complex language is able to make individual and elaborated speech acts and can elaborate more fully on his thoughts about various persons, objects, and events when confronted with a situation that does not allow him to use his own restricted code.

Agreeing with other theories of child-rearing effects on educational achievement and of the interrelationship of language usage and social control, Bernstein sees the two social strata as marking different goals for their children, the lower class relating to more immediate needs and the middle class toward future rewards. The language of the middle-class parent sensitizes the child to an organization of words that implies nuances of relativity, future status, and self-regulation of behavior. It is a language that requires precision, in order to distinguish fine differences among elements and one that presumes subjective intent as relevant.

The parent–child relationship of the lower-class family is distinguished by a language in which intent is verbally explicit. The verbal forms used are expressive and direct and transmit a sense of immediacy, maximizing "the direct experience of affective inclusiveness rather than verbally conditioned emotional and cognitive differentiation" (Bernstein, 1961, p. 297).

While all classes develop verbal interactions that are implicit, immediate, and direct, it is the middle-class child who experiences both the informal language form and the elaborated verbal form just described, and who can, when faced with the formality and expectations of the schools, conform to these requirements. The lower-class child's language development has deeper roots in his immediate environment, which frequently fails to prepare him for the subtle verbal expressions he encounters in the school.

For the bilingual child of lower-income status, the discrepancy between formal school language and his own can be very great. The linguistic forms prevalent in the speech of lower-income persons are combined with a dual-language usage, additionally complicating the child's relationship to the school's expectations. It has been suggested that the cognitive development of the lower-income child may be affected by the forms of the language he uses; for the bilingual child, the issue becomes even more complicated because his thought processes may not be immediately associated with either of his languages. While there is generally no inferiority of bilinguals' performance on tests of nonverbal tasks, lowered performance on tests requiring verbal responses suggests the impact of this verbal confusion. The lack of precision between his language and his thought may be the most significant cause of the bilingual's depressed performance on intelligence tests.

Implications for bilingual children who are learning to read

BILINGUALISM AND SOCIAL CLASS

The convergence of a bilingual mode of expression and a socioeconomic status that relegates large numbers of bilingual children to a state of poverty is seen as the major problem in the bilingual child's ability to meet early school expectations. Each aspect—language or social class—can be, in itself, a contributing factor toward potential school failure. But for the bilingual child, each aspect must be recognized as containing additional burdens.

Although it would be difficult to assess the weight of each of the factors contributing to difficulty for the lower-class bilingual child, the impact of low socioeconomic status is well documented for all children of such strata. The middle-class bilingual child is sensitized to language forms that are consistent with the overall aims of most middle-class school systems. His or her language may have, in fact, been acquired in ways that permit separateness between the two languages. In addition, the middle-class bilingual child is essentially more socialized toward the norms of school life than his lower-class counterpart, despite potentially similar problems in language confusion.

Since learning to read depends heavily upon language and thought, it appears that a higher level of linguistic competence would be beneficial to the beginning reader. What may be of even greater importance, however, are those aspects of cognition that are required to clue into a system of values upon which the school system is predicated, values that delay gratification, address the future, and recognize subtle differences among persons and events, allowing the individual to make subjective decisions about his own actions. Since these values also contribute to the capacity to think in relative terms, they have a place in both the cognitive and affective dimensions of a person's life. Communities that use language variations different from those in the schools do not always provide opportunities for children to acquire language forms necessary for dealing with school expectations.

BILINGUALISM AND READING TEXTS

When a bilingual child enters school, he is confronted with reading materials that are written, for the most part, in the school dominant language rather than the home dominant language. In addition, the content of the reading materials reflects the values and mores of the dominant culture and may cause the bilingual child to have difficulty in relating to the content, as well as the language, of the book he is given to read.

Recently, some publishers have made an attempt to produce materials that reflect an urbanized or ethnically balanced picture of society. This, in itself, does not appear to be the answer to the reading problems of bilingual children, but it is probable that the effort toward revising content, combined with more knowledge about the language and the reading processes, could provide a basis for better instructional strategies. Since the problem of low achievement among lower-income bilingual children is a very complex issue, it is assumed that the solution of that problem will come about by attending to several facets of the issue.

BILINGUALISM AND PREDICTION IN READING

As has been suggested by recent theories into the reading process, the reader relies on his language sense in order to make predictions about what he reads. The more he is able to do so, the less he depends on early reading skills and the more he is able to comprehend. When one uses a language system that includes different cues from those presented in the standard text, one is confronted with innumerable barriers to one's intuitive expectations, which leads one to a state of confusion. The harmony between expectation and actuality is the condition that permits the reader to attain competence. The disharmony created by failure to predict slows the reader to a painful process of word-by-word decoding. Although this latter approach may help implement a beginning reader's task, it stands in the way of fluent mastery of the text, and, more importantly, it diminishes comprehension.

The bilingual child deals with both a different vocabulary and a different syntax system from which he must make his predictions. He also may have a different set of connotations for some of the vocabulary words he encounters in texts written in English. Without sufficient early success, he is likely to withdraw; certainly he is not likely to become competent in the process that he is trying to acquire.

Our educational system does not allow for much freedom for children in the primary grades, where skills acquisition is considered paramount and learning is considered to take place in one mode. The child learns early that making mistakes is deplored, and he develops mechanisms to avoid the criticism that he feels he will encounter. These behaviors may act to inhibit the child from creating a personal environment in which he learns productively. Involvement with the school dominant language is curtailed for the young bilingual child. The degree of experimentation permitted could be related to the degree of success the bilingual child is likely to have. Smith (1971) points out that the child acquires mastery over a very complex system of language in a very short time, requiring minimal input. Much of this mastery has occurred because the child is permitted to discover the rules that govern the relevant sound, structures, and meanings of his language.

When the child approaches beginning reading, he has had considerable cognitive experience in dealing with language. Smith (1971, p. 225) asserts that there are additional knowledges that the child must acquire in order to read, but that this information can be given the child in a form so that he may create generalizations from the knowledge he already possesses:

> He needs to learn what are the distinctive features of written language and their relations to letters and words and meanings. He needs to know what makes and what does not make a difference in reading.

While some of these differences can be taught, Smith believes that a child cannot be shown the significant differences of written language; he has to discover them for himself.

In an instructional situation in which the child is permitted to make generalizations about the written features of language, the teacher's role shifts from one of direct instruction to one that provides feedback. Essentially the child has to arrive at a point in learning where he can make rules, try them out, and evaluate and revise them, based on the responses he receives. The teacher can become one source of feedback, thereby allowing the child to know if he is on the right track. If given when needed, feedback can stimulate a child to continue learning. When the child is learning to read in an atmosphere that permits mistakes, he will risk them for the sake of creating rules and categories that help him become a fluent reader.

The bilingual child could benefit from the kind of instruction that allows discovery of the school dominant language in both oral and written forms. Encouragement in listening and conversing in that language should take place with the permissive notion of discovery. The child should be given the opportunity to "do" the language, with just sufficient feedback to help him continue. Similarly, when he reads in a language over which he is still gaining control, he will require a setting that allows for experimentation and emphasizes comprehension rather than word calling. The risk he takes will probably be in direct relationship to the teacher's attitude.

We must naturally assume that there will be some conflict between the child's natural language and his second one. The importance of developing a compatible relationship between the two need not be underestimated. It should be assumed that the child associates important attitudes and values with his natural language and that these must be retained while the child is using his second language. The conflict that arises between the use of the two languages has little to do with inherent attributes of either, but rather with the societal attitude that devalues one and prefers the other. Clearly, young children cannot be expected to comprehend this unnatural attitude toward their language. On the contrary, it can lead only to confusion and a diminuition of their self-concept. With a sufficient sense of loyalty to their families and community, this confusion reverts to one of distrust for the dominant culture and its language preference.

A rich language program is implied as a beginning solution to the bilingual child's problem. That solution probably can take place only in classrooms where involvement and experimentation are valued and where it is understood that language is internalized when creative use is encouraged. In order for children to read the language, they must be able to begin to think in the language. If we are going to take seriously the notion that language is a measure of thought and that language and thought are strongly interrelated, then these ideas must be incorporated in the curriculum development of the schools.

Specific programs in beginning reading instruction can be analyzed in terms of the time available for creative oral usage. The child's experiences should become the basis for learning to read. O'Brien sums up the complexity of the task when she recognizes that "the reading act is so intricately enmeshed in the entire process of language, culture and social experience that it is very difficult to determine the manner in which a child first perceives written symbols as meaning" (1973, p. 103). A reading approach that links the child's language production to the reading process is an attempt to create a situation in which that perception can be made.

One such method is the language experience approach in which the child's dictation becomes the basis for reading. This is an instructional strategy that allows the child to provide his own semantic and syntactic components. All of the words and structures he is asked to read will be part of his own oral language usage. The approach offers the child an opportunity to realize the relationship between spoken and written symbols. Until a child recognizes that relationship, he is not actually reading.

A further advantage of the language experience approach is that it involves the child actively in a process in which his own experiences are given overt value. It is assumed that a highly individualized and "ego-involved process" will be useful to the bilingual child in trying to bridge the gap between home and school.

An alternative approach to teaching the bilingual child to read in his second language would bring the child into the reading process through his first or natural language. A basic premise of this approach is that reading is a thinking process, based on secure control over the language. The process itself is the aspect that counts. Once the reader can become a competent reader in the language he understands well, the transfer toward reading in another language is facilitated. There are many factors to consider in this approach, among which are teacher staffing; the traditional role of the school as representative of the majority culture; and the relationship between the short-range and long-range goals of a reading program in the schools.

Of immediate concern, however, is the relationship of the reading process to the child's language development. One concern that any reading program must consider is that the child may have inconsistent or inadequate control of either of the two languages he is acquiring. The bilingual communities of the United States are integrated with a dominant culture that pervades the daily life of the community. The language spoken by its members reflects the convergence of these two cultures. Adult models, representing complex language usage and a high level of literacy, are not always available. Therefore, it is important to provide the child with opportunities to acquire some competence in both of his oral languages before proceeding to the reading process.

Although the problems of social class factors will still be operant, a reading approach that uses the child's natural language and places a value on the subculture's natural language system, while increasing the child's ability in the dominant culture's language, will provide the bilingual child with just those supports necessary for success in beginning reading. Once some competence has been acquired in both languages, reading in both languages will become possible for the bilingual child.

References

Bernstein, B. Social class and linguistic development: A theory of social learning. In A. H. Halsey, J. Floud, and C. A. Anderson (Eds.), *Education, economy and society*. New York: Free Press, 1961.

Bruner, J. S. The course of cognitive growth. *American Psychologist*, 1964, *19*, 1–15.

Carroll, J. B. *Language and thought*. Englewood Cliffs, N.J.: Prentice–Hall, 1964.

Chomsky, C. *The acquisition of syntax in children 5 to 10*. Cambridge, Mass.: MIT Press, 1969.

Dulay, H. C., and Burt, M. K. Goofing: An indicator of children's second language learning strategies. *Language Learning*. 1972, *22*, 235–252.

Dulay, H. C., and Burt, M. K. Should we teach children syntax? *Language Learning*, 1973, *23*, 245–258.

Dulay, H. C., and Burt, M. K. Errors and strategies in child second language acquisition. *TESOL Quarterly*, 1974, *8*, 129–136. (a)

Dulay, H. C., and Burt, M. K. A new perspective on the creative construction process in child second language acquisition. *Language Learning*, 1974, *24*, 253–278. (b)

Fishman, J. A. Domains and the relationship between micro- and macro-linguistics. In J. Gumperz and D. Hymes (Eds.), *Directions in sociolinguistics*. New York: Holt, 1972.

Gibson, E. J., Shurcliff, A., and Yonas, A. The role of grapheme–phoneme correspondences in the perception of words. *American Journal of Psychology*, 1962, *75*, 554–570.

Gibson, E. J., Shurcliff, A., and Yonas, A. Utilization of spelling patterns by deaf and hearing subjects. In H. Levin and J. Williams (Eds.), *Basic studies on reading*. New York: Basic Books, 1970.

Goodman, K. The psycholinguistic nature of the reading process. In K. Goodman (Ed.), *The psycholinguistic nature of the reading process*. Detroit: Wayne State University Press, 1973.

Gumperz, J., and Hernandez-Chavez, E. Bilingualism, bidialectism, and classroom interaction. In C. Cazden, V. P. John, and D. Hymes (Eds.), *Functions of language in the classroom*. New York: Teachers College Press, 1972.

John, V. P. The intellectual development of slum children: Some preliminary findings. *American Journal of Orthopsychiatry*, 1963, *33*, 813–822.

Klein, J. *Samples from English culture*. Vol. 2. *Child rearing practices*. London: Routledge, 1965.

Lawton, D. *Social class, language and education*. London: Routledge and Kegan Paul, 1968.

Loban, W. *The language of elementary school children*. NCTE Research Report No. 1. Champaign, Ill.: National Council of Teachers of English, 1963.

McClelland, D. C. *The achievement movement*. New York: Appleton, 1953.

Nisbet, J. Family environment and intelligence. In A. H. Halsey, J. Floud, and C. A. Anderson (Eds.), *Education, economy, and society*. New York: The Free Press, 1961. Originally published 1953.

O'Brien, C. *Teaching the language different child*. Columbus, Ohio: Charles E. Merrill, 1973.

Piaget, J. *Language and thought of the child*. London: Routledge and Kegan Paul, 1959.

Smith, F. *Understanding reading—A psycholinguistic analysis of reading and learning to read*. New York: Holt, 1971.

Strickland, R. G. The language of elementary school children. *Bulletin of the School of Education* (Indiana University), 1962, *38* (4).

Vygotsky, L. S. *Thought and language*. Cambridge, Mass.: MIT Press, 1962.

Wardhaugh, R. Theories of language acquisition in relation to beginning reading instruction. In F. Davis (Ed.), *The literature of research in reading with emphasis on models*. New Brunswick, N.J.: Rutgers Graduate School of Education, 1971.

Weaver, W. W., and Kingston, A. J. Modeling the effects of oral language upon reading language. In F. Davis (Ed.), *The literature of research in reading with emphasis on models*. New Brunswick, N.J.: Rutgers Graduate School of Education, 1971.

Relationship of "Life-Space" to Human Aggression: Implications for the Teacher in Bilingual–Bicultural Education

JOAN C. DYE, Hunter College of the City University of New York

This chapter is based on the premise that a teacher needs to be sensitive to the total learning environment of his students, both the psychological and the physical. It is divided into three sections. The first contains a clarification of the terms *aggression* and *life-space*, as well as a discussion of the relationship between these two concepts. The second consists of an examination of this relationship in the school setting and suggestions for ways to alter the school environment. The third provides ideas for the study and experimentation in a school setting.

Life-space and human aggression

AGGRESSION: A BIOLOGICAL UNIVERSAL

Aggression has been described as "attacking" or "initiating" action (Morris, 1967, p. 175). Its function, ecologically speaking, is to permit an organism to deal with its natural surroundings, its *oikos* (household), which includes all other animals and plants. In animals, aggression is generally a form of physical activity that fulfills a need, such as killing an animal of another species to satisfy hunger, competing with a member of the same species for sexual gratification, or battling to establish territory when the population is too dense to sustain life for all. According to Konrad Lorenz (1968), aggression is ongoing in a healthy animal. This permanent urge leads to a state of unrest and random activity or "purposive searching" if it is not directed toward the fulfillment of needs.

This state of unrest or turbulence is identified by Morris (1967) as a physiological preparation for attack, common to man and animals. It is relieved through taking action (the act of aggression), the goal of which is domination over another being or over the environment. In human beings, as in animals, if aggression does not culminate in some physical struggle with a resolution that will eliminate the tension, it is directed toward some appeasement or displacement activity (redirected to another person, object, or activity)—or toward escape.

When there is no resolution, or if the expression of aggression is completely blocked, it may be turned inward to fear, anxiety, or depression, or perceived as coming from a source outside the self. In extreme cases of aggression turned inward in self-hatred, the resolution may take the extreme form of suicide. In all cases, however, the physiological preparation of the organism is the same. More adrenalin is secreted, the senses become more alert, and, generally speaking, the organism has more power potential.

What Morris describes as a "state of turbulence" is described by Elton McNeil (1965, p. 28) as a human restlessness essential to life. It is a necessary apparatus for aggressive responses and is present at birth, although it is subject to individual differences. In animals, aggression can be increased experimentally through repeated success in fighting and decreased through repeated defeats or by lack of encounters—a sort of programming for violence or for docility. According to Redl and Wineman (1957) children can also be programmed for violence.

Patterns for directing aggressive behavior inward as fear, anxiety, and self-hate are also fixed in childhood (McNeil, 1965). Aggression, whether turned inward or outward, is heightened by frustration, which occurs when there is a discrepancy between an individual's desire to resolve a problem and his or her inability to do so. The bulk of human aggressiveness may be caused by frustration, a thwarting of the constructive drive necessary for self-defense.

If the accumulated aggression ("action-specific energy") is not discharged through a motor pattern, if it is dammed up and "subjected to long stagnation by withholding all releasing stimuli," then it "strains to break through" (Kuenen, Lorenz, Tinbergen, Schiller, & Von Uexküll, 1957). When the internal pressure of accumulated energy reaches such a high level that it breaks through all inhibitions, the motor pattern goes off by itself, like a reflex action. This extreme form of aggressive behavior, aggression released fully and abruptly in a state of high energy arousal, can be described as *violence.*

Whenever aggression is discharged, whether or not its intensity has been heightened by frustration, the release from tension leads to a feeling of well-being or equilibrium. The form, however, in which this tension is released depends on the past experience and training of the individual, as does the level of tolerance for frustration and for the conditions that lead to frustration. Aggression can be discharged through such diverse activities as shouting and raging, committing murder, creating a work of art, scrubbing a floor, wrestling with an intellectual problem, and beating oneself (Storr, 1968).

LIFE-SPACE: AN INDIVIDUAL PERCEPTION

As noted earlier, the organism has a household, *oikos*, which includes all other animals and plants. Edward Hall (1969) has suggested that the way this environment is perceived and the individual's reactions to it are culturally conditioned. He has written that different cultures have different perceptions of spatial boundaries as well as different concepts of time. Furthermore, he has noted that speaking distances vary across cultures and what feels comfortable to a Spanish speaker may make an American irritable without his being consciously aware of why.

A modification of the idea that cultural orientation is the chief factor in conditioning speaking distance was suggested by Stanley Jones, a researcher who worked for 2 years in various areas of New York City. He produced evidence that conditions of poverty forced people to change their ethnic–cultural orientation to a stronger "culture of poverty." In overcrowded areas, he found that everyone stood about 1 foot apart regardless of ethnic background—closer than the usual distance of 2 feet ascribed to Americans (Fast, 1970, pp. 186–187).

In addition to the conditioning effects of both culture and environment, factors relating to interpersonal relations can affect perceptions and reactions. Although Hall (p. 148) gives an illustration of culturally conditioned territorial needs in the situation of mother and daughter in the kitchen, the factor of who will dominate is also settled there. Someone who is exerting his dominance will take over more of the territory or have priority over more of the available space. What is more important than whether an individual maintains, shares, or gives up his territory or "preserve" is his control over what happens to his claim (Goffman, 1971, p. 60).

It would seem that not only can the relationship between actual physical space needs and aggressive behavior be seen to vary among individuals, but also that the heightening of aggression may be related as much to the individual's perceptions as to the actual physical space involved. For instance, in cases of overcrowding in an urban situation, the feeling of being overcrowded may be a feeling of being trapped in a socioeconomic situation. In cases where desperate people are driven to suicide, one often reads that they cannot be approached closely except by someone who has established some relationship of trust, indicating physical and psychological interaction. Even normal people, when angry, seem to signal others to keep a greater physical distance.

The idea of "life-space" can be seen to be a matter of individual perception when one examines the physiological aspects of space perception. According to Robert Wallis, the concept of space is developed through a form of programing, a "progressive fashioning of the mind," which is essentially temporal and interacts "with the organism which is at the same time spatial and temporal" (1968, p. 21). Physical space and time condition the mind through sight, hearing, touch, and muscular movement.

In his book, Wallis' purpose is to study the relationship of temporal disturbance to behavioral psychoses. His premise is that the brain is a relatively closed system and that time is what permits an internal action to develop. He sees the concept of space as being related to the sense of distance between desire "revealed by the sense of sight" and the "muscular movement necessary to attain it," which implies that the "sense of distance" is temporal. "Action and temporal function are made and unmade together" (Wallis, 1968, p. 228). As José Delgado (1969, p. 234) expressed it, "time and distance appear to have different meanings to different observers."

The individual's "life-space," therefore, appears to be a personal construct of how he is placed in space and time and with relation to others. This construct, culturally conditioned and idiosyncratically experienced, seems to be a psychological and physiological concept, including both inner and outer reality. A person can require "room to grow" intellectually as well as physically. Someone can intrude on another's personal space by staring or speaking in a "penetrating" way as well as by bodily invasion. A person "confined" to a wheelchair can have "flights" of the imagination that take him on a tour of the world.

RELATIONSHIP OF AGGRESSION TO LIFE-SPACE

If life-space is considered both a psychological as well as a physiological concept, it can include psychological as well as physical opportunities for the release of tension created by the turbulence of aggression, an essential life element. Turbulence will be increased when either physical or psychological conditions prevent an organism from taking a resolving action, be it fight, flight, displacement, redirection, or sublimation. Inadequate life-space may be conceived as whatever prevents the actualization of the self and the integration with others. Being deprived of life-space can be a cause for heightened aggression.

Frustrations occur for everyone but it is likely they will occur more frequently when an individual's usual behaviors for directing aggression (action for well-being) are thwarted, misunderstood, or do not achieve the expected results. This situation can occur whenever an individual is not familiar with the environment. Taking Hall's concept of variations across cultures of acceptable conversational distances, for instance, one can see that an individual's need for closeness and connectedness could be thwarted if the other individual seems to be signaling rejection by retreating backwards during a conversation. If there is no conscious awareness on the part of a child of how different cultures use space in this situation, he could feel anxious and unhappy, and perhaps develop a sense of alienation.

In a New York City neighborhood, Irish and Italian residents expressed antagonism and resentment at the "invasion" of their territory by "Hispanic aliens," through physical, acoustic, and olfactory spatial intrusion—"crowding the sidewalks with their stalls of merchandise, filling the air with loud music and spicy smells" (Cowan & Cowan, 1975, p. 8). The established residents seem to have been demonstrating what sociologists and anthropologists have documented as the hatred-producing power of neighborhood tensions, social inequality, social disorganization, and crowding, particularly in areas of poverty. They also seem to have been exhibiting the degree to which social customs and cultural mores can increase or decrease "the sum total of aggression engendered in the members of a society" (Redl & Wineman, 1957, p. 21).

Sidney Mintz (1970) pointed out that aggression expressed as rage or hatred against others is not the whole story. In a discussion of the struggle of black Americans against the restrictions of slavery, both the physical conditions and the removal of personal identity, he explained that much of the struggle was "hidden and subtle and is still little understood." He cited activities such as malingering, self-destruction, poisoning, and so on as techniques that "desperate people employ to keep their sanity when confronted with an inhuman social system" (Mintz, 1970, p. 19).

Although the suggestions contained in this chapter are directed towards improving the conditions of the individual's external reality, there are techniques that can be used to improve the individual's inner reality (self-perception) as well. Several innovative approaches have come from the "human potential" movement, which John Mann (1972) has comprehensively reviewed. The purpose of these techniques is to help the individual know himself, learn his strengths, appreciate his own worth, create and maintain strong bonds with others, and work to adjust his external environment. They can also help children set realistic goals for themselves and to experience success in achieving these goals, as well as to help them gain a feeling of competence and independence. These techniques help children learn how to deal with frustration as well as how to direct aggression into positive action.

Implications for the teacher

SCHOOL: A PSYCHOPHYSICAL ENVIRONMENT

Because of the interaction between mind and environment described earlier, school can be considered as a total environment, in which not only the interaction between people, but also the physical setting and ordering of time can be factors that influence aggressive behavior. This idea is confirmed in a description of a treatment center for very aggressive children that seems applicable to group living in a school classroom (Redl & Wineman, 1957, p. 284). Factors to which these aggressive children show great sensitivity include the architectural design, the space distribution, the arrangement and type of furnishings, the equipment, and even the style of housekeeping.

In a school setting, research has shown that the way the classroom is organized can affect students in a positive or negative way. A gloomy, barren, messy room helps create negative feelings that can result in disruptive behavior (Davis, 1974). Disorderliness in storing materials, which makes it difficult to find materials, and poor maintenance of equipment can also lead to disruptive behavior, by discouraging student interest. If the school setting has such a strong effect on learning, perhaps there should be more interdisciplinary research involving architects, interior decorators, educators, sociologists, psychologists, and parents.

An important consideration, according to Redl and Wineman (1957), in arranging an environment for children being treated for overly aggressive behavior is that the climate should not be too drastically different from their natural habitats. This may also be an important consideration for arranging a comfortable school for the child whose cultural background is different from that represented by the school, as a "newcomer suffers from a clouded perception of his environment and paralysis of self-confidence" (Thompson, 1973, p. 41). Arrangement of a familiar place can include such items as the use of color, which is "part of an individual's microspace that shapes him and which he manipulates to reach a better accommodation with his environment" (Thompson, 1973, p. 77).

Another part of the environment considered important in designing a physical setting is the amount of touching of others to which people are accustomed (St. Marie, 1973, pp. 15–16). In a "contact" culture, such as the Spanish, Italian, and French cultures, there is much physical contact, while there is little in a "noncontact" culture, such as the American, English, and Swiss cultures. Where greater contact is desired, chairs can be placed closer together to allow touching and more open space can be provided for greater personal interaction. Or, chairs can be placed far apart and small areas closed off, to provide privacy and to keep people apart.

Although there are differences in spatial perception that seem to be culturally conditioned, a person's individual needs can be influenced by his emotional states. A student in a high state of arousal, no matter what his culture, seems to need a greater distance between him and someone perceived to be an antagonist, such as the teacher (Thompson, 1973). The perceptive teacher can probably tell how close he can be to a student (or students) without making the student feel uncomfortable. He can become aware of nonverbal signals of withdrawal when personal space has been violated—such as the closing of eyes, withdrawal of chin chestward, moving backward, and general agitation, such as rocking, leg swinging, and tapping.

It is not only the students' spatial needs of which the teacher needs to be aware. A non-Hispanic teacher of Latin American students may find himself backing away from a student to reestablish his own personal boundaries if his cultural background has conditioned him to greater social distance. Both awareness and sensitivity are needed to discover both cultural and idiosyncratic variations in such subtle areas of personal interaction.

ORDERING SPACE

In addition to the adjustments of spatial relationships among people, adjustments based on principles of interior design in the physical environment can be made to meet student needs in the classroom. These adjustments include the manipulation of materials that provide sensory information in the three areas that make up a person's perception of space: (1) motion of the body (kinesthetic); (2) touch (tactile), including hearing, as eardrum and receptor cells in the skin "feel" vibrations; and (3) sight (visual) (Hochberg, 1964).

As the spatial sense is perceived by man in a simultaneous way, with the three types of spatial perception interacting (Kuenen *et al.*, 1957), space can be created or evoked by "all manner of associations among colors, textures, sounds, and their intervals" (McLuhan & Parker, 1968, p. 6). It appears that spatial perception can be influenced by aspects of the environment that involve all the senses. Some examples of ways in which the environment can be designed to influence spatial perception follow.

Creating a feeling of open space

Furniture can be folded, stacked, and pushed against the wall. Chairs can be pushed under the tables (most effectively if the backs fold down). Equipment can be hung on wall pegs, stored away in cupboards or hidden behind screens. Walls and furnishings can be painted light colors to give an impression of more space. Vertical lines and wall arrangements can be used to make ceilings seem higher, and horizontal lines can be used to give an impression of greater width. Large, mirrored areas or shiny, reflecting metal or plastic can be hung to give the illusion of additional space. Large windows with a view can be left free of curtains, and pictures with the illusion of depth can be hung to create a sense of openness.

Creating a feeling of closed-in space

Areas can be closed off and separated by barriers such as carrels, bookcases, folding screens. Fabric can be draped to form a canopy. Walls or partitions can be painted dark colors, shades drawn at windows, and rooms partially lit. Different colors, designs, and patterns can separate a large open area into smaller units.

Defining space

Areas can be marked off by storage cubbyholes or by clothing pegs. Personal possessions can be marked by unique decorations or by identifying colors or designs. White lines can identify boundaries between related groups of objects, as well as tie them together on a shelf. Large circles can be drawn in chalk on the floor to establish temporary boundaries.

Inviting close contact

Large open areas can be provided where several students can work together at a time. Chairs can be placed close together so their occupants will be within touching distance. Round tables can be used and chairs can be placed in a circle. Furniture can be arranged in special ways to influence the flow of conversation. Chairs can be placed around an activity area, such as an art or sewing table. Large areas can be painted in warm yellows or orange to help stimulate social participation.

Providing spatial flexibility and variety

Movable furnishings, including partitions, can be rearranged to accommodate changing spatial needs. Objects that are opposites in color, size, and shape can be placed near each other to provide greater spatial contrast. For instance, a light object can be placed against a dark background to make the object seem closer to the viewer. A tall, narrow cabinet can make a long, low bench next to it look closer to the floor. Objects placed at various levels can provide more stimulation than those lined up on one level, depending on the objects. Sounds coming from different directions and from different levels can also create the illusion of spatial changes. Sounds that grow gradually louder seem to be approaching, while those that grow softer seem to be fading into the distance.

Facilitating work

Supplies can be placed near the site of activities and storage organized for easy retrieval of equipment. Chairs can be placed far apart, not facing each other, to make it easier for students to work independently. Large areas can be colored green or blue-green to help relax tensions and to reduce muscular activity, as an aid to concentration. A spotlight or a vivid color, such as red, can draw attention to a particular area or object.

Reducing sensory stimulation

For eliminating noise, cork can be placed on shelves to eliminate the sounds of items being placed on them. Doors can be equipped with rubber bumpers to keep them from banging. Clothes closets and bookcases filled with books can line walls to insulate a source of noise. Headphones can be used for individual listening. Papers and books can be cleared from tables and desks. A curtain or blind can cover a bulletin board or other display area, as well as a window, to eliminate distractions.

Some general precepts that can be followed in designing physical space for students who are overly aggressive include: obtaining furniture designed and arranged to invite use; providing books and equipment made of sturdy material and placed where they are easy to obtain; arranging space that provides for both active and quiet activities; arranging several activities to occur at the same time; making allowances for wear and tear; offering a sense of order, but not a rigid order; and providing a setting related to sociological or cultural patterns.

ORDERING TIME

It is important not only to provide space that works toward eliminating tensions, but also to organize time through routines that relax and reduce anxiety. The organization of time is related to the perception of space. A disturbed child (in this case, over-aggressive) may perceive time as being of longer duration than may a child who is enjoying something (Redl & Wineman, 1957, p. 120). If time is perceived differently by a child whose culture is different from that of the school environment, he may also experience some disturbance or disorientation.

Important to timing are such considerations as how to gauge the optimum time to allow for different activities, how to arrange the sequence of activities, and how to flow from one activity to another. The teacher can help smooth transitions by having materials ready for the succeeding activity before interrupting students in what they are doing. It is also important that children see routines as a way to facilitate life rather than as a "potential challenge for goodness or badness" (Redl & Wineman, 1957, p. 295).

Routines that are just used for order's sake should be avoided. The purposes of routines should be "for ego-support, for providing for individual and group needs, for creating a climate of stability in expectations" (Smith & Geoffrey, 1968, p. 162). Routines also should be flexible. Limitations of space and of group size require rules and regulations that are inevitable, such as taking turns for sharing equipment. The classroom calendar can also be seen as a form of routine, with daily and weekly recurring activities (Smith & Geoffrey, 1968, p. 162).

In addition to using routines and regulations that promote order and security rather than fear and frustration, the teacher should prepare in advance the materials necessary for an activity. He can also prepare students for each step in order as well as provide suggestions for alternatives to achieve goals. By anticipating students' needs, he can help reduce emotional upsets (Smith & Geoffrey, 1968, p. 101).

The use of ritual can help reduce hostility by providing a "cooling-off" period. An example of how this technique was applied in a situation in the classroom was described by Smith and Geoffrey (1968, p. 82). They explained that a conflict occurred, when seats were changed, over who should sit near the teacher's desk. This conflict was resolved by the use of an elaborate procedure or ritual. First, those who wished to sit near the teacher's desk put their names on the board. Then these names were put into a hat, with some time used in finding the hat. After that, there was a vote to determine who should pull out the winning name; a classroom visitor was selected. By the time the decision was made, there was no more group hostility and there was no further argument about the seating arrangement.

Techniques such as these can be used to advantage in the special situation of the classroom. In this controlled environment, a setting can be arranged to help a child develop a sense of psychological relativity as well as to help him practice behaviors appropriate for a variety of situations. This goal can be accomplished in the classroom without the conflicting pressures of the outside world.

Delgado (1969, p. 237) has suggested that social integration might be improved through an understanding of psychological relativity. Such an improvement is important, because society forms the basis of each individual and because "personal destiny is related to, and in large part dependent on the destiny of the whole group." He noted that a person cannot be separated from his sensory world, since that world also forms the basis of each individual. New environments as well as encounters with other people can change perceptions and expectations. Perhaps Delgado's suggestion should be expanded to include an understanding of physiological relativity as well.

According to McLuhan and Parker (1968, p. 253), people tend to assimilate new sensory information in familiar ways. They may not even "receive" new information in some cases. McLuhan and Parker point out that people from different cultures screen sensory information in different ways, so that "experience as it is perceived through one set of culturally patterned sensory screens is quite different from experience perceived through another." When someone is confronted with new sensory information, therefore, it is processed in familiar ways, just as a man from Earth landing on the moon would have to "translate all lunar experience into familiar terms."

Ideas for study and experimentation

GATHERING INFORMATION

Like the man landing on the moon, the new student "lands" in the classroom and experiences some disorientation in time and space, particularly if this is the first experience of a classroom. For the bilingual student, the adjustment may be even more complicated, as he will be expected to function in two different environments. Although it is possible he will not become "bi-proxemic," that is, able to adapt spatially to two different cultures, he needs to feel comfortable at least.

It would seem that the teacher can most help a student become comfortable and feel less anxiety in the school environment if the teacher knows something about the student's "familiar" way of reacting to and interacting with the external environment. Such information can be obtained by observing the student's behavior and by asking questions. Some things the teacher may need to discover include the following.

Where does the student spend more time—in large, open areas or in closed areas?

Where does the student prefer to sit—in the rear of the room, at the side, in front, near a window, by himself, or with others?

Does the student generally seek to be in close contact with others, move his chair closer, lean toward, and touch them?

Does the student usually avoid close contact with others—lean or turn away?

Does the student keep his papers organized or is his desk cluttered? Does he pile up his papers or spread them out? Does he like to be surrounded by possessions or discard them?

Are there objects with which the student interacts—such as books, scientific or technical equipment, or art displays?

Does the student seem to prefer to sit in the same place or to shift places?

How does the student react if his accustomed seat is taken?

Does the student seek out some colors and reject others?

Does the student usually prefer working at a desk or table? Does he perch on a table or sprawl out on the floor? Does he get up and move around often?

Can the student ignore what is going on around him when he needs to concentrate on work or is he distracted by the environment?

Does the student tend to put things away after he uses them or does he leave them lying around? Does he become involved with several things at once or one at a time? Does the student relate to several people or one at a time?

Does the student feel uncomfortable when furniture or other objects are moved and rearranged or does he enjoy and seek change?

Does the student claim a larger territory than others by using more space physically, marking areas with his personal possessions, and making more noise? Does he claim a smaller area than others? Does he allow others to come into his space or does he discourage intrusions?

Does the student seem to indicate a preference or demonstrate a particular awareness in one area of sensory stimulation over others, such as visual, acoustic, or motor?

What type of room does a student design, using pictures from a magazine or making a personal sketch?

STRUCTURING THE ENVIRONMENT

When the teacher has obtained some information about students' individual identities and their present orientation to the external environment, he can begin to develop, with their cooperation and involvement, some ways to help them feel comfortable in new environments. He can help diminish the intensity of "cuture shock" by helping students make a gradual orientation to different ways of perceiving and interacting with different environments by beginning from the students' present orientation.

Such a gradual approach might help someone from a so-called "contact"culture feel less alienated and distressed in a "non-contact" setting. Very brief initial periods of exposure to a non-contact setting can be less devastating than total immersion. In addition, close contact through visual and acoustic means might be used to compensate for reduced close physical contact. Some cultures have been identified as "contact" and "non-contact" on the basis of how much physical touching takes place. It is possible, however, that some non-contact cultures may "touch" through other means, such as visually (their eyes met), or acoustically (her voice "caressed" him).

Specific techniques and strategies that a teacher and students may devise to help strengthen and develop the ability to function in various environments will depend on the ages of the students, size of the group, individual personalities and group interaction, the physical properties of the room, time spent there, and the educational activities that must be carried out. Therefore, the following ideas are not a list of techniques but of procedures that might be followed.

Identify needs (Step I) by answering such questions as the following:

What basic human needs are to be satisfied—such as a sense of identity and connectedness and feelings of competence and achievement?

What educational activities must take place? What additional optional activities are desirable? What is needed to carry out the activity, including the amount of time. How many people will be involved? Will there be group and individual activities?

How do individuals interact? Are some combinations more effective than others? How does the group function?

What are the various individual needs that students have expressed, in words or by their actions?

What are the different cultural settings in which students will be expected to function? What objects might be important to create a sense of cultural authenticity?

Analyze the existing space (Step II) by answering such questions as the following:

Will the same space be used to represent two different cultures or are separate rooms involved?

How large is the room or rooms? Where are the windows, doors, and closets?

How much time is available?

What furniture and equipment are available? Which ones serve more than one purpose?

What additional furnishings might be needed? Can they be purchased, borrowed, or improvised? How much, if any, money is available?

Design the environment (Step III) by keeping in mind that the real objective is not to create a setting into which the students must fit, but one with which they can identify and that can help them meet their basic needs. This objective will involve making decisions on furniture arrangement, color and design, storage and maintenance, and schedule of activities that reflect the needs of a particular group of students.

When planning the *furniture arrangement*, make several copies of a scale drawing of the room or rooms to be used. Indicate doors, windows, and built-in furniture such as closet, cupboards, laboratory equipment, sinks, and so on. Make scale cutouts of all movable furnishings available, (make several sets so that older students can participate in the planning). More than one plan will be needed if the setting does not always remain the same.

Decide on two or three basic arrangements of furniture depending on the types of activities to be carried out. Display the plans so that students and/or aides can help with the rearranging. One plan can indicate the usual arrangement of the room. Another can indicate a way to vary the usual plan to accommodate special activities as well as those engaged in fairly frequently. A third plan might indicate a way to gain maximum floor space for vigorous physical activity or for some special event. Be sure to consider needs for privacy as well as for interaction, for group and independent work, for flexibility, for transferring from one activity to another, and for safe traffic flow.

In deciding on *color and design,* try to accommodate needs and desires of the group and its individual members. If some things are not possible, seek alternatives. If walls cannot be painted the desired color, perhaps partitions or large sheets of heavy colored paper can be used. Colored light bulbs may be used for special effects. If one room is used as a setting for two distinctly different environments, perhaps reversible screens, table mats, and wall hangings can help change the setting, as well as can shifting the furniture. If the areas cannot be separated by barriers, they can be identified by unity of color, design, or shape (perhaps a graphic on the wall—which can also change the shape of the room).

In selecting *objects for display,* try to use those with which students can identify and that will enhance their feelings of well-being as well as help create a cultural ambience. These will probably include items made or contributed by the students themselves. The decision on where these should be placed can wait until the furnishings and work equipment have been ordered.

In planning for *storage and maintenance,* students can help make decisions on where and how things will be stored. There should be room for their personal possessions as well as for school materials. In elementary grades, it may have to be decided where and how to keep small animals. Some part of the planning should include the designation of responsibility for upkeep. If no one wants to water plants, for instance, there might be a decision to gain the same effect by using artificial ones.

Design should involve *scheduling,* as classes are usually large and thought needs to be given as to when activities might take place as well as to how materials and equipment will be shared. Small group activities of a special nature may have to be scheduled at a particular time or arrangements made for the time of the visiting specialist. Certain activities can be carried on simultaneously and others cannot. It may be important to have the whole group come together at certain times. At the end of the day or of a scheduled class time, some time has to be allowed to put equipment away or perhaps to rearrange furniture.

Improve the design (Step IV) by observing how the students interact and react to the environment created. Determine where adjustments need to be made to further encourage harmony of the group and to reduce individual tensions and anxieties. The following questions may be used by the teacher to guide his observation of the situation.

Is there space for the whole class to gather comfortably together or does there seem to be much pushing and shoving because of too little room?

Are some spaces overcrowded and others not used? What seems to be the factors that attract students to the favorite places?

Is friction being caused by inadequate traffic flow patterns? Can students get at supplies without interfering with other students?

Do students constantly rearrange the furnishings? Although flexibility and spontaneity may be desired, constant change may signal a need to change the basic design.

Is a student demonstrating more hostility in one cultural setting than in another? Is there anything that can make him more comfortable? For instance, if he shows a need for more contact, can he be seated near a traffic flow pattern, a door perhaps, or in a central location?

Are there visual or acoustic factors that seem to annoy? Do students react adversely to some colors, noises? (Note the negative, even agonized, expressions on students' faces when chalk makes noise on the board. Also some people are bothered if a picture is hanging crooked.)

Does a student seem angry because of a lack of status? Perhaps he can be given a job in which people come to him or an opportunity to fill more space by displaying art or written work or some other personal objects?

If a student is feeling especially pressured and frustrated by the demands of time, what spatial arrangements, colors used, ordering of activities, can be designed to provide a sense of tranquility?

What arguments and disagreements can be settled or avoided by arranging for more privacy, changing seating patterns, adjusting rules for taking turns, separating activity areas, changing the combinations of activities going on simultaneously, increasing or decreasing the number of participants in activities, and clearly defining personal territory?

The handling of space is seen by Abbey (1973, p. 14) as "one of the most critical elements in the total communication which goes on in schools." He refers to such items as interpersonal distances, the arrangement of furniture and the way people are positioned in relation to others. He, McLuhan and Parker (1968) and Mortensen (1972) emphasize the psychological affects which can be seen in relation to the physical setting. Mortensen (1972, p. 317) suggests that the "physical attributes of a communicative situation" can even affect the "psychological orientation, perception, [and] motivations," as well as "overt interactions" of the participants. The physical setting of the classroom, it seems, is more than a trivial matter of concern for the teacher.

References

Abbey, D. S. *Now see hear! Applying communication to teaching.* Toronto: The Ontario Institute for Studies in Education, 1973.

Cowan, P., and Cowan, R. For Hispanos, it's still the promised land. *The New York Times Magazine,* June 22, 1975, pp. 8–11, 39, 46–50.

Davis, J. E. *Coping with disruptive behavior.* Washington, D.C.: National Education Association, 1974.

Delgado, J. *Physical control of the mind.* New York: Harper & Row, 1969.

Fast, J. *Body language.* New York: M. Evans, 1970.

Goffman, E. *Relations in public.* New York: Basic Books, 1971.

Hall, E. T. *The silent language.* Greenwich, Conn.: Fawcett, 1969.

Hochberg, J. *Perception.* Englewood Cliffs, N.J.: Prentice–Hall. 1964.

James, M., and Jongeward, D. *Born to win: Transactional analyses with gestalt experiments.* Reading, Mass.: Addison–Wesley, 1971.

Kuenen, D. J., Lorenz, K., Tinbergen, N., Schiller, P., and Von Uexküll, J. *Instinctive behavior* (C. H. Schiller, trans.). New York: International Universities Press, 1957.

Lorenz, K. *On aggression* (M. K. Wilson, trans.). New York: Harcourt, Brace & Row, 1968.

Mann, J. *Learning to be: The education of human potential.* New York: The Free Press, 1972.

McLuhan, M., and Parker, H. *Through the vanishing point.* New York: Harper & Row, 1968.

McNeil, E. (Ed.). *The nature of human conflict.* Englewood Cliffs, N.J.: Prentice–Hall, 1965.

Mintz, S. W. Creating culture in the Americas. *Columbia Forum,* 1970, *13,* 22–26.

Morris, D. *The naked ape.* New York: McGraw–Hill, 1967.

Mortensen, C. D. *Communication, the study of human interaction.* New York: McGraw–Hill, 1972.

Redl, F., and Wineman, D. *The aggressive child.* Glencoe, N.Y.: The Free Press of Glencoe, 1957.

St. Marie, S. S. *Homes are for people.* New York: Wiley, 1973.

Smith, L. M., and Geoffrey, W. *The complexities of an urban classroom.* New York: Holt, 1968.

Storr, A. *Human aggression.* New York: Bantam Books, 1968.

Thompson, J. J. *Beyond words: Nonverbal communication in the classroom.* New York: Citation Press, 1973.

Wallis, R. *Time: Fourth dimension of the mind* (B. B. Montgomery and D. B. Montgomery, trans.). New York: Harcourt, Brace & World, 1968.

Bilingual Interaction Analysis:
The Development and Status

DARRYL R. TOWNSEND, The University of Texas at Austin

Despite an apparent controversy as to whether education is an art or a science, the profession itself is increasingly relying on objective measures. This trend can be seen in curriculum design as well as in attempts to analyze instruction. Wright (1960) found that only 8% of the empirical studies in child development that he analyzed in 1960 appeared to have any observational data base. This finding is in sharp contrast to the type of studies currently being reported in journals and texts.

One area in which reliance on observable data has markedly increased is the analysis of classroom behavior patterns. This procedure, commonly known as *interaction analysis,* attempts to quantify the behaviors of teachers and students for at least four purposes: (1) to describe the current practices operative in classrooms; (2) to monitor instructional systems, programs, or curricula; (3) to investigate relationships between classroom activities and the growth, progress, or change of the students affected; and (4) to train or augment the training of teachers.

The development of the philosophical bases on which objective observation currently rests stems from deep historical roots. Psychology, sociology, anthropology, child development, philosophy, and education have all made their contributions. Brandt (1975), in describing an historical overview of systematic approaches to school observation, cites four major sources as contributors: ecological psychology, ethnological research, interaction analysis, and behavior modification. Research developing from each of these four areas figure in the development of today's trend toward the use of objective observation systems. Brandt more than adequately relates the philosophical and theoretical aspects of these approaches.

The modern history of interaction analysis as a method of observing classroom behaviors began in the late 1950s with Ned Flanders. His work focused on the categories of behavior that would show relationships between teacher behavior or style and student learning. Since that relatively recent beginning, well over 200 individuals have contributed to the data base currently available.

In order to conduct his research, Flanders (1970) devised a 10-category system that would encode every conceivable verbal pattern that could occur in the classroom. Herein lies the theoretical base on which the interactionist works. From the pool of all possible behaviors, a set of categories is selected. These categories must be readily distinguishable and must reflect aspects of the classroom interaction process that are most relevant to the problem being explored. Behaviors are then recorded in the context of the theoretical framework that has been constructed. Finally, analyses are performed to determine the presence or lack of relationships among categories. Brandt (1975) emphasized the importance of the theoretical base by stating that "Theory is essential, therefore, in isolating important variables to be investigated, deriving meaningful categories for those variables, and providing a rationale for later interpretation" (pp. 23–24).

The diversity to which this theoretical base has been extended is staggering. More than 120 different classroom observational category systems have been identified (Simon & Boyer, 1967). Medley and Mitzel (1963, pp. 298–303) offer a convenient way to dicihotomize these instruments: (1) *category systems*, and (2) *sign systems*. The Flanders system is a category system. Each category is mutually exclusive, but collectively they represent all possible behaviors. A sign system identifies a discrete number of categories that are precisely defined and noted if they occur. No attempt is made to describe all interaction; a time period is set at the end of which the recorder notes which, if any, of the specified behaviors have occurred. The sign systems usually have a larger number of categories that are more specific, while the category systems will have fewer divisions, which are defined more broadly.

A third type of instrument is known as a *rating system*. Unlike the previous two, the rating scale proposes a continuum between two apparent opposites, e.g., strict–lenient, warm–cold. The recorder observes the interaction for a specified period, and records, usually on either a 5-point or 7-point scale, the degree to which each behavior was evident. Kent (1966) identified 133 forms of such rating systems. It seems safe to estimate that over 200 must be available today.

There are several differences among the various types of instruments. One difference is the type of recording procedure used. As mentioned, the category systems record each interaction as it occurs. A provision is usually included whereby if one behavior is prolonged, multiple recordings are made. The time period most often used is 3 seconds. Therefore, if one particular interaction lasts 12 seconds, four consecutive recordings will be made. With the sign systems and rating systems, the recording follows a period of observation, and, in most cases, there is no variation in recording if the event occurs once or 10 times.

Another difference concerns the items included. The distinction involves the use of high-inference or low-inference terms. The former describes terms that require the recorder to exercise considerable judgment in determining how or where to record a behavior. Examples include terms such as "kind," "helpful," "warm," and so on. The description *low-inference*, of course, refers to easily definable terms such as "teacher asks question," or "teacher sits down."

A third difference involves format. This difference refers to the particular dimension of classroom interaction on which the instrument focuses. Possible considerations in this category include teacher behavior, verbal or nonverbal; content or subject matter; language involved; and level of conceptualization. A recent development, since 1968, or so, has been the idea of multiple or multidimensional coding. An instrument designed for multiple coding, simultaneously records data on two, three, or four dimensions.

With respect to the sources from which categories are derived, there is also some disparity. Rosenshine and Furst (1973) developed four classifications based on authors' descriptions of their own variables. These four are: (1) instruments with explicit theoretical or empirical base (usually derived from learning theory or developmental sequences); (2) instruments with implicit theoretical or empirical base, but for which no specific person or research was credited; (3) modification or syntheses of existing systems, such as the Flanders system or others; and (4) author-originated category systems, containing categories the author believes to be important, but for which no origin is specified. In their article (1973, pp. 138–145), Rosenshine and Furst classify 73 of the systems described in *Mirrors for Behavior* (Simon & Boyer, 1970) according to these criteria.

Additional items concerning observational systems and their use can be found in a number of sources (Flanders, 1970; Good & Brophy, 1973; Weinberg & Wood, 1975; Rosenshine & Furst, 1973). Of most concern in this chapter is the relationship between interaction analysis and bilingual education. What are the applications? What has been done? What could be done? If interaction systems have a theoretical base, and if they are adaptable to different formats, levels, language, and so on, can they be used in bilingual education as they have been used in monolingual classrooms?

Only four studies have been identified that fall into the general category of what could be called *bilingual interaction analysis*. Probably the most comprehensive study undertaken in this area was conducted by the United States Commission on Civil Rights and reported in *Report No. 5: Mexican-American Study—Teachers and Students: Differences in Teacher Interaction with Mexican-American and Anglo Students* (1973).

Previous studies conducted by the commission had pointed out that schools in the Southwest had generally failed to adapt their curricula and programs to the interests, skills, and language with which Mexican-Americans enter school. The 1973 study was designed to investigate possible disparities in the way teachers treat Mexican-Americans and Anglos within the same classroom. In the introduction, it is reported that various factors influence the educational experience of a child. These factors include school facilities, textbooks, and the training and experience of teachers. The report contends, however, that "educational opportunity is primarily affected by what goes on in the classroom" (p. 7). The report further indicates that the most important aspect of the educational process is the interaction between teacher and student.

In preparing for the 1973 study, the commission determined that the aspect of classroom interaction had been omitted in all the studies concerning the equality of education opportunities afforded to minorities. As a result, five members of the Commission staff received intensive training in the use of a modified version of the Flanders Interaction Analysis System (FIAS), and undertook the task of encoding classroom behavior in three states. The areas included were the Santa Clara County area of California; four areas in the state of Texas, including San Antonio and Corpus Christi; and two areas in the state of New Mexico, including Albuquerque and the area near El Paso, Texas. Teachers were notified prior to the visit of the commission members. The observer generally sat in the back or the side of the room for approximately one hour. During that time, one 10-minute period was encoded according to the Flanders System. The remainder of the time was spent observing other aspects of the classroom, the teacher, and the students.

In order not to bias the results, a per-pupil measure was calculated for each time each type of behavior occurred. In other words, it was not sufficient to compare the number of times that a single item occurred. These measures were obtained for Anglo and Mexican-American students in the following way:

> The number of times each behavior occurred for Mexican-Americans was divided by the number of Mexican-Americans in the classroom, and a similar calculation was made for the Anglo pupils. The difference in the way the teacher interacts with Anglo and Chicano pupils is measured by the disparities in the Anglo and Chicano per pupil measures (United States Commission on Civil Rights, 1973, p. 15).

The statistical analyses of the results indicated that of the twelve categories assessed, statistically significant disparities were found in six of the categories. In each case, Anglo students received a greater concentra-

tion of the desirable behavior. The six categories in which the disparities were statistically significant were: praising or encouraging, acceptance or use of student ideas, questioning, positive teacher response, all
noncriticizing teacher talk, and all student speaking. This finding was
interpreted by the study (pp. 17–18) to mean that

> Mexican-Americans received significantly less praise and encouragement
> from the teacher and less often hear the teacher accept or use the ideas
> they express. Teachers also spent significantly less time in asking questions
> of Chicano pupils than of Anglo pupils.

Mexican-Americans also received less positive response from teachers
and received less noncriticizing teacher talk. It was also determined that
Mexican-American students spoke significantly less during classroom
time than did Anglo students.

Following a chapter describing the overall disparities of the teacher–
pupil interaction, the remainder of the study elaborates on the six significant disparities. Included in the discussion are possible reasons for the
disparities, possible explanations of why they have been perpetuated, as
well as some suggestions on how they might be eliminated. Also included
in the report are explanations of bias that may affect the report itself. Explanations are given concerning the commission staff members' efforts to
overcome the three types of possible bias: coding biases of the observers,
obtrusive biases caused by the observer's presence, and sampling biases.

Another study, conducted by Hughes and Harrison (1971) while
working in the Harlandale Independent School District (Texas), used a
modified Flanders System to record the amount of pupil talk in Spanish
and English occurring in classrooms of 18 student teachers. Baseline data
were recorded in October with subsequent recordings in April. During
the 6-month interim period, students were instructed in the use of interaction practices. A comparison of the two interaction patterns showed a
significant increase in the amount of student participation at the .01
level of confidence.

Studies conducted by Townsend (1974) and Zamora (1974) were
designed to compare verbal and nonverbal interaction patterns of bilingual teachers and assistant teachers. The setting for both studies was
the José Cárdenas Early Childhood Center in San Antonio, Texas. The
studies were conducted in consecutive years (1973, 1974) on 56 early
childhood teachers and assistant teachers, 53 of whom were Mexican-
American. The children in the center were 3 and 4 years old; approximately 98 percent were Mexican-American and over 90 percent were
either Spanish-speaking monolinguals or were Spanish-dominant bilinguals with very limited ability in English. Teachers were defined by the

center as those primarily responsible for the children. In all but three cases, they were college graduates, and in all but two cases, they had some level of certification in Texas. Assistant teachers were assigned to help teachers. The educational background of the assistants ranged from high school dropout (two cases) to one college graduate; most had graduated from high school, and many had had some college. Their background in early childhood and their training in instructional methods were derived exclusively from inservice training.

A number of questions were researched in the studies. Most of the concerns centered around the following questions:

1. Do verbal and/or nonverbal behaviors of bilingual teachers differ from those of assistant teachers?
2. Do bilingual teachers and assistant teachers exhibit different interaction patterns verbally or nonverbally as they teach similar subject matter in two languages?

To gather data for the studies, the System for Coding Interaction with Multiple Phases (SCIMP) was used (Townsend, 1974). The system consists of five phases for examining various dimensions of classroom interaction. The verbal study used Phase II, Instructional Behaviors, coupled with the system's bilingual overlay. Phase II is a 17-category system with a Flanders-type format; the bilingual component adds separate columns in which to record the language being used. The nonverbal analysis used Phase III, Affective Behaviors. This system consists of a 9-category format using opposite poles of four nonverbal dimensions, and a "void" category, which is defined as the absence of nonverbal behavior. The categories include positive touching or negative touching, positive nodding of head or negative nodding of head, positive use of eyes or negative use of eyes, and smile or frown.

Each of the 56 subjects (both studies) was coded on four occasions. Two codings took place during Spanish lessons and two during English lessons. Lessons averaged 10 minutes in length. Recordings for the verbal study were made every 3 seconds or with each change of interaction (whichever occurred first). A time-sampling procedure was used for the nonverbal study by recording one observation every 5 seconds. Both studies used an analysis of variance with repeated measures to determine significant differences.

The findings indicated that there were significant differences in teacher–assistant-teacher behaviors, and in the behaviors of all subjects as they taught in the two languages. In the verbal dimension of teacher versus assistant teacher behavior, four significant findings were most apparent: (1) teachers had a higher indirect–direct ratio (.005 level), indicating they tended to be more indirect by using more praise, acceptance, encouragement, and so on; (2) assistant teachers had greater percentages of interaction in the "teacher talk" category (.01 level), which includes lecture, telling, or idle conversation; (3) teachers allowed a greater percentage of student response (.005 level); and (4) assistant teachers were more inclined to switch from one language to the other during lesson presentations (.05 level).

There were five significant findings in the nonverbal dimension: (1) assistant teachers had a higher percentage of "void" behaviors (.01 level); (2) assistant teachers demonstrated more "negative nodding of head" (.05 level); (3) assistant teachers demonstrated more "negative use of eyes" (.05 level); (4) assistant teachers demonstrated more "combined negative nonverbal behavior" (.05 level); and (5) the teachers showed a much higher percentage of "combined positive nonverbal behaviors" (.005 level).

With respect to differences in behaviors when using one language or the other, significant differences were found only in the verbal dimension. The nonverbal behaviors of teachers and assistant teachers were consistent across both languages, whether considered as separate groups or as one large group. However, at least seven categories showed significant differences between the use of certain verbal behaviors in one language as compared to the other. During lessons taught in Spanish, there was a greater percentage of questions asked (.005 level); a greater percentage of student responses (.001 level); a greater percentage of rejecting a student's answer (.05 level); and a greater percentage of incidents in which a student response was followed by teacher acceptance (.0001 level). Also, though not statistically significant, the indirect–direct ratios averaged .3720 higher for lessons taught in Spanish than English.

While teaching lessons in English, subjects had a greater percentage of direction-giving behavior (.005 level); a greater percentage of incidences in which a student response was followed by teacher praise (.05 level); and a greater percentage of the use of two or more consecutive reinforcing behaviors (.005 level).

When compared to the vast number of studies conducted in monolingual classrooms, this is a very limited amount of research. An adaptation of interaction analysis in a dual-language setting has been conducted in foreign-language classrooms, however. Since 1966, Gertrude Moscowitz has been conducting studies using a modified Flanders instrument known as the *Foreign Language Interaction System* (FLint). The instrument, designed for foreign-language supervisors, uses all of Flanders' categories, but makes finer distinctions among them, subdividing 8 of the categories by adding letters (2, 2a; 3, 3a). In addition, Category 10 was expanded by adding separate numbers for laughter and confusion, making a total of 12 categories. The dual-language aspect is accommodated in the following way: It is assumed that the interaction in the class will occur in the target language of the class, i.e., Spanish for a Spanish class. If it does not occur in that language, a small "e" is noted beside the number depicting the interaction. As an example, "4" indicates a question in the target language, "4e" indicates a question in English. Moscowitz (1968) found, in comparing an experimental group that had used FLint in their training with a control group that had received no training in interaction analysis, that the experimental group finished the semester with a significantly more positive attitude toward foreign-language teaching as determined by an attitude questionnaire. In analyzing teaching sessions from both groups, it was also found that the experimental group used more indirect interaction, specifically praise and encouragement.

A similar system was established by Wragg (Instrument 79 in Boyer, 1970, vol. 13). Wragg's system consisted of using the Flanders system and adding a "1" before any category in which the interaction was in a foreign language.

In an article by Ernesto García (1970) entitled "Modification of Teacher Behavior in Teaching the Mexican American," he states that there is a need for teachers to improve in two ways. The first is seeking ways of improving teaching by learning how to plan for, produce, and evaluate behavior change. Four specific categories are stressed: having a variety of teaching strategies available, using behavioral objectives in instruction, using interaction analysis instruments to detect both verbal and nonverbal interaction, and understanding and using the contingencies of reinforcement. With respect to interaction systems, he refers specifically to the Flanders System for observing verbal behavior. He also refers to the principle of raising the level of instruction through the use of interaction analysis systems.

In another article similar to that of García, Klingsledt (1972) discusses indicators of effectiveness for teachers of Mexican-American children in middle schools. After discussing what he considers to be seven of the most important traditional indicators of teaching effectiveness, among which is found the use of interaction analysis and the ability to control the pattern of interaction so optimal learning and growth takes place, he concludes that there is no single indicator of effective teaching, for teachers of Mexican-Americans or for anyone. He then refers to an article by Arthur Combs (1964) in which Combs says that the best teacher is one who has developed a style that actualizes his own personality.

What are some of the major findings of interaction studies conducted in monolingual classes? Despite Medley's (1973) conclusion that almost no single teacher characteristic has been discovered that consistently makes a significant difference in what a child learns, Rosenshine and

Furst (1973) identified nine variables for which there seemed to be some empirical evidence that their presence increased student achievement. Those items are as follows:

1. the clarity with which the teachers made presentations
2. the variability or flexibility of the teacher
3. enthusiasm, defined as vigor or power, of the teacher
4. task-oriented and/or businesslike teachers (accounted for achievement on at least one measure in six of seven studies)
5. criticism (resulted in significant negative relationships)
6. teacher indirectness (as defined by Flanders, seems to consistently yield positive correlation)
7. student opportunity to learn criterion material, or that subject matter over which the student will be tested
8. the use of structuring comments to preview what is going to happen or to review what has happened
9. the use of multiple levels of questions or cognitive discourse, especially where the multiple levels remained separated for statistical analyses.

The above findings all relate to the relationships between classroom activities and the progress of students. Other findings relate to the monitoring of programs and the training of teachers. As an example, Seifert (1969) compared the teacher patterns for Weikert's Moderately Structured Language Program for Preschoolers with the Bereiter–Engelmann Preschool Program, which has a high degree of structure. This comparison was made using Medley's instrument, known as OScAR. Despite described differences, the interaction patterns of the teachers and pupils showed very few differences, and the behavior of the children showed no differences at all. In another study made in a preschool setting, Smothergill (1971) analyzed the effects of elaborative versus nonelaborative teaching style on the children involved. The term *elaborative* was defined as encouraging children's comments and involvement, while the term *nonelaborative* was defined as communicating only necessary task information and not encouraging child involvement. Results showed that those children taught under the elaborative style gave more task-relevant elaborations and made significant gains from pre- to posttests on verbal similarity tasks and story telling tasks. Both Soar (1972a) and Stallings (1974) have conducted research concerning the relationship of program models one to another. Soar found that students in classrooms with a moderate amount of control, rather than too little or too much pupil freedom, made significant gains on achievement tests.

With respect to the training of teachers, Flanders (1970) and Soar (1972b) have both shown significant positive relationships between the behavioral style of a teacher and student outcomes. The work of Moscowitz (1968) in training foreign language teachers to be more indirect has already been mentioned.

Questions

A few questions need to be asked at this point. Is it reasonable to assume that the numerous findings in monolingual settings are directly transferable to classrooms in which two languages are used for instructional purposes? Are there peculiarities in the dual-language setting that necessitate specific investigation? Are there interaction patterns that are more productive in one language than in another language? Evaluators continually preach that empirical findings in one setting are not directly transferable to another setting. It does seem safe to assume, therefore, that the same methodology that has been used to secure findings in monolingual settings could be equally applicable to findings in a bilingual setting?

The system

The remainder of this chapter is devoted to a system that can be used to gather information geared to answer the questions just posed. As stated at the outset, there are four major areas in which interaction studies have been conducted: program description, program monitoring, comparing interaction patterns to student growth, and teacher training.

Starting with the last item first, there always appears to be a need for teacher training. During the 1974–1975 school year in Texas, the Texas Education Agency (TEA) reported that 1790 teachers involved in bilingual education were bilingual and 786 were monolingual (TEA, 1974–1975). During the 1975–1976 school year, state funding was approved for kindergarten through second grade, with optional funding available for third through fifth grades. Well over three times the number of bilingual teachers will be reported during the 1975–1976 year. For the following year, bilingual programs for kindergarten through third grade will be required, with optional programs for fourth and fifth grades (TEA, 1976). This effort is intended to accommodate some portion of the state's 671,013 Mexican-American students, a figure representing 23 percent of the students in Texas.

What are the state's resources for finding teachers to meet this growing demand? The first option is to use Mexican-American or Spanish-speaking teachers, provide them with inservice training, and employ them in bilingual programs. The second method is to train teachers at the preservice level. At the end of the 1974–1975 year, 25 colleges and universities offered TEA-approved programs, enabling graduates to receive an emphasis, a concentration, or a major in bilingual education.

Whichever method is selected, there is a continued need for inservice training. Teachers need to understand better the interaction processes in their classes. In order to collect data that may be useful in understanding the processes, the System for Coding Interaction with Multiple Phases (SCIMP) was devised (Townsend, 1974).

SCIMP consists of five phases or instruments with the option of four other interaction overlays. The phases are as follows:

I. A basic, 5-category, Flanders-type system
II. An expanded, 17-category, Flanders-type system
III. A 9-category system to record affective behavior of the teacher
IV. A 54-catgory sign system to record student behavior along an approach/avoidance continuum
V. A follow-up instrument, designed to record a child's out-of-class behavior relative to specific objectives.

In addition to the five instruments, four overlays were developed to provide more specific information concerning the nature of the interaction, especially in Phases I and II.

A. Concerns the bilingual component, recording the language of the interaction
B. Concerns the subject matter orientation of the interaction, whether it is task-oriented or nontask-oriented; whether it can be grouped into a hierarchy; or whether subject subdivisions exist into which the interaction can be grouped
C. Concerns the moral–conceptual framework for use in childhood studies on the concept of God
D. Concerns the interaction identification by specifying or naming the participants in the interaction or the object of the teacher's interaction.

Through unique combinations of phases and overlays, over 50 types of instruments can be assembled to record the wide variety of available classroom data.

SYSTEM FOR CODING INTERACTION WITH MULTIPLE PHASES (SCIMP)

Phase I: The basic system

A teacher who is beginning to look at classroom interaction patterns should have sufficient data to make the study meaningful, but should not be overwhelmed with so much data that the system becomes burdensome. Most of the systems with 10 or more categories seem to provide more information than is necessary for the beginner. The 5 categories of Phase I provide basic information to the teacher concerning four aspects of his or her behavior and frequency counts on student participation. A dash (−) is used to represent "silence," but is not one of the numbered categories. The 5 categories of Phase I are as follows:

Category
1. Teacher asks a question pertaining to content or personal concerns. Answer expected.
2. Teacher accepts, praises, rewards, or compliments a student or a student response. Repeating student response.
3. Teacher rejects, opposes, or ridicules a student or a response. Denies something, says no, managing or correcting student behavior, or justifies authority.
4. Other teacher talk. All talk not included in above categories. This includes directions, lectures, idle comments, or explanations.
5. Student talk. Anything said by a student.
(−) Silence.

The categories are intended to be all-encompassing, meaning that anything that takes place in an instructional setting should fit into one of the categories. As is apparent from the categories, this portion of the system centers primarily on activities of the teacher. The number beside each category is the code number that is recorded as the behavior is displayed. This procedure means that if a teacher asks a question, a "1" is recorded; if the student responds, a "5" is recorded underneath the "1"; if the teacher praises the student's response, a "2" is recorded. This pattern can be demonstrated by the following sequence of interaction:

Sample coding procedure

1	1	5
5	1	2
2	5	4
4	3	4
4	1	4

The above sequence would indicate that a question was asked (1); a response was given (5); the response was praised (2); some teacher talk ensued (4, 4); two questions were asked (1, 1); a response was given (5); the teacher opposed it or stated it was wrong (3); another question (1); a response (5); praise (2); and more teacher talk (4, 4, 4).

Important Tips for Encoding.   When learning to use an encoding system, a number of items should be kept in mind. Listed below are six considerations in learning to use an interaction system:
1. *Memorizing the categories.* The most important aspect of learning

a system is to memorize the categories. An observer needs to have every definition totally memorized; a response to any statement needs to be automatic. Learning to encode is like learning to type, take shorthand, or play the piano—it takes practice. The only way to do it is to do it. Once the system is memorized, then speed and accuracy increase with practice. The beginner could first look at written dialogues, move to tape-recorded dialogues, and finally move to live classroom interaction.

2. *When in doubt.* When in doubt concerning the number that should be assigned a specific interaction, a decision should be made quickly. If the decision is a legitimate concern between two categories, the recorder should make a rule in his or her mind on which a decision can be made. As long as a rule is made in the observer's mind and is consistently followed from that point on, the system will work fine.

3. *If one gets lost.* If an encoder loses track of the interaction pattern, and has missed several interactions, he or she should try not to be confused or frustrated. The encoder should draw a thick black line under the last number indicating that the interaction has been broken, wait for the next discernable interaction, and begin recording anew. Several studies have shown that missing a few interactions is not important to the overall pattern that will emerge.

4. *Prolonged interaction.* If one type of interaction continues for a prolonged period, e.g., a student gives a 15-second answer to a question, then multiple numbers are recorded. The rule of thumb is that another number is recorded in the sequence for each three seconds that the same interaction persists. So, if a child's answer continues, the encoder would record a "5," slowly count to three, record another "5," count to three, record another "5," etc. The same is true for extended interaction in every category, even silence "(−)." This procedure allows the tallies to be more representative of actual elapsed time, rather than just representing the changes in interaction.

5. *Special adaptations.* The purpose of collecting classroom data for teacher training is to assist the teacher in whatever area is felt to be essential. Therefore, teachers or encoders are given free license to make whatever adaptation will facilitate more meaningful data. As an example, a consecutive list of 5's does not differentiate as to whether that is one child with a long answer, numerous children with very short answers, or several children with medium length answers. Any kind of little note can be made to indicate which is taking place. One suggestion is to join those 5's that are continuous; another is to put brackets or circles around those that are continuous.

Using the Data. It is not necessary to encode lengthy segments of classroom interaction in order to compile data that will serve as useful feedback to classroom teachers. Much information can be accumulated in short lesson segments of 4 to 10 minutes. After encoding a lesson or a lesson segment, there are two types of analyses that can be made. The first method is to analyze the data in continuous form. This analysis consists of looking through the various sequences, determining how many times a student response was followed by praise or by criticism, or raising any other questions that may be asked of the data. The second method is to summarize the data. The following is an example of a summary format that may be used:

Categories	Number of tallies	Percentage of total
1	24	24
2	9	9
3	4	4
4	30	30
5	30	30
—	3	3
	100	100

A number of questions can then be asked of the data:

1. What is the total amount of teacher talk versus the amount of student talk? In this case the teacher talk is the sum of Categories 1–4, equaling 67 tallies; the student participation, as shown in Category 5, is 30 tallies. This is a 97-tally sum, meaning that teacher talk represented 69% of the interaction and student talk represented 31% of the interaction. The three tallies listed under "silence" do not figure in that computation.

2. What is the ratio of reward or praise responses (Category 2) to negative or critical responses (Category 3)? In this example, there were more than twice as many tallies in Category 2 as there were in Category 3.

3. What is the ratio between questions asked and student responses given? In this example, there were 24 questions asked and 30 student responses given. When the number of student responses is close to the number of questions, this result indicates that the majority of the questions asked were answered in less than 3 seconds. When the number of questions exceeds the number of student responses, this result indicates that the teacher is asking two or more questions in order to receive a response. When the number of student responses far exceeds the number of questions, this result usually indicates that the questions asked are of a higher cognitive level and require more than 3 seconds to respond, or that responses are sought from numerous students before the teacher asks another question.

4. What is the ratio between the number of questions asked and the amount of teacher talk? In this example, teacher talk exceeded questions asked 30 to 24.

The list of questions, of course, could be extended. The important thing is that questions be asked that supply the teacher with information relevant to his or her classroom interaction pattern. Such feedback will provide information on which desired changes can be based.

It is essential to remember that there is no value judgment implied in the reporting of objective data. To say that a teacher acquired 90% of the tallies as opposed to 10% for the students is not to place a judgment on that finding. It merely states that the recorded interaction ratio was 90% to 10%. The value judgment, meaning the decision as to whether that should or should not have been the case, is left to the teacher. After analyzing the results of a lesson, the teacher is the one who can say "that is the way I intended it to be," or "I did not intend for it to happen that way." When recorded behavior differs from intent, decisions can be made that will alter behavior in subsequent lessons. When intent coincides with behavior (as recorded on the interaction instrument), then behavior patterns are reinforced.

Phase II: The expanded system

Phase II of SCIMP is designed for teachers and researchers who want to progress beyond the 5-category system. It is intended to allow for finer distinction among classroom behaviors. The 17 categories included in Phase II, as in Phase I, are intended to be all-encompassing, meaning that anything that takes place in an instructional setting should fit into one of the categories. This phase, as with Phase I, primarily focuses on the activities of the teacher. In most cases, the categories represent extensions or subdivisions of the categories contained in the Flanders System. The categories and their definitions are as follows:

Phase II

1. *Preparatory, stage-setting activities.* Questions or statements intended to heighten interest, arouse curiosity, or introduce a topic or activity.

   a. *What do you think I have behind my back?*
   b. *Today we're going to talk about something very interesting.*
   c. *What do you think we're going to do next?*

2. *Dealing with feelings.* Questions or statements that deal with a student's moods, joys, sorrows, etc. Display of empathy. Concerns for the personal well-being of students.

a. *I'll bet that really hurts.*
b. *You sure look happy today, Tom.*
c. *Don't you feel well, Diane?*
d. *I realize that they are hard problems.*

3. *Questioning.* Any question concerning subject matter or other material that does not fall in a more specific category. These are only questions for which an answer is expected. Also included are statements with a question intonation for which answers are expected. This category also includes repeating a question for purposes of reiterating or in case students did not hear; also includes saying a person's name, which is, in effect, re-asking a previous question to that person. Various models on levels of questions have been developed that can be used in conjunction with this category, if desired. This is done by marking an exponent to denote the level. For example, 3^2 is a question at Level 2.

a. *Which hand is this?*
b. *Why did he do that?*
c. *How would you solve this problem?*
d. *Bill?* (Bill answers) *Mary?* (Mary answers)

4. *Extending, elaborating, encouraging, and building on student ideas.* This category includes any statement or question that is used to "stay with" a student that is unable to make a desired response on the first attempt. Any type of assistance or prodding or giving clues, etc., that is designed to be of help to the student. It might entail asking a second question to get a more specific or more lengthy answer, especially after getting a wrong answer. The category is also used when student ideas are used by the teacher as building blocks or in referring to what a student has said to clarify or point out something to the class.

a. *I'm sure you can get it. Keep thinking.*
b. *We talked about this animal yesterday.* (clue)
c. *Tell me some more.*
d. *What do you mean?*
e. *Like Janie said, there are lots of things that are red.*
f. *Bill, you just answered that question a minute ago; could you repeat your answer?*

5. *Accepting, acknowledging, or receiving student answers.* Any statement or verbal expression that communicates to a student that an answer has been heard, received or accepted, without any specific judgment being pronounced. This category also includes repeating a student answer for the purpose of showing the student that the teacher accepts an answer.

    a. *O.K., Uhum.*
    b. *Fine, good,* etc. (when they are procedural rather than praising)
    c. Question: *What is this?* (3)
       Answer: *It's blue.*
       Response: *It's blue.* (5)

    6. *Praising, reinforcing, and building student confidence.* Any statement, phrase, or question designed to praise the student for appropriate behavior, a good response, a thoughtful answer, etc. The difference between this category and Number 5 is that here the child feels personally rewarded. Behavior can be in response to something or spontaneous praise.

    a. *That was really great.*
    b. *You really worked on that one.*
    c. *Have any of you seen such a pretty picture?*

    7. *Student response.* Any verbal response that a student makes to a statement, question or direction. Any response to another student such as answering a child's question.

    a. *There are at least five.*
    b. *How should I know?*
    c. *My favorite is blue.*

    8. *Student initiation.* Any verbal statement or question made by a student that is self-initiated. It may be directed toward the teacher or another student. It could be a joke, a wisecrack, an unrelated procedural statement, or a question. It may be spoken out or said after having been recognized by the teacher.

    a. *May I sharpen my pencil?*
    b. *Bill just hit me.*
    c. *I don't see why it's seven.*

    9. *Activity.* Whenever the students are engaged in a general activity, such as a film, story, song, game, written assignment, etc., this category is used. It only needs to be written once and may include a note in the margin as to what happened, and possibly how long it lasted. It is also used to show nonverbal acts such as performing some specific task as directed by the teacher.

    10. *Teacher talk or response, procedural or nonsubstantive statements.* Any type of information imparted by the teacher. Includes lecture, jokes, rhetorical questions, teacher answers to student questions (positive or negative), unrelated teacher talk, and other teacher utterances that are not classifiable in other categories.

    a. *The capital of Utah is Salt Lake City.*
    b. *It's sure hot in here.*

   c. *Yes, you may sharpen your pencil.*
   d. *No, you may not get a drink.*
   e. *And why didn't they come? Because they weren't invited.*

11. *Teacher directions.* Any instructions, in question or statement form, given to students preparatory to, during, or in terminating an activity. It may also include procedural directions given at any time during a lesson.

   a. *Open your books to page 16.*
   b. *Would you close the door, please?*
   c. *Return to your seats after you have done it twice.*

12. *Behavior control.* Questions or statements intended to stop or correct a student behavior judged by the teacher to be inappropriate or disruptive. It may be directed toward individuals or an entire class. Also includes prescribing punishment.

   a. *What do you think you're doing?*
   b. *Don't say another word.*
   c. *Jim, how many times do I have to tell you? Stand in the corner until I tell you to leave.*

13. *Rejecting a student answer.* Any specific response that tells a student his answer is wrong or unacceptable. A question intended to reject a student answer. This response does not reflect on the student's intelligence or imply he is stupid for being wrong. It is feedback.

   a. *No, it's not 12.*
   b. *"B" is incorrect.*
   c. *Nope.*
   d. *Don't you want to rethink that?*

14. *Criticism or self-justification.* Includes "talking down" to a student, in any way degrading a student, or relying on authority as teacher as a reason for doing something. Anything that in the opinion of the coder embarrasses the student. Also includes derogatory statements about a student.

   a. *We're doing it like this because that's the way I said to do it.*
   b. *I knew you wouldn't be able to answer it.*
   c. *Tom, are you ever going to do anything in here?*

The last three categories give a general assessment of the state of the classroom.

15. *Confusion.* Any time two or more codable activities are occurring at once. Also includes excessive student talk, times when a general murmur covers the class, or when a specific interaction is not detectable because of the noise level in the class.

16. *Laughter.* Laughter or giggling by the class or a part of it. It may be with the teacher, at the teacher, or among the students.

17. *Silence.* Any absence of verbal interaction. It may follow a scolding, a question, or may be a pause in the activity. May also be used as a device or method by teacher to silence children.

As discussed previously, Phase II is an extension or elaboration of Phase I. The categories represent finer breakdowns of the possible classroom activities.

Categories of Instructional Behaviors

Teacher Behavior: Indirect
1. Preparatory, stage-setting activities
2. Dealing with feelings
3. Questioning
4. Extending, elaborating, encouraging, building on student ideas
5. Accepting, acknowledging, or receiving student answers
6. Praising, reinforcing, and building student confidence

Student Behavior
7. Student response
8. Student initiation
9. Activity

Teacher Behavior: Direct
10. Teacher talk or response, or nonsubstantive statements
11. Teaccher directions
12. Behavior control
13. Rejecting a student answer
14. Criticism or self-justification

Nonsubstantive Behavior
15. Confusion
16. Laughter
17. Silence

The following chart shows the conversion from Phase I to Phase II:

Phase I	Phase II
Category 1 ⟶	Category 3; possibly 1, 2, and 4
Category 2 ⟶	Categories 5 and 6; possibly 2
Category 3 ⟶	Categories 12, 13, and 14
Category 4 ⟶	Categories 1, 2, 4, 10, and 11
Category 5 ⟶	Categories 7, 8, and 9
— ⟶	Categories 9 and 17

Categories 15 and 16 of Phase II are not encoded with Phase I.

In reviewing results, the same types of analyses used in Phase I are also applicable. For more in-depth processing of data, one can determine the percentage of direct versus indirect tallies. In his initial work with interaction analysis, Flanders assigned categories into two classifications depending on "teacher centeredness" (direct) or "student centeredness" (indirect) of the behaviors. The block of categories from 1–6 are classified as indirect; the block from 10–14 are classified as direct. By totaling the number in each block the figure can be expressed as a fraction known as the *I/D ratio.*

For example, if the total number of tallies for a given recording period in categories 1–6 was 150 and the total number in the block from 10–14 was 50, the I/D ratio would be expressed as 150/50. By dividing the fraction, this I/D ratio equals 3. A teacher who consistently has an I/D ratio greater than 1 can be classified as having an indirect style. A teacher who consistently has an I/D ratio of less than 1 (such as 137/274), could be said to have a more direct teaching style.

As with Phase I, the determination of the teacher talk versus student talk is easy to determine. The teacher talk is the sum of the tallies in Categories 1–6 and 10–14; student tallies are the sum of Categories 7 and 8.

As mentioned above, no conclusions concerning the quality of any lesson can be made on the basis of an I/D ratio or percentages of teacher versus student talk. These are only variables that should be compared to a teacher's intentions, the students in a particular class, their age level, and a number of other circumstances.

A more extensive graphic interpretation is also possible using the categories in Phase II (see Townsend, 1974). The applications of a graph are primarily, but not exclusively, for research. The advantage of the graphic interpretation is that sequential behavior is considered in addition to tallies by categories. A graph considers the behavior that precedes and follows each entry. Results are then interpreted in the context of 10 areas that represent sequential combinations of behaviors.

Phase III: Affective behaviors

From the work of Galloway (1971), Hodge (1971), and others, it has been demonstrated that a teacher's nonverbal, affective behavior can play a very important part in his or her effectiveness.

To provide for this variable and to incorporate it into the overall analysis of interaction, Phase III was created. There are nine categories that represent a continuum running from a hypothetical plus (+ or + 4) through 0 to a minus condition (− or − 4). There are two ways to use Phase III: as a separate entity, or in conjunction with either or both of the preceeding phases.

When used alone, the Phase III recording sheet enables an observer to mark tallies beside each of the categories as a particular behavior occurs. Instead of a running account, it is suggested that a specific time interval be set and the behavior be recorded at the end of each time period. The intervals can be determined on the basis of the overall length

RECORD SHEET—PHASE III (only)

Observer _____ Teacher _____ Time interval _____ Other _____

BEHAVIORS	TALLIES	TOTALS & %
SMILING A +		
POS. PHYSICAL CONTACT C +		
POS. NODDING-HEAD N +		
POS. USE OF EYES B +		
VOID OF VISIBLE AFFECT V		
NEG. USE OF EYES B –		
NEG. NODDING-HEAD N –		
NEG. PHYSICAL CONTACT C –		
SMIRK, FROWN A –		

209

of the recording period. If a lengthy recording is anticipated, longer intervals of time can be selected; for shorter periods, the recordings need to be more frequent. Time intervals may run from 5 seconds through 30, 45, or even 60 seconds. As a general rule, 10 seconds is a comfortable interval.

The recorder enters on the sheet the time interval he has selected, uses a sweep second hand or a stop watch, waits x seconds and records the behavior that is being exhibited at that second. This procedure is repeated every x seconds, depending on the interval that has been selected.

At the conclusion of the recording period, the total number of tallies is determined, the number of tallies in each category is determined, and the percentages are figured for each category by dividing the total number of tallies into the number for each specific category.

When used in conjunction with the preceding phases, the affective designation is made beside the number recorded. When using Phase III with Phase I or II, instead of deciding on a time interval, one decides that for every three or four entries for Phase I or II, the affective designation is recorded beside that third or fourth number. Using every third entry on Phase II, the tally sheet would look like this:

```
3              8
3              10
7 N+           10 V
7              8
5 ·            12
6 A+           12 N –
```

It must be remembered, that regardless of what interaction category is taking place, it is the teacher's affective behavior that is observed and recorded.

At the end of the recording period, numbers of tallies and percentages can be determined as described earlier. In addition, seeing the affective behavior paired with the interaction behavior reveals another dimension that is not apparent when tallies are recorded alone.

During use in a major study (Zamora, 1974; Townsend & Zamora, 1975) the definitions of the nine categories were slightly revised during field testing and data gathering. The definitions, as revised by Zamora, are as follows:

Code   Definition
A +   Smiling
C +   Positive contact of a physical nature: hugging, shaking hands with students; patting the back, head, or shoulders; guiding the student.
N +   Positive nodding of head (encouraging or urging student to continue).
B +   Positive use of the eyes: eye contact, any attempt to make eye contact;

sweeping eye movement (taking in the group of students); focusing eyes on the material being taught.

V   No visible affective behavior in the categories described.

B —   Negative use of eyes: staring, glaring; stern looks of disgust or anger; nonuse of eyes (lowering eyes while teaching).

N —   Negative nodding of head; shaking head "no" as in disagreement.

C —   Negative contact of a physical nature; pushing students; pinching; hitting; slapping.

A —   Smirk (sarcasm); frown.

Phase IV: Student interactions

To this point, all of the emphasis has centered on the teacher, his or her behaviors and activities. The object of the teacher's interaction has not been considered, except concerning the student's participation in a lesson. Phase IV is designed to consider such questions as the following: (1) What does a student do during a lesson? (2) Is he "with" the teacher or not? (3) Does the student ever talk? and (4) What specific activities does the student engage in during the lesson?

There are three divisions within Phase IV: Approach, Potential, and Avoidance. Approach indicates that a student is attending to or participating in a lesson or activity that is judged to be appropriate by his teacher. Avoidance indicates that the student is not attending, is disrupting, or in some way is not following prescribed or appropriate behavior patterns. Potential is the small middle area that shows neither attention nor disruption. The categories are self-explanatory. Spaces are left at the bottom of each section on the recording instrument to insert other specific behaviors that a recorder feels are not covered in the definitions or ones that should be remembered with greater specificity. The context of each category should be adjusted to the appropriate age level. For example, reference to "seat" could be interpreted as a child's place on the floor in an early childhood setting.

Recording with Phase IV is based on a set frequency with no attempt to record every change in interaction. To observe one child, a record sheet is secured and completed. The item labeled *Time Interval* is the period of time that will elapse between the recording of each tally. A stop watch or sweep second hand should be used to allow for a consistent passage of time. If, as an example, 10 seconds were chosen as the interval, a behavior would be recorded, 10 seconds would be allowed to elapse, and another tally would be made. It must be remembered that it is the time between observations that is important. With this 10-second interval, if it took a recorder 6 seconds to locate the appropriate category and record the tally, only 4 seconds would remain during the interval. At the end of the 4 seconds, the next observation would be made and

APPROACH

Listening
Listening—doing something else
Desire to be recognized—raise hand, etc.
Student initiates—recognized question
    —recognized statement
    —unrecognized question
    —unrecognized statement
Student responds—recognized question
    —recognized statement
    —unrecognized question
    —unrecognized statement
    —in a physical manner
    —in choral or class response
Interaction with a near pupil—verbal (resp. or initin.)
    —physical
Attempts to engage teacher on personal basis—verbal
    —with personal contact
Shows evidence of being proud of self
Laughs, giggles in support, with teacher or class
Working alone
    —with another
    —with teacher
Free play—alone
    —with another
    —with teacher
Engages in a classroom activity
Leaves seat with permission
Does favor, errand, act, or direction for teacher

POTENTIAL

Daydreaming
Lies down, lays head down, closes eyes, or sleeps
Restlessness
Being quiet, waiting
Other type of act.—blows nose, ties shoes, etc.

AVOIDANCE

Attempting to avoid being called on or noticed
Ignores teacher
No response
Says "don't know" when called on
Purposefully not doing what class is doing
Stands up without permission
Leaves seat without permission
Pursues his own activities
Spontaneous, disruptive talk; joke, wisecracks, etc.
Yells for disruptive effect
Teasing, poking horse-play with other students
Gets mad at student—verbal
    —with physical contact

Cls/rm _____ Note _____ Setting _____ Student _____ Time Interval _____ Recorder _____ Date _____

(continued)

	Madness or hostility at teacher—verbal
A V O I D A N C E	—with physical contact
	Calls teacher a bad name
	Shows evidence of rejection, embarrassment, left out
	Laughs, giggles that are disruptive
	Cries, pouts
	Glories in having disrupted
	Attends to stimulus outside room

recorded. With some practice one can learn to time the looking and recording period to last as long as the specified interval. The recorder looks up every 10 seconds and spends the interval locating the category and recording the tally. At the conclusion of the recording period, the tallies are totaled and recorded in the column on the right.

Another method of recording is to observe more than one student at a time. This procedure is done by securing and completing a record sheet for each child to be observed and arranging them in a pile. Then, in a systematic way, the first child is observed, his behavior is recorded, and his sheet is put on the bottom of the stack. The second child is then observed, his behavior is recorded in like manner, and his sheet is moved to the bottom. When each child has been observed, one cycle is completed, and the sheet for the first child is on top again. The process is then repeated. Obviously, the larger the number of students one observes the fewer the number of observations one can make. With practice and some familiarity with the sheet, a cycle can be completed for five children about every 20 seconds. This rate would allow three observations per minute, which would be sufficient for most recordings. The number of students observed should be adjusted in accordance with the following factors: (1) the purpose for the data, (2) the anticipated length of the recording session, and (3) the type of activity of the class (in a very open setting, one might spend 3 to 5 seconds just locating a child for observation).

A few suggestions are presented here concerning the instrument, data gathering, and the use to which the data can be applied.

1. If more than one observation is made on a single child, a separate sheet should be used on which to keep a running, cumulative total in each category. This way, trends can be observed and objectively noted.

2. The instrument can be used to collect baseline behavior data prior to an intervention program, and then used to collect the postdata to determine if there has been any significant change in behavior.

3. The data can be used as a barometer of classroom affect.

4. If a teacher feels a child is misbehaving or is disruptive, the data from this instrument can be used to either support or refute his/her

accusation. In conjunction with this point, the data can be shown to parents as an objective indication of the child's behavior patterns.

5. If recorded by an outside observer, data from the instrument can indicate children who are never talking, are never initiating, are always playing alone, or any number of situations of which the teacher may not be aware.

6. The use of the instrument may provide the teacher with data concerning likes or dislikes of certain students if it can be observed that a consistent behavior pattern is altered each time a certain type of lesson is presented.

Obviously, this list can be extended to include many other applications. Again, no value judgment is implied by any category. By objectively reporting and summarizing these data, one is only to infer that such a behavior pattern was displayed. Implications, value judgments, and alterations should all be considered with the student and/or the student's parents.

Phase V: Lesson follow-up

The observation instruments reviewed to this point all describe the classroom activities of the teacher or the student. The education of the child, however, goes beyond the confines of the classroom. What is done in the classroom setting could be futile unless there is some transfer to the behavior patterns of the child in the "real world." Phase V is intended to be an aid to parents, teachers, or other interested observers to see if lessons, objectives, or commitments alter a child's behavior. This instrument records a child's behavior based on a given set of input.

The form is used to observe a child's behavior following a lesson. The period of observation, however, can vary from a few minutes to many days. If used by a parent, he or she needs the help of a teacher in completing the first part of the form before any observation begins. If used by a teacher, he or she must take care to observe a child in a setting other than a classroom. The instrument was designed to be used cooperatively by parents and teachers in order to be able to integrate the educational goals of the child and his out-of-class behaviors. As an example, if a teacher could fill out the portion that applies to himself or herself, give it to the parent for a period of observation, then have the completed form returned, the assembled data could be a resource for further diagnosis and individualization.

With the exception of the name of the observer, the teacher completes the form down through and including "Commitments or promises made by child." The specified behaviors that either indicate adherence to or opposition to objectives or commitments can be described with as much

```
                    PHASE V—RECORD SHEET
Name of student _____ Observing Period _____
Name of teacher  ——————————  Class/Rm _____
Name of observer_____

Subject of lesson _____
Teacher's behavioral objective for children _____
_____

Commitments or promises made by child.
1.
2.
3.
Observed behaviors that indicate adherence to the objective(s) or commit-
ment(s) and place and date observed.
                    Behavior            Date              Place
1.
2.
3.
4.
5.

Observed behaviors that contradict the objective(s) or commitment(s) and
place and date observed.
                    Behavior            Date              Place
1.
2.
3.
```

detail as is felt necessary. The important aspect is that the description be made in behavioral terms, e.g., "He wrote his name five times on his blackboard while playing alone." This statement could be contrasted to a nonbehaviorally stated comment, e.g., "He was good the entire afternoon."

Overlay A: Bilingual interaction

Each of the overlay components are designed to augment, expand or further clarify the data collected with Phases I, II, and III. Overlay A is designed to couch interaction in terms of the language being spoken. When used in conjunction with Phases I or II, data is obtained regarding the specific behaviors that take place in each language. As an example, it might be recorded that a bilingual teacher does most of her praising in one language and not in the other, or that she often switches the language of interaction for a specific kind of lesson. The recording sheet for this overlay has two columns, one for each language. This sheet, of course, could be expanded if there were a need for a third language. Sequential recording then takes place by entering the number of each behavior in the column that identifies the language in which it was spoken. The following is a sample interaction sequence:

SP	ENG		SP	ENG
10			7	
10			7	
	1			11
	3			7
7				3
5			7	
6			13	
	3			3
	3			7
7				6

When interpreting results gathered from a bilingual classroom, there are at least three dimensions of concern:

1. To count the number of tallies in each column to see the relative percentages devoted to each language. This count can be made for an entire lesson, or it can be computed separately for teacher talk and student talk.

2. To perform an analysis of the data in each language by separately adding tallies in each category for one language, then repeating the process for the second. This procedure enables a recorder to state a finding such as the following: With respect to questions asked, 17 were asked in Spanish and 9 were asked in English.

3. To consider the sequential effect of switching languages by examining interaction that preceded each switch. An encoder is able to determine if the teacher continues in the language to which a student has switched, or if the teacher returns to the other language. One is also able to determine if any specific teaching patterns provoke switches.

An important consideration when using Overlay A is that the encoder be adequately proficient in both languages of instruction. It is obvious that if a recorder does not sufficiently understand the interaction, the data obtained would be of no use. The person, then, must both know the system and be bilingual.

There is a provision whereby this overlay can be used without reference to any of the phases described earlier. In order to do so, the columns are identified and the speaker is noted with no reference to the behavior. In other words, each time a teacher behavior occurs in Spanish, a "T" is recorded under the column marked Spanish. If a child answers a question in English, an "S" (for student), or a "B" or "G" (for boy or girl), is recorded in the English column. The number of tallies for each language can be analyzed as language totals or specific breakdowns for "T" and "S" can be made for each language.

Overlay B: Subject matter framework

Just as Overlay A focuses on the language of the interaction process, Overlay B enables recorders to identify subject matter or other categorical classifications in which interaction takes place. A wide variety of possibilities are available for use with this overlay. The overlay is intended to be used with Phases I or II, and is recorded in the same multicolumn method as the language interaction is recorded in Overlay A.

Some of the considerations that may be used for this part are as follows:

1. The most simple dichotomy would be one that describes the orientation of a lesson. The categories could be "lesson orientation," and "nonlesson orientation." All behavior that is specifically related to a subject being taught would be recorded in one column, while procedural statements, unrelated questions and comments, interruptions, asides, etc., would all go into the other column.

2. Specific content titles or subject headings can be used. For an early childhood social studies lesson, for example, such categories as "family," "workers," and "community" might be involved. For a reading lesson, one might identify the various aspects of reading that are being considered in the lesson. Columns might be headed "initial consonants," "medial vowels," "terminal consonants," "diagraphs," "blends," etc. The level of sophistication into which subjects can be broken down is infinite.

3. Various hierarchies and/or taxonomies can also be used. Such classifications as "cognitive," "affective," and "psychomotor" can be used. With these three headings, the actual behavior is recorded with Phase I or II in the column that identifies the domain of the interaction. Other possibilities include "convergent," "divergent," "evaluation" and "other"; "high level," "low level"; or "product," "process," and "evaluation." One might use some developmental stage categories such as Piaget's sequences of "perception," "operations," and "transition from perception to operations." His developmental categories could also be used: "preoperational," "concrete operations," and "formal operations." One would need to take special care to operationally define each term to facilitate encoding (Furth, 1969, p. 58).

In essence, any classification system that focuses on categorical differences is applicable. It should be remembered that, with any system selected, it is helpful to include an "other" category in which to record nonsubstantive behaviors.

Some examples of possible recordings are shown below:

Phase I		Phase II		
Task	Nontask	Cognitive	Affective	Psychomotor
1			1	
5		3		
	5	7		
	3		8	
1			2	
	5	11		
5				9
2				9
				6
		11		
		10		

The types of analyses that can be done with the data are similar to those listed under Overlay A:

1. Column totals can be made to show that there were five "task" tallies and three "nontask" tallies.

2. Row totals for each column can be made for each category. This total would show the following for the above example on the left. Questions, 2 task; Praising, 1 task; Teacher Authority, 1 nontask; no category 4s; Student Interaction, 2 task and 2 nontask.

3. The sequential effects involved in moving from one column to another can be analyzed.

Overlay C: Moral–conceptual framework

The purpose of this overlay, which could be conceived as an extension of Overlay B, is to describe column overlays that could be used in the teaching of lessons related to the concept of God. The overlay was developed for an early childhood study that sought to determine the stages of progression in children's concepts of God.

As in Overlay B, the column headings are identified as a sequential or categorical system. The four columns under which entries are made are as follows:

1. *Self-Concept-Related Subject Matter.* These are discussions that deal with the person's opinion of self, characteristics, or attitudes; anything requesting introspection or self-evaluation, even if it pertains to a moral principle.

2. *God-Related Subject Matter.* Any sentence or phrase that contains the word "God," "Jesus," "Godhead," "Deity," or refers directly to the subject of God, his attributes, characteristics, powers, virtues, etc.

3. *Moral-Related Subject Matter.* Any sentence or phrase that contains or relates directly to any of the following:

a. anything dealing with or concerning "rightness" and/or "wrongness;"
b. anything concerning principles of "moral," "correct," "righteous," or "virtuous living;"
c. stories that contain a moral relating to any of the principles noted in (b);
d. teachings that relate to one's conscience;
e. hypothetical situations that request judgment as to "right" or "correct" behavior; and
f. teachings about other related religious themes.

4. *Other Subject Matter.* Any subject matter that does not relate to any of the three categories above.

When an interaction could be classified in two or more categories, it is always recorded in the applicable column with the lowest number; in other words, the column farthest to the left. Following is an example of an interaction sequence recorded using Phase II and Overlay C:

Self-Concept	God-Related	Moral	Other
	1		
	3		
		7	
		5	
	10		
	3		
	7		
			8
			12
			17
		3	
		7	
	3		
	7		
	6		
1			
1			
3			
	7		
3			
7			
6			

This overlay can also be used independently of either Phase I or Phase II. Just as with Overlay A, the record sheet can be constructed and tallies indicating teacher and student, (boy or girl) can be entered in the appropriate columns instead of coding the behavior. These data, while they do not describe the specific interaction, do describe the content orientation of the lesson and the relative amount of interaction among participants.

This particular instrument can be useful in Sunday School classes, parochial school classes, Bible study classes, and other lessons related to the concept of God. The rationale behind the construction of the columns is that the intent of a teacher of religious instruction should be to move the lesson orientation to the left. Stories concerning moral behavior or relating to the attributes of God seem to be most useful when they are internalized into a student's self-concept.

Overlay D: Interaction identification

When encoding a student response or a student initiated behavior with Phases I and II, the recorder only identifies the respondent as being a student. When more specific data are needed or requested, individual students can be identified with the use of Overlay D. This identification is made by recording, beside the student behavior code, either the student's initials or seat number. The same method can be expanded to include students who are the objects of a particular teacher interaction, by recording, beside the behavior interaction category, the initials or seat number of the student involved. The following is an example of a sequence that uses interaction identification:

Overlay D, using student initials	Overlay D, using seat numbers
3–JD	3/12
7–JD	7/12
6–JD	6/12
3–DT	3/4
7–BR	7/5
12–BR	12/5
7–DT	7/4
6–DT	6/4

In this example, Jack Dow (JD) sits in Seat 12; David Tripp (DT) sits in Seat 4, and Betty Robbins (BR), in Seat 5.

Three other categories are useful when this overlay is employed. They are as follows:

W—*Whole class:* Interaction directed at the whole class, responses solicited from the whole class, or a response given by the whole class.
S—*Small group within the class:* More than one person but less than six, seven, or eight. Such things as the second row, the five boys on the left side, the girls in the back, etc., might be included.

L—Large group within the class: More than six, seven, or eight persons but less than the entire class. Might include such things as the left side of the room, two or more rows or clusters of chairs, all the girls in the class, etc.

Other specific identifying numbers, letters, or codes can be assigned to distinguish between specific small groups. For example, four students in the front of a class might always be responding to the teacher's questions. This group could be labeled "S_1." Each time the group responded or a question was directed toward the group, the entry S_1 would identify them.

To analyze the data from this overlay, when it is used in conjunction with Phase I or II, there are at least two options:

1. To mark on a seating chart the number of interactions recorded for each student. Such information would provide basic ideas regarding students who never interact with the teacher and those who continuously do. It could also be used to determine if the teacher interacted more with boys or with girls, or whether one side of the room was favored over the other.

2. After determining (or while determining) the total number of interactions, the specific kinds of interactions can be determined for each child. Such questions as the following could be answered:

    a. Who answers the most questions?

    b. Who never answers questions?

    c. Are there children whose only interaction with the teacher is in a behavior control setting?

    d. Which students initiate interaction?

    e. Which students receive praise?

    f. Which students do not receive praise?

The complete system

It was mentioned previously that over 50 instruments could be constructed by using and combining phases and overlays in unique ways. This flexibility allows teachers and researchers to look at aspects of classroom interaction that are of particular interest to them. The most complete combination allows for five separate aspects of interaction to be analyzed simultaneously. On one record sheet, the following information can be gathered on one specific event: the subject matter or task orientation, the language involved, the specific behavior of the teacher or pupil, the affect of the teacher, and the student or students who are addressed or interacting. It should be obvious that such a system

The Complete System Record Sheet for SCIMP Phases II, III;
Overlays A, B, D

Task Oriented						Non-Task					
Spanish			English			Spanish			English		
Beh	Affect	Pupil	Beh	Affect	Pupil	Beh	Affect	Pupil	Beh	Affect	Pupil
			1	A+	W						
			10		W						
			3		SG						
7	N+	CT									
6		CT									
						8		JS			
									8	A−	JS
3		W				12		SG			
			7	V	W						
			6		W						
			10		W						
			3	A+	W						
			7		LB						
7	A+	JS									
6		JS									
			3		LB						
			7		FR						
						10	V	W			
			3		FR						
			7		FR						
			6	A+	FR						
6		FR									
6		SG									

would probably only be used for sophisticated research rather than for immediate teacher feedback, and that interaction could not be encoded live but would need to be done with the assistance of a video recorder (see the sample of the record sheet used in the complete system).

INTEGRATING PHASES AND OVERLAYS

The purpose for having numerous options from which to choose is that teachers should be entitled to encode the behavior that will be most meaningful to them. SCIMP provides a teacher or teacher trainee with multiple recording options from the most basic to the most complex. It is not intended that any of these categories be rigid or confining. Teachers, in fact, are encouraged to be selective in determining the data that they wish to encode.

This, or any system of interaction analysis, is most useful if it is used consistently. The most successful arrangement for real inservice growth seems to be pairs of teachers, both of whom are well versed in the coding system that is being used. For 5 to 10 minutes per day one teacher goes to the other teacher's room and records the interaction that takes place. The interaction tallies are totaled and the teachers can stay 5 to 10 minutes after school reviewing what took place. The following day the situation is reversed, and the teacher who was observed the day before becomes the observer. Nothing critical is mentioned during these visits. As stated previously, objective recording instruments do not transmit value judgments; they only record interaction. The data are then compared with the teacher's intent and it is the teacher who decides how he or she might alter interaction to more closely approximate intent. The teacher may, of course, seek advice, answers, or other resources, but the decision is his or hers to make.

If a "buddy system" cannot be arranged, other personnel within the school may be available to assist in the recording if they are willing, especially with Phase I, and/or Overlay A, B, or C when used independently of the phases. Such individuals include principals, counselors, librarians, parents, aides, student teachers, district supervisors or administrators, custodians, secretaries, or any number of other individuals. If none of these is willing or able, small cassette recorders can also be used. A teacher can record a segment and encode the lesson himself at a later time. Again, teachers should be encouraged to encode only small segments of lessons. By encoding 5 to 10 minutes, a teacher can receive sufficient feedback to compare his behavior with his intent.

THE INTERACTION LESSON PLAN

When an athlete videotapes or films a performance, he or she often spends hours watching and studying each aspect of the behavior exhibited. The position of each body part is analyzed with respect to placement, timing, and execution. This type of study provides the athlete with valuable feedback that is translated to behavior change and subsequently to an improved performance. A teacher who realizes that an interaction record sheet is a graphic representation of his or her performance in the classroom is able to benefit in a similar way.

The last aspect of the behavior change cycle is the plan to improve.

```
┌─────────────────────────────────────────────────────────────────────────┐
│                    SCIMP INTERACTION LESSON PLAN                          │
│  Name of Teacher          Jami Powell                                     │
│  Kind of lesson (skill, discussion, lecture, etc.)      Discussion        │
│  Subject matter or skill area     Social Studies     Date     10/19       │
│  Number of children   9    Instrument(s) to be used   Phase II, Overlay A │
│  Anticipated length of lesson    12 min.   Place   Zavala School, Room 419│
│  One area I want to develop during this lesson is as follows:  Greater    │
│                                                                  student   │
│  involvement; consistent use of Spanish                                   │
├─────────────────────────────────────────────────────────────────────────┤
```

This will mean I will try to encourage tallies in the following categories:

<table>
<tr><td>7</td><td></td><td>8</td></tr>
</table>

A typical interaction sequence to encourage might be as follows:

3		3
7	or	7
7		8
7		7

One area I want to avoid is as follows: Answering my own questions; cutting off student talk

This means I will try to minimize tallies in the following categories:

10		13

A typical interaction sequence to avoid might be as follows:

3		3
17	or	7
10		13
10		10

Goals: I will have at least 50 tallies in category 7

I will have not more than 20 tallies in category 10

Notes or comments:

First, data are gathered; second, analyses are preformed; third, results are compared with intent; and, fourth, a plan is formulated whereby one can bring about the desired change. The Interaction Lesson Plan is intended to assist in this process. It is intended to help remind the teacher desirous of changing that there is more than the content aspect of lesson preparation; there is the interaction aspect.

On the planning sheet the teacher records some details concerning the lesson to be taught, e.g., kind of lesson, number of students, etc., and then describes the interaction that is to take place. It is here that the teacher describes his or her intent, against which the results will be compared. Items included are as follows:

1. an area or category on which to concentrate;
2. an operational description of that category;
3. an area or category to avoid;
4. an operational description of that category;
5. a place to set goals (if desired);
6. a place for notes or comments.

After completing the sheet, the lesson is taught and the interaction is encoded and summarized. Those data are then compared with the predictions on the sheet and any discrepancies are noted. Obviously, the comparison will never be perfect, nor are predictions intended to be restricting. If something arises during the lesson, and the teacher decides to alter his/her intended approach, she/he need not feel bound by the predictions. It can be helpful, however, to assist a teacher to plan a specific interaction pattern, teach a lesson, and then determine if a goal was reached. Observed, unintentional deviations can then become the basis for subsequent change. (See the example of a completed Interaction Lesson Plan using Phase II.)

References

Brandt, R. M. An historical overview of systematic approaches to observation in school settings. In R. A. Weinberg, and F. H. Wood, (Eds.), *Observation of pupils and teachers in mainstream and special education settings: Alternative strategies.* Minneapolis, Minn.: University of Minnesota, Leadership Training Institute/ Special Education, College of Education, 1975.

Combs, A. The personal approach to good teaching. *Educational Leadership,* 1964, *21* (6), 369–377.

Flanders, N. A. *Analyzing teacher behavior.* Reading, Mass.: Addison–Wesley, 1970.

Furth, H. G. *Piaget and knowledge.* Englewood Cliffs, N.J.: Prentice–Hall, 1969.

Galloway, C. M. Non-verbal: The language of sensitivity. *Theory into practice,* 1971, *10* (4), 310–314.

García, E. F. Modification of teacher behavior in teaching the Mexican American. Albuquerque, N.M.: Southwestern Cooperative Educational Laboratory, 1970. (ERIC Document Reproduction Service No. ED 057 971).

Good, T. L., and Brophy, J. E. *Looking into classrooms.* New York: Harper & Row, 1973.

Hodge, R. L. Interpersonal classroom communication through eye contact. *Theory into practice,* 1971, *10* (4), 264–267.

Hughes, B. E., and Harrison, H. Evaluation report of the bilingual education program: Harlandale Independent School District; San Marcos Independent School District; Southwest Texas State University, 1970–71. Harlandale, Texas, 1971. (ERIC Document Reproduction Service No. ED 055 686).

Kent, L. Student Evaluation of Teaching. *Educational Record,* 1966, *47:* 376–406.

Klingsledt, J. L. Teachers of middle school Mexican-American children: Indicators of effectiveness and implications for teacher education. Washington, D.C.: U.S. Office of Education (Health, Education, and Welfare), 1972. (ERIC Document Reproduction Service No. ED 059 828).

Medley, D. M. Closing the gap between research in teacher effectiveness and the teacher education curriculum. *Journal of Research and Development in Education,* 1973, *7:* 39–46.

Medley, D. M., and Mitzel, H. E. Measuring classroom behavior by systematic observation. In N. Gage (Ed.), *Handbook of research on teaching.* Chicago: Rand McNally, 1963.

Moscowitz, G. The effects of training foreign language teachers in interaction analysis. *Foreign Language Association,* 1968, *3:* 218–235.

Rosenshine, B., and Furst, N. The use of direct observation to study teaching. In R. M. W. Travers (Ed.), *Second handbook of research on teaching.* Chicago: Rand McNally, 1973.

Seifert, K. Comparison of verbal interaction in two pre-school programs. *Young Children,* 1969, *24:* 350–355.

Simon, A., and Boyer, E. G. (Eds.) *Mirrors for behavior: An anthology of classroom observation instruments,* Philadelphia: Research For Better Schools, 1967.

Smothergill, N. The effects of manipulation of teacher communication style in the pre-school. *Child Development,* 1971, *42:* 1229–1239.

Soar, R. S. An empirical analysis of selected follow through programs: An example of a process approach to evaluation. In I. J. Gordon (Ed.), *Early childhood education.* The seventy-first yearbook of the National Society for the Study of Education. Chicago: NSSE, 1972. (a)

Soar, R. S. Teacher-pupil interaction. In *A New Look at Progressive Education, 1972 Yearbook.* Washington, D.C.: Association for Supervision and Curriculum Development, 1972. (b)

Stallings, J. *An implementation study of seven follow through models for education.* Paper presented at the Annual Meeting of the American Educational Research Association (59th, Chicago, Ill. April, 1974).

Texas Education Agency. Application for operational expenses allocation for state bilingual education programs. Annual summaries available from TEA, Austin, 1974–1975, 1975–1976.

Texas Education Agency. *Texas public schools law bulletin.* Austin, Tex.: West Publishing Co., Section 21.453 (B), p. 173, 1976.

Townsend, D. R. *A comparison of the classroom interaction patterns of bilingual early childhood teachers.* Unpublished doctoral dissertation at The University of Texas at Austin, 1974.

Townsend, D. R., and Zamora, G. L. Differing interaction patterns in bilingual classrooms. *Contemporary Education,* 1975, *46:* 196–202.

Weinberg, R. A., and Wood, F. H. (Eds.), *Observation of pupils and teachers in mainstream and special education settings: Alternative strategies.* Minneapolis, Minn.: University of Minnesota, Leadership Training Institute/Special Education, College of Education, 1975.

Wright, H. F. Observational child study. In P. H. Mussen (Ed.), *Handbook of research methods in child development.* New York: Wiley, 1960.

United States Commission on Civil Rights. *Teachers and students: Differences in teacher interaction with Mexican American and Anglo students, Report V: Mexican American education study.* Washington, D.C.: U.S. Government Printing Office, 1973.

Zamora, G. L. *A comparison of the nonverbal communication patterns of bilingual early childhood teachers.* Unpublished doctoral dissertation, University of Texas at Austin, 1974.

Part IV

GENERAL TOPICS AND REVIEW OF THE LITERATURE

12

Bilingual Education and the Future of Language Teaching and Language Learning in the United States[1]

JOSHUA A. FISHMAN, Yeshiva University

An exciting field

Language teaching is an exciting field. During the past third of a century, there has been as much innovative theory, curricular and methodological rethinking, and sophisticated debunking in the language-teaching field as in the much-stressed fields of mathematics and science. This ferment says a great deal about the intellectual vitality of language teaching and clearly distinguishes it (as well as math–science) from the social sciences and the other areas of the humanities, which, regrettably, have remained comparatively unrevised in terms of instructional theory or methodology. Indeed, the growing relationship between the language field and the math–science field on the one hand (in terms of the forces that shape American life and American education), and the shrinking relationship between the language field and humanities–social-science field on the other hand, is related both to the heights and the depths that American language teaching has experienced since the beginning of World War II.

Extrasocietal and external societal influences

During and immediately after World War II—war needs themselves being among the most dramatic influences that American language teaching has ever experienced—the most influential ideas shaping American language teaching methods were derived from linguistics and from psychology. I refer to these as *extrasocietal* influences since neither the view that gave primacy to syntax and phonology over lexicon and use,

---

[1] This chapter is a revised version of an article originally appearing in *ADFL: Bulletin of the Association of Departments of Foreign Languages*, 1975, 6 (3), 5–8, and also appears in the author's *Bilingual education: An international sociological perspective* (Rowley: Newbury House, 1976).

nor the view that gave primacy to listening comprehension and to speech over reading and writing, had any societal image, purpose, or function explicitly in mind. Neither approach attempted to cope with the question, "What should be the role of subsequent languages in the life of the learner and in the life of society?" There was absolutely no conscious "language-in-society" model underlying either of these powerful methodological approaches, both of which are still very much with us today.

Although the same extrasocietal designation is not true with respect to the second most powerful force influencing American language teaching during the past third of a century (here I refer to the post-Sputnik panic and the realization that language expertise was vital for defense-related purposes), that force was an external societal factor rather than an internal one. The threat of Soviet technological modernization imposed itself on us from outside our own boundaries, and even when language instruction responded to that threat with all the "nondeliberate" speed at its command, it never (well, hardly ever) linked its contribution to national defense with the indigenous language resources internal to American society. The Language Resource Project that I headed from 1960 to 1963, and that resulted in my book, *Language Loyalty in the United States (1966)*, tried to provide such an internal societal link, but it offered an idea whose time had not yet quite come. The common American approach to language learning (and, indeed, the common approach of the language teacher per se to the commodity he was "pushing") was that additional languages are useful or crucial for our national well-being particularly if such a language is (a) learned in school rather than in the context of home and community, (b) learned as a mature adult (in college or in graduate school), (c) learned as a target, in itself, rather than as a process for the mastery of other material, and is (d) exotic to the American content in terms of easy access to the learner.

The ascendancy of societal concerns

Let us quickly skip over everything that the concentration on external threat enabled foreign language teaching to accomplish. The rapid expansion (indeed, duplication) of programs, increase in positions, and mushrooming of student incentive funds have been recounted many times. Let us turn immediately to the realization that during the past decade (1965–1975) most of the impetus for change in language teaching and language learning has had strong indigenous societal roots, although the former external exposure is also still present. In this past decade, language teaching in the United States has had to respond, as never before, to internal social needs such as the needs of the urban disadvantaged, alienated youth, the ethnic minorities, the needs bred by rebirth of ethnicity among some whose parents fancied that they had escaped from it, and, most recently, the needs created by the fiscal crunch. Many of these societal needs and reemerging lost continents have hit language instruction directly, in that the high priorities given to them have left proportionately fewer taxpayer and foundation dollars for other needs. In addition, the educational establishment's reaction to those needs and pressures have often hit language instruction indirectly by permitting greater latitude to the student choice of subjects to be studied, greater opportunity for "alternative" forms and contents of education, and, correspondingly, lesser insistence on language learning, as new subjects and as new populations enter our high schools, colleges, and universities

For one reason or another, language enrollments have generally been dropping, language requirements have been fading, and the attack on language learning has been mounting. As in all times of strife and disappointment, the time and mood are ripe for a new savior. Language teaching in the United States needs a new panacea, a good bet, a stimulating idea, a rallying cause, or, at the very least, a straw to clutch at in the form of an unbeatable method. It is at this point that bilingual education enters the picture to save Little Red Riding Hood from the Big Bad Wolf.

Bilingual education and compensatory education

There is a growing recognition in language teaching circles—as in education circles more generally—that a sizable proportion of the disadvantaged lack facility in English (not to mention standard school English), and that if their educational progress is not to be appreciably delayed and diluted, they had best be taught most subjects in their non-English mother tongues, at least until English-as-a-second-language (ESL) gets through to them. The recent *Lau* decision of the Supreme Court may soon foster a nationwide approach along these lines; yet with all its welcome relief for all children whose English is really insufficient for the burden of educational effort, I doubt that this decision will do much for language instruction. Bilingual education is merely compensatory, merely transitional, is no more than a desperate attempt to fight fire with fire. If a non-English mother tongue is conceptualized as a disease of the poor, then, in true vaccine style, this disease must be attacked by the disease bacillus itself. A little bit of deadened mother tongue, introduced in slow stages in the classroom environment, will ultimately enable the patient to throw off the mother tongue entirely and to embrace all-American vim, vigor, and vitality.

My own evaluation is that compensatory bilingual education is not a good long-term bet either for language teaching or for bilingual education per se. The multiproblem populations on whose behalf it is espoused—populations that are underprivileged, unappreciated, alienated —cannot be aided in more than an initial palliative sense by so slender a reed as compensatory bilingual education. Populations that present well-nigh insuperable problems to our schools and to all of our establishment institutions, even if they were monolingual English speakers, will not cease being such problems merely because they are offered a year or two of introductory education primarily in their non-English mother tongues. Their problems and ours are not that simple to overcome.

Bilingual education "sold" as a compensatory promissory note will disappoint us all, teachers and citizens alike. It will not solve the basic societal problems of the non-English-speaking poor and therefore will not solve their basic educational problems. It will soon be just another educational panacea gone sour, and language teaching as well as bilingual education as a whole will both suffer needlessly as a result of having another bad bet.

Bilingual education and ethnic legitimacy

There is another rationale for bilingual education, one that may be of somewhat greater interest to language teachers and to American society at large. Thanks to our recent ethnicity binge, this rationale recognizes that non-English mother tongues and cultures in our own midst are things of beauty, to be maintained and treasured forever and ever. It recognizes these languages and cultures not for manipulative, compensatory, and transitional purposes, but as basic ingredients of a healthy individual self-concept and of sound group functioning. Groups that are deprived of their languages and cultures are dislocated groups. Such groups have no alternative but to dump dislocated and alienated students on the doorsteps of the school and of all other institutions of the larger society. Greater self-acceptance among non-English-mother-tongue children (including acceptance of their parents and their traditions and their immediate societies), and greater mutual acceptance between such children and the American mainstream, will also foster greater genuine school progress. Bilingual education under this rationale is oriented toward group maintenance, and as a result is not merely a compensatory, transitional "quicky" (Fishman, 1972).

Note, however, that this rationale, too, has an unstated assumption—namely, that bilingual education is needed only for the "unmeltable ethnics." Such a view is still patronizing—although patronizing "once-removed"—in that it assumes that nonethnics are beyond or above bilingual education and "all that." Language and ethnicity are still assigned to the "outer fringe," beyond the propriety of white Anglo-Saxon Protestantdom. Enlightened patronization would not be a propitious approach to strengthening the impact of mathematics or history in American education or in American life, and I predict that, welcome though it may be among the Navajos, it will do little or nothing for the place of language learning in our schools and in our society more generally.

Bilingual education for enrichment

In various parts of Canada (and not only in French Canada) economically comfortable English-speaking parents are voluntarily sending their eager youngsters to primarily-but-not-entirely French schools. Such "immersion schools" for societally favored youngsters also exist in France, Germany, Latin America, the Soviet Union, the Arab World, Italy, and Belgium, not to mention many parts of Africa and Asia. These schools bring together two languages of wider communication rather than one pitifully small language and one gargantuanly large one. They involve the populations most able to pay for a good education and most likely to succeed educationally and societally rather than those least favored in these respects. Immersion schools require the most advantaged to stretch further educationally, and thus are really an enrichment for the rich. They continue, albeit at a somewhat more accessible level, the bilingual education tradition practiced by most elites since the days of the ancient Egyptians and Greeks and Romans. They are eminently successful and therefore attract the best students, teachers, and administrators; and because they attract the best personnel, they become even more successful. Regrettably, such schools are almost unknown in the public sector of American education.

Of course, bilingual education for enrichment also involves some unspoken assumptions, just as does compensatory and group-maintenance bilingual education. Bilingual enrichment education assumes not only that the well-off particularly stand to gain from an additional cultural exposure but also that, indeed, they are the very ones for whom such an exposure is an acceptable and even a powerful motivating argument. My own view is that enrichment (or immersion) bilingual education is the best way of demonstrating the academic and societal advantages of bilingual education. I am sure that immersion bilingual education could become the most reliable prop for language teaching in the United States, just as it has become in some of the countries I have mentioned. Such a prop would be more than a fad, more than a nostrum, were it ever to catch on. It represents bilingual education not only at its best, but at its broadest. However, I am not sure that "middle America," in whose image most of our secondary and higher educational institutions are shaped, is quite ready for it, or ever will be.

Bilingual education in sociolinguistic perspective

Let me close by considering both bilingual education and language teaching in a sociolinguistic perspective. If there is anything that bilingual education can contribute to language teaching more generally, it is the maximization of language learning for the communication of messages that are highly significant for senders and receivers alike, both in their individual as well as in their actual and potential societal capacities. There is simply no way in which language teaching that focuses on language as a *target* of instruction can fully capture the total impact on the learner that is available to language teaching that also capitalizes on languages as a *process* of instruction. Because bilingual education *does* use language as a process—particularly in its enrichment guise, but also in its compensatory and group-maintenance guises (which definitely have a validity of their own, although of a more temporally or demographically restricted nature)—it provides a powerful and worldwide boost to language teaching. However, like every potential solution, it poses potential problems as well.

Is the American public mature enough for enrichment-oriented bilingual education? Are we and our colleagues in the language-teaching profession mature enough to move toward it rather than reject it because of our own personal inadequacies and societal biases? My own tendency is to view the future in optimistic terms. I see future language teaching and language learning in the United States as including a greater variety of rationales, goals, and methods than has hitherto been the case. I forsee bilingual education among these methods, and I forsee more language teachers able to engage in it than previously, whether for compensatory, group-maintenance, or enrichment purposes. Indeed, I foresee American bilingual educators as being able to engage in various kinds of bilingual education, rather than merely in one kind or another, depending on the students and communities to which they are addressing themselves. Finally, I forsee more secondary-language teachers also able to engage in bilingual education, and more bilingual educators being able to engage in second-language instruction, rather than two quite distinct groups of language practitioners, as is most often the case in this country today.

As for bilingual education itself, it cannot be the panacea for all the ills that plague American language teaching today. It is but one opportunity among many to revitalize language teaching. It is itself internally diversified into compensatory, group-maintenance, and enrichment streams and must not be viewed as one undifferentiated blob. It has its own problems of training and funding. It can no more remake society, education, or even language teaching than can any other partial solution to all-encompassing and multifaceted problems It should not be underrated, but it should not be oversold on false premises. It has functions that go above and beyond language teaching. However, I know that it is here to stay as a worldwide phenomenon today, with outcroppings in well over a hundred countries, and I trust that America will profit from it and contribute to it in the days to come.

References

Fishman, J. A., *et al. Language loyalty in the United States.* The Hague: Mouton, 1966.

Fishman, J. A. *Language and nationalism.* Rowley, Mass.: Newbury House, 1972.

13

What the Child Brings and What the School Expects: First- and Second-Language Learning and Teaching in Bilingual–Bicultural Education

JUDITH T. GUSKIN, Kenosha, Wisconsin

Introduction

Bilingual-bicultural education has emerged at an exciting time. It is a time when theories and practices regarding language learning and teaching are being challenged; values and goals related to the education of minorities are topics of heated argument; public reexamination of the role of ethnicity and language maintenance is encouraging soul searching that starts with personal histories and broadens to interpretations of our history and of our goals as a nation. Interdisciplinary efforts, involving links between linguists, sociologists, psychologists, anthropologists, and educators, are giving birth to new journals focused on language learning and bilingual education.

Just as our knowledge is being increased and challenged, educators find themselves enmeshed in the complexity of implementing new programs with all the multitude of decisions required for such implementation—for example, decisions about parent involvement, teacher selection and training, interpretation of legislative mandates, and the development of materials and tests to fit local goal definitions. We need to sift through competing philosophies and conflicting theories and data and to create images that can guide educators as they plan, act, evaluate, and dream.

This chapter is an attempt to forge a coherent conception of language learning from a selective review of first- and second-language acquisition in the hope that a dialogue will develop between those breaking new ground in the study of how children learn and use language in social settings and educators attempting to conceptualize and create learning environments to increase the communicative competence of children. Given the interdisciplinary efforts involved, it is difficult to keep abreast of new studies. It is also a challenge to try to weave these studies into some pattern that identifies and highlights similarities and that places them within a broader conception of human learning. Yet, as educators, we must aim to find ways to use new knowledge of human learning and to integrate this knowledge into a more general conception of human learning that can guide us as we search for goals, methods, and evaluation techniques. Research should lead us to confirm or reexamine our assumptions about learning as well as about the institutional arrangements created to foster it. Both what the child brings to the learning environment and the social expectations he adapts to in the school setting need to be included, for a human being is a social creature, always creating and being created by his or her interaction with others.

Any attempt of this kind is likely to reflect an author's general approach to learning, highlighting certain findings and choices in composition and arrangement that help pull the picture together. In addition, limitations regarding scope are required. My subject, therefore, is limited to young children, and my orientation is primarily that of Piaget. I hope that the picture that emerges of language learning will prove useful to those planning bilingual–bicultural programs.

What the child brings

FIRST-LANGUAGE LEARNING

Language is one of the most basic processes of human socialization. When we say that a child brings to school some knowledge of his first language, we must understand how he has acquired it in order to take full advantage of the kinds of learning startegies already demonstrated by the child.

Born into a social group, the child has acquired socially meaningful behaviors, one of which is language. Language has helped him to be integrated into the daily patterns of everyday life in his home. He has learned the appropriate ways to talk about the comings and goings of others, just as he has learned to predict when others will come and go. Without being directly taught, motivated by his own needs for food, cleanliness, love, and attention, he has learned by looking, touching, and making people and things react. Piaget (1970) has referred to the active process of taking in the new and building on the old as a form of self-regulation. Throughout this process the child is not passive, and while he may imitate and repeat, he is the architect of his knowledge of the world.

If I had to find one short expression to characterize the essence of this learning, I would choose "finding patterns." The world to the young child must be incredibly confusing. Yet, through the repetition of patterns of interaction with others as they respond to his needs, his expectations and understandings grow. He learns to pick out, from the multitude of stimuli that impinge on him, from the strange symphony of everyday noises, those that will help him to anticipate actions and the consequences of actions. Eyes, mouth, hands, skin, and his sense of inner pain or satisfaction, as well as the sounds of others and his own sounds, aid him in developing his understanding of language. As George Herbert Mead (1934) has said, this culturally situated language will then provide the key to the development of a socially adequate identity. He will understand what he can do and how others interpret what he can do.

Given a responsive environment, the child reaches out to the confusing realities of unknown objects, people, and relationships, and develops a sense of trust in others and in his own behaviors. He enjoys inventing new ways to act and to get reactions. Both Piaget (1970) and Chomsky (1972) stress the active invention and construction that must take place if language is to be learned. Certainly bits and pieces of language and of other behaviors are learned, but they are learned not as isolated meaningless items, but rather as parts of the bigger puzzle that contains both language and social interaction.

In a recent paper by Labov and Labov (1974), this testing and defining process by which a young child learns his first words is shown through careful documentation of the modifications the child makes in testing the application of words. The child uses intonation patterns to ask for a confirmation of his meaning. For example, the child proceeds to ask which of the animals in a zoo belonged to his category "cat," which at first meant only a household pet. Words are *categories* that change. At first they may be broad, then become narrower in scope. As learning about objects, events, and people continues, categories and their relationships to each other mesh, divide, and are born anew. An active child and a responsive environment make this possible.

Simple language and social routines, linked together, give meaning at one point in the history of the child's development, then become transformed into more complex utterances and social routines. What starts as a simple wave coupled with the words *bye-bye* ends as a sophisticated repertoire of ways to interpret and manipulate the openings and closings of conversations in a number of different situations. Just as we all start as simple cells and become transformed into complex organisms before birth, so does our understanding grow and change in our social environments.

The categories the child constructs and the ways he uses them will not be identical to those of adult members of his community. They are likely to be overextended meanings, starting points for social interaction. As Eve Clark (1973) indicates in her review of early semantic development, common perceptual features, like shape, may lead the child to create a category that later is changed. Words that sound similar to the child may be thought to be similar in meaning.

The selection and modification of words, since words are concepts or categories, are not entirely a function of what the child hears or what the others in his environment intend him to learn. While certain words will reflect names of people and objects he has experienced, the cognitive level of the child is an important consideration. Roger Brown (1973), in reanalyzing an extensive corpus of child language data, has stressed that a common level of cognitive development seems to account for the appearance of certain early meanings: the meanings of *more,* the meaning of negation, of *allgone,* of possessives such as *mommy's shoe* and locatives such as *on* and *in,* as well as of a number of simple requests such as *give me.*

As the child develops more ways of understanding his world, his language will reflect this knowledge. Slobin's (1973) data indicate that children with a better understanding of the meaning of future time, also have more ways of talking about it. In her recent study of the use of *before* and *after* by young children, Keller-Cohen (1974) confirms this point. Piaget for some time has stressed the need to understand child logic before we can really understand what children mean when they talk.

While knowledge of the level of cognitive development can provide certain expectations about language use, each child not only has had unique experiences with people and events, but also has his own style of learning, which will be reflected in his language development as well as language use. Roger Brown (1973) feels that, based on his studies, some children are "word gatherers," intent on increasing their vocabularies, while others enjoy playing with patterns and thus advance more quickly in syntactical development. Some are willing to risk being misunderstood more than are others, and may therefore try out new insights more often.

Human languages are wonderfully flexible instruments in that meaning can be expressed even if the grammatical structure is simplified. All of us who have tried to communicate in a foreign environment without having mastered the foreign language are grateful for this flexibility. So is the child. The fact that we learn how to guess meaning through context, our general understanding of what is logical or acceptable behavior, and our modification of our listening and speaking skills when faced with different kinds of speakers, all work to the advantage of the young child who cannot master all of the obligatory and optional patterns of his language right away.

The young speaker will use *what* he can *when* he can, and it is clear to those who interact with him that he has not mastered all of the com-

binations of the various elements of a   ses the phrase.
For example, the child will use I do'   ⌐ has mastered the
use of do in all constructions (Brow   . he will understand and use
the words ask and tell long befo.e ne will consistently select the right
one (Chomsky, 1969). Temporary compromises, ways to cope with
complexity, and ways to figure out simplifications—all are important to
the young learner and to those who interact with him.

To sum up, first-language development is a process whereby the child
is constantly increasing his ability to adapt to his world by creating intermediate strategies of communication. His strategies are based on his
current grasp of the logic of the behavior of people, objects, and events,
which is a function of his cognitive development and the cultural realities that have molded his expectations and values. In addition, his own
unique learning style, his motivation to risk sharing with others his best
"guesses" of the moment, and the grammatical complexity of the language with regard to the specific form used by adults to express a particular meaning—all of these help produce his language behavior.

SECOND-LANGUAGE LEARNING

Is the process of second-language learning very different? Certainly
where and when the child learns a second language will affect the speed
of his learning. How much opportunity he has to use the language in
socially meaningful situations will be particularly important. There is
more diversity in the where and when of second-language learning than
there is in first-language learning and we have much to learn about the
differential effects of this diversity. However, certain strategies used by
the second-language learner seem similar to those of the first-language
learner.

The strategies of the second-language learner are: the identification of
patterns; attempts to simplify and use words and phrases even if the
meanings and structures are only partial approximations; the finding of
ways of figuring out socially embedded language not only as a means of
gaining confirmation of meaning but also as a way of learning culturally
appropriate patterns; and the flexibility and risk-taking behaviors of
trying to use analogies with his first language, knowing that these analogies may be only partially correct in meaning and structure. In addition,
there are individual styles of learning, differences in emphasis on learning vocabulary or structure, and differences in motivation and the desire
to understand and/or identify with speakers of the language.

The child who uses two languages has an advantage in that he has
already learned that words represent categories that need to be checked
for applicability. Also, he has quite a number of categories available to

him. The more use he can make of what he has already learned about words and about the encoded realities they represent, the easier it will be for him to remember and expand meaning. This understanding leads the learner to try to use what he knows even if he needs to be corrected.

Studies of second-language learning among children (Ervin-Tripp, 1973b; Hatch, 1974) indicate that children will try hard to substitute first-language meanings for words in the second language. They will depend on feedback to clarify differences. Sometimes meaning will be clarified by expanding what the child said, sometimes by asking for repetition, by acknowledging understanding, or by just behaving appropriately. The child will actively seek confirmation of meaning. The focus will not necessarily be on correctness, but rather on appropriateness or the ability to impel action.

Hatch presents an interesting example of the process involved when a second-language learner tries to gain confirmation of meaning. She describes two young preschoolers building towers with blocks. One of the boys is a native speaker of English, the other is not. The native speaker says: *Quit making it so tall.* The other boy asks: *What is /sulta/?* Ignored by his companion, he begins to talk to himself aloud: *He says /sulta/. There is no /sulta/. He is wrong. /Sulta/ doesn't mean anything.* Most likely, when the tower comes tumbling down, our nonnative speaker will figure out the meaning of /sulta/.

Hatch (1974, p. 15) summarizes her data on second-language acquisition as follows:

> From what we have learned from the data so far, it seems that communication is the goal of all learners and parts of the language system which are not important to communication are learned slowly. However, if a structure is extremely frequent in the input data, the learner will produce it. Effects of frequency are modified in a number of ways. If a form requires a change in word order, it will be learned late. If there are a variety of forms for a structure (e.g., plurals with /s/, /z/, and /ez/ forms) it will be acquired late.

The child learning a second language, just as the child learning his first, may make the mistake of assuming that similarity of sound means similarity of meaning. Just like the first-language learner, he will learn certain set phrases, perhaps overextend meanings, and use these phrases before becoming fully able to use the elements in the phrase in grammatically correct and appropriate ways. For example, the first language learner uses *do* in *I don't know* before he can say *Do you know it?* or *He laughs like I do.* Some second-language learners may learn to use *don't* but may overextend its meaning to include *is not* and *couldn't* and *wouldn't* (Cancino, Rosansky, & Schumann, 1975). Both the first- and second-language learner have communication as their goal. If the structure requires a change in word order, or some other modification that creates complexity, it will be simplified or experimented with until the learner understands and learns to control the complexities.

The learning of whole phrases without clear understanding of how to separate, limit, and order these constituents in a variety of constructions does not indicate that the language learner is just parroting, but rather indicates that he is using intermediate strategies, parsimonious first steps, taken because they are the most useful steps to take at that point in the learning process.

We have much to learn about all of the kinds of strategies the second-language learner uses. An analysis of errors can help us to gain insight into these strategies. Corder (1974), Schumann and Stenson (1974), Dulay and Burt (1974), Richards (1974), and others are attempting to assess the types of errors second-language learners make. Some errors certainly reflect the second-language learner's attempt to apply inappropriately a word or construction from his first language when using his second; some reflect developmental stages sometimes similar to those of first-language learners; some errors reflect a failure of memory; and others reflect the complexity of the material to be mastered. Learners are guided by their previous knowledge of language and situations, their current level of cognitive development or semantic understanding of the "what" of the utterance, and their current hypothesis about the new language they are learning. Also, they bring with them strategies of a general nature—how to listen, use an analogy, and perceive patterns, as well as the courage to rely on their own ingenuity to guess a meaning and appropriate ways to express it.

We need more data on how different degrees of bilingualism contribute to strengths and weaknesses of language learning. On the one hand, some bilinguals may have greater perceptual skills, perhaps caused by more practice in reorganizing their processing system and in finding similarities and differences. A study by Cohen, Tucker, and Lambert (1967) indicates that bilinguals perceived unknown consonant clusters with fewer errors than did monolinguals. On the other hand, the presence of more overlapping categories allows meaning and structures to be confused. Some of these confusions can lead to oversimplifications in both languages being learned. In addition, the exposure to speakers who are still mastering two languages could lead to other kinds of difficulties as well as strengths. Studies by Lance (1969) and others indicate that for both bilingual adults and children, many different kinds of errors are found. Much more research is needed on the interactions between degree of bilingualism, types of exposure to other learners, and the age and levels of mastery of bilingual students. Also, a longitudinal perspective is needed in order to identify learner strategies and the effects of different learning environments on these strategies. Hopefully, studies of bilingual education will increase our understanding of language learning.

APPLICATIONS FOR BILINGUAL PROGRAMS

As we review first- and second-language learning for the purpose of developing bilingual programs, the following general issues emerge.

1. Programs desiring to help young learners to master two languages need to be built on a philosophy based on the meshing of language with everyday social relationships. Knowledge of what the child brings should include the degree of use of both languages in everyday life. Which relationships and patterns of his life aid the child in developing which language? Which language has served as the medium through which his social identity has evolved? His vocabulary, his understanding of certain social situations, and his feelings of comfort in talking in these situations and about them constitute the network of language patterns he brings with him along with his level of grammatical mastery. He will use what he has in order to create new patterns and guess at new meanings. We will understand what he does in school better if we know what he brings as well as how he is currently using language in school and outside of school.

2. For young learners, cognitive level should be constantly checked, since assumptions about the logic underlying certain aspects of language use may be unclear. One major advantage of bilingual–bicultural education is that cognitive development can grow hand in hand with language development, since knowledge of the world is taught through language.

Children organize their world through language and try to create a reasonable fit between their present capabilities to understand and the ways they can communicate this understanding. This process involves guessing about meaning of words or expressions. For the young child, as meanings about the way objects and people behave become more differentiated, vocabulary and structure also become differentiated. Sometimes only the structures are difficult, requiring a new word order, agreement rules, or more choices with regard to patterns. However, the focus will be on meaning, and meaning is always growing, expanding, and becoming more elaborate. Assumptions about logic and behavior underlie the construction of sentences and these assumptions may be hidden if only grammar is considered. Emphasis on understanding the logic of behavior of people, objects, and events should go hand in hand with language learning.

3. Strategies brought by a child will reflect individual differences in approaching problem-solving and language learning. Some children are "word gatherers," others seem to work harder on structure. Bilingual–bicultural classrooms may have more diversity of competencies and styles than other classrooms. Planning that allows for diversity with regard not only to skills but also learning strategies would benefit the children. Recognition of different styles and skills will prevent children from being discouraged and lead to more individualized instruction.

4. An active learner uses intermediate strategies to make basic desires known, takes risks, and expects that his listener will guess his meaning and respect his efforts. Attempts to use vocabulary from one language while speaking another, to repeat phrases that have been heard as a way of talking with limited mastery of grammar, and to keep a conversation going by learning "fillers" and alternative ways to say something to avoid difficult structures—these are not necessarily marks of lazy learners. Rather, the more daring the learner, the more he is willing to try to keep speaking, and the more rapidly he will progress in learning language. Language is fun to the extent that personal meaning can be expressed. Only programs that create situations where speaking is desired, where a reason for communication exists, and where social identity will not be hurt by making errors will create speakers.

What the school expects

School settings are appropriate places for the extension of first- and second-language skills in many ways—for increasing vocabulary, developing scientific language and thought, demanding clarification of implicit meanings, and for teaching children how to take turns in group discussions, how to use people and books as resources, and of course, how to read and write. Appropriate concern for teaching these skills is important for bilingual programs, if we expect the child to be able to use both languages to learn and communicate.

Whether concerned with first- or second-language learning, good teachers do expand a child's repertoire of language skills by building on a basis of knowledge and respect for what the child brings. They know that the child has been actively engaged for several years in creating patterns of meaning which have been embedded in cultural patterns and that his identity has been constructed out of the reflections of others' reactions to what he says and does. As long as he received confirmations that were responsive and positive, the child tried out new behaviors. If the school provides another setting in which he can experience a satisfying mutuality of relationships, he will continue to test, to take risks, and to order and integrate new objects, new ideas, and new people. He will continue to learn and to grow.

Good teachers of very young children treat language as an integral part of the growing cognitive development of the child. They know that the child understands more than he can say, and his meaning is not exactly the same as an adult's meaning. Good teachers are aware that a child may ask for clarification even if he knows the answer because language has many social functions, one of which is attention getting. Teachers will modify their speech in certain ways, check on meaning, encourage peer conversations, allow verbalization to accompany actions, and generally encourage the child to try out a variety of ways to express his meaning.

Just as parents (Gleason, 1973) modify their language with young children, often supplying the answers or the context for the child, so do teachers. Parents become aware that children use different styles to talk to their peers or younger children and good teachers use knowledge of style differences to increase the child's repertoire of useful language. Simplification of adult speech, repetition of phrases, expansions, and filling in omissions are natural ways adults interact with young children both prior to school age (Ervin-Tripp, 1973a) as well as in school.

However, as language becomes a more explicit "subject" in the curriculum, and as teacher–student interaction becomes more controlled and teacher dominated, the gap between home and school language expectations grows. Intellectual growth is often less explicitly linked with learning language skills, and social relationships, identity and cultural patterns are less explicitly linked with the type of verbal interactions expected for school success. Correct answers to questions that teachers determine (within prescribed boundaries that dictate both "what" to respond and "how" to do so) become the dominant form of communication (Barnes, Britton, & Rosen, 1971).

Outside and inside the classroom, controlled adult–child communication accounts for only a part of the communication experiences of the child. Peer interaction, valuable for social development as well as language learning, continues to be important. Learning environments that do not use and enrich the social interaction between children are ignoring a valuable opportunity for increasing language skills. Especially for bilingual–bicultural settings, creative ways to capitalize on peer interaction for language learning should be tried. The motivation for taking risks in communicating, for expressing personal meaning, and for using situational contexts to guess at meaning will be enhanced by imaginative organization of classroom environments and programs to promote language communication among children. Approaches like the open classroom, with tasks requiring peer cooperation, may encourage student communication skills as well as fit cultural patterns of behavior familiar to students.

Professional assumptions involved in teaching include the assumption that children must only hear "correct" answers and "correct" speech. Yet, if meanings grow and change, and if language learning is a gradual process of figuring out patterns, learning rules, and trying out analogies, does this not raise some questions about the desirability of allowing partially correct responses in a context of mutually growing competency? It is not that "being wrong" is desirable, but that the encouragement of a continuing flow of communication and a decreasing dependency on the teacher are desirable goals.

Another assumption often made is that teachers should insist on maintaining the "purity" of the langauge they are teaching. Sometimes this assumption means exclusion of dialect variations; sometimes it means exclusion of the "mixing" of two languages. However, such variations are a part of the living language of the children, especially those who are living in multicultural, multilinguistic communities and societies where members of a family differ in their degree of competency. In real social situations, even the bilingual teacher concerned with "purity" is likely to switch from one language to the other to express meaning more appropriately. While efforts to learn new vocabulary and standard grammar are important, such efforts should not communicate disrespect for the language the child brings. The classroom should expand the child's understanding of the communicative skills involved in appropriately modifying "purity" for the sake of relationships and meaning. After all, relationships and meaning are what make language the delightful human enterprise that is it!

Another expectation usually held in schools is that the order of teaching that texts and teachers have prescribed is the most efficient order of learning. The most logical arrangements, or even the apparently easiest sequences, may not be the best for every learner. The child is used to knowing only a part of reality—he has had to make use of a limited vocabulary and limited ways to express his meanings for many years. While providing an organized language program certainly should aid him in acquiring certain rules more quickly, he is quite used to storing information that is temporarily tagged in his memory with question marks. If the need arises for him to use the auxiliary system in order to say something, he will learn a part of it. Errors are to be expected, but will, over time, begin to disappear as more information, from both inside school and outside it, lead him to try new alternatives. Some flexibility and individualization in following the curriculum and greater opportunity for situational needs to produce the impetus for learning may encourage learners to look for and remember patterns that only later become more fully clarified as part of the rules of the language.

Rule learning and rule using is a gradual affair. Young children may need more implicit learning, more observational learning, more trial-and-error learning. Children who are not yet in third grade cannot easily monitor their own speech (Cazden, 1972), and may not even understand why they should be judging it (DeVilliers & DeVilliers, 1972). This fact does not mean that feedback should be avoided, nor does it mean that corrections are unnecessary. However, we do not want *mere* repetition of patterns, nor do we want learners who can spout rules but are incapable of using them. The child has already learned important rules by acting and getting reactions, by asking for confirmation and taking risks, both in terms of language learning and other types of social learning. As Wilga Rivers (1972, p. 55) has aptly stated, our classroom environment should encourage such behaviors also.

> The student will acquire this realization of the possibilities of application and combination of what he is learning, not by listening to lengthy abstract explanations . . . but by using the structural patterns he is learning, in combination with what he has learned, for some purpose of his own. It is not sufficient for him to use a pattern to complete an exercise or to answer as the teacher requires; he must practice selection from the earliest stages of instruction, in an attempt to combine what he knows and what he is learning in the expression of a message he has personally chosen. (It is in this activity that, under the teacher's guidance, he learns the extent of pemissible extrapolation or analogy.) No matter how simple the pattern, it is important in the communication system for its possibilities of occurrence and combination, and it takes its place in the second-language system the student is building up as soon as it becomes a medium of communication, rather than a simple manipulative operation.

Often the expectations for teaching performance require that a certain number of lessons be covered. Time constraints thus put the teacher in the bind of closing off *exploration* in favor of *telling* and covering the curriculum. In addition, the size of the class, the expectation that the teacher is the only authority, and the unclarity of goals all lead to produce what Rivers has termed "pseudocommunication." This kind of communication lacks both the motivation that impels personal expression and the richness of meaning that is created in situations where cultural connotations allow for levels of understanding. A reexamination of the basic goals of the curriculum is necessary in order to prevent constraints from becoming excuses for failure.

Seelye (1974) has asked for just such a reexamination of the goals of language instruction. He is convinced that the failure to fully incorporate cultural understanding into language instruction has helped to create this situation of pseudocommunication. Culture, he insists, is not a frill, but a necessity to the understanding and use of language, for it includes not only art and music but also the patterns, assumptions, and values of everyday life. Also, bilingualism itself does not insure cultural understanding or respect. A more explicit approach to the teaching of culture and language use is needed. Of course, such an approach is not easy, and Seelye's good suggestions for teachers still require that the teachers have the insights, knowledge, self-confidence, and institutional rewards necessary for them to implement such an approach.

Rarely have teacher-training programs provided models or the knowledge base necessary for teaching language use meshed with cultural patterns and values. Holidays are usually the way culture is taught in schools. A bilingual teacher recently told me that she was teaching "Anglo" culture to Greek immigrant students by having them make valentines for Valentine's Day. Clearly, this approach to teaching culture is not sufficient. What aspects of a complex culture should be taught? How can the *dynamic,* changing nature of culture be communicated? How can cultural values and expectations be taught without attempting to replace one set of values and expectations with another? Will Woodsworth's (1973) suggestion that we start with cultural meanings for language teaching aid language learning as well as cultural understanding? How do teachers understand biculturalism and what do they perceive to be its relationship to bilingualism and language learning? There are many difficult questions and only attempts to try and to evaluate different models of integrating language and culture will provide us with some answers. We certainly need greater efforts to ensure that cultural expectations become a part of learning to speak and that cultural understandings become a part of living together in a multicultural society and world.

The motivation to learn something as complex as another culture and language is critical to success. Lambert and Gardner (1972) have shown how students' motivation may vary according to family background, social class, societal values, and political and economic events. Motivation to try to teach language and culture in new ways is also complex. The teacher's own personal history of language learning, feelings about acculturation, and interpretation of school and societal goals are likely to influence the goals and methods the teacher accepts and effectively implements (Guskin, 1975). In addition, the teacher needs opportunities to try out new behaviors as well as rewards for the greater effort involved. Motivation and attitudes deserve attention in the planning and implementation of change in schools. A complex change such as bilingual–bicultural education involves examination not only of the motivations and attitudes of the learners and the teachers, but also of the parents and other learners, teachers, and citizens in the community. Language learning as well as intergroup relationships will be improved by greater concern about attitudes and motivation.

Ultimately, the implementation of educational change will depend on the motivations, values, and expectations of a society at a particular point in history. The fact that schools today do not yet have materials, methods, and rewards necessary to support language teaching that is inextricably entwined with the teaching of cultural understanding and cross-cultural communication does indeed reflect the past history of public education as well as intergroup relations in this country. It is appropriate that, as part of our bicentennial celebration, we reexamine the past. How has our history shaped our goals regarding language teaching? How has it affected the motivation of our citizens for language learning and language maintenance? How has it shaped the social, political and economic relationships between ethnic minorities on our farms and in our cities?

We have had, in the past, a two-pronged policy with regard to language teaching and learning. On the one hand, we gave early recognition to the learning of languages by elites as a means of increasing their intellectual powers and marking their social status. On the other hand, we gave early condemnation to the maintenance of language and cultural differences, which condemnation helped increase the economic and political power of elites and those who changed themselves to fit their mold. Certainly one aim of this policy was to create a stable and unified nation with a common language and common assumptions about appropriate behavior. While this is a critically important goal for any society, it is not clear that we needed to pay the dual price of the loss of a rich heritage by so many, and the ethnocentrism and arrogance that often seems to interfere with interethnic communication at home and abroad.

Respect for what the child brings should be the basis for building an environment for learning that will motivate and educate; respect for differences in culture and language should be the basis for building a society in which motivation for communication and cooperation is a major goal.

References

Barnes, D., Britton, J., and Rosen, H. *Language, the learner and the school*. Middlesex, England: Penguin Books, 1971.

Brown, R. *A first language: The early stages*. Cambridge, Mass.: Harvard University Press, 1973.

Cancino, H., Rosansky, E., and Schumann, J. *The acquisition of the English auxiliary by native Spanish speakers.* Paper presented at Teaching of English to Speakers of Other Languages, Annual Conference, Los Angeles, 1975.

Cazden, C. *Child language and education,* New York: Holt, 1972.

Chomsky, C. *The acquisition of syntax in children from 5 to 10.* Cambridge, Mass.: M.I.T. Press, 1969.

Chomsky, N. *Language and mind.* New York: Harcourt Brace Jovanovich, 1972.

Clark, E. What's in a word? On the child's acquisition of semantics in his first language. In T. Moore (Ed.), *Cognitive development and the acquisition of language.* New York: Academic Press, 1973.

Cohen, S., Tucker, G. R., and Lambert, W. E. The comparative skills of monolinguals and bilinguals in perceiving phoneme sequences. *Language and Speech,* 1967, *10,* 159–168.

Corder, S. P. The significance of learner's errors. In J. Schumann and N. Stenson (Eds.), *New frontiers in second language learning.* Rowley, Mass.: Newbury House, 1974.

DeVilliers, P., and DeVilliers, J. Early judgments of semantic and syntactic acceptability by children. *Journal of Psycholinguistic Research,* 1972, *1,* 299–310.

Dulay, H., and Burt, M. Errors and strategies in child second language acquisition. *TESOL Quarterly,* 1974, *8,* 129–136.

Ervin-Tripp, S. Some strategies for the first two years. In T. Moore (Ed.), *Cognitive development and the acquisition of language.* New York: Academic Press, 1973. (a)

Ervin-Tripp, S. Structure and process in language acquisition. In S. Ervin-Tripp, *Language acquisition and communicative choice.* Stanford, Cal.: Stanford University Press, 1973. (b)

Gleason, J. Code switching in children's language. In T. Moore (Ed.), *Cognitive development and the acquisition of language.* New York: Academic Press, 1973.

Guskin, J. *Understanding bilingual teachers: A sociolinguistic analysis.* Paper presented at the American Educational Research Association, Washington, D.C., March, 1975.

Hatch, E. Second language learning—Universals? *Working papers on bilingualism,* Issue 3. Toronto: The Ontario Institute for studies in Education, June, 1974. Pp. 1–17.

Keller-Cohen, D. *The expression of time in language acquisition.* Paper presented at the Linguistic Society of America, New York City, December, 1974.

Labov, W., and Labov, T. *The grammar of "cat" and "mama."* Paper presented at the annual meeting of the Linguistic Society of America, New York City, December, 1974.

Lambert, W., and Gardner, R. *Attitudes and motivation in second language learning.* Rowley, Mass.: Newbury House, 1972.

Lance, D. *A brief study of Spanish–English bilingualism.* Research Project Orr— Liberal Arts 15504. College Station, Tex.: Texas A&M University, 1969.

Mead, G. H. *Mind, self, and society.* Chicago: University of Chicago Press, 1934.

Piaget, J. Piaget's theory. In P. Mussen (Ed.), *Carmichael's manual of child psychology* (3rd ed.). New York: Wiley, 1970.

Richards, J. Error analysis and second language strategies. In J. Schumann and N. Stenson (Eds.), *New frontiers in second language learning.* Rowley, Mass.: Newbury House, 1974.

Rivers, W. From skill acquisition to language control. In W. Rivers, *Speaking in many tongues.* Rowley, Mass.: Newbury House, 1972.

Schumann, J., and Stenson, N. (Eds.). *New frontiers in second language learning.* Rowley, Mass.: Newbury House, 1974.

Seelye, H. N. *Teaching culture: Strategies for foreign language educators.* Skokie, Ill.: National Textbook Co., 1974.

Slobin, D. Cognitive prerequisites for the development of grammar. In C. Ferguson and D. Slobin (Eds.), *Studies of child language development.* New York: Holt, 1973.

Woodsworth, J. On the role of meaning in second language teaching. *Language learning,* 1973, *23* (1), 75–88.

14

Assessing the Scholastic Achievement and Cognitive Development of Bilingual and Monolingual Children

THOMAS M. IIAMS, Educational Research Associates

One of the weaknesses of many federally and locally funded bilingual programs is the lack of any hard data showing how well the bilingual child is functioning in terms of academic achievement and cognitive development (United States Commission on Civil Rights, 1975). Inventories have been made of the affective concerns of bilingual–bicultural schooling and the positive gains in pupil self-confidence and school attitudes (Beatty, 1969). The purpose of this chapter, therefore, is not to review such attitudinal assessments but rather to focus on what many feel to be the nitty–gritty of bilingual education: Is a bilingual youngster, or an English-handicapped student enrolled in a bilingual–bicultural program, likely to do as well, academically, as immigrant school children of his age group and similar socioeconomic status assigned to the regular classroom?

At the outset it must be clearly understood that only a handful of bilingual children are presently studying in bilingual–bicultural classrooms. Indeed, most coordinate bilinguals (that is, those speaking a second language and the mother tongue interchangeably) will be found in the regular classroom, having been denied admission to the bilingual program because of demonstrated proficiency in English, as measured in reading scores, or because of parental fears that instruction in the vernacular will result in less attention to English composition and grammar. In some of our Nassau County (New York) schools, for example, fluency in English is grounds for exclusion from the bilingual classroom, whereas a Spanish- or Italian-surname child, illiterate in his parents' native language but with no greater English speaking disability than a disadvantaged monolingual Anglo, is unaccountably eligible for a "bilingual" course of study. Indeed, at the present time, a non-English-speaking ethnic scoring above average on every cognitive test given in his or her mother tongue may be enrolled in the same transitional bilingual program as an English-handicapped, minority youngster with no reading and writing skills in any language because a dialect is spoken at home.

For those school administrators with even a handful of non-English-dominant pupils in their care, the problem of whom to assign to the bilingual program is complicated by the many myths associated with bilingual learning generally and with bicognitive development in particular. Computerized record keeping, self-concept tests in the vernacular, and bilingual syntax measurements may help in the assignment of children for instructional purposes but educators would also like to know if bilingualism is healthy in terms of individual cognitive development. Moreover, they need some reassurance that putting youngsters into a special bilingual classroom is not going to have a greater negative effect on their academic performance, as compared to those of similar background struggling along in mainstream classrooms.[1]

One positive indication of the current revival in bilingual studies is the rediscovery of a 40-year-old monograph by Seth Arsenian entitled *Bilingualism and Mental Development: A Study of the Intelligence and the Social Background of Bilingual Children in New York City.* Curious to learn more about the interaction between bilingualism and intelligence, Arsenian chose as his thesis advisor, Rudolf Pintner of Columbia Teachers College, originator of the Pintner nonlanguage test for intelligence. It was Pintner who first drew Arsenian's attention to the work of men like D. J. Saer (1923), E. Jamieson and P. Sandiford (1928), and F. Smith (1923), whose research on simultaneous language learning carried the suggestion that some mental confusion and lowering of IQ occur during the development period.

The Saer experiments are interesting because his subjects were 1400 relatively homogeneous Welsh school children. Analyzing his data, Saer discovered that the predominantly bilingual rural children showed less academic aptitude than the largely monolingual city children. Because they fell further behind with each grade level, Saer reasoned that some mental confusion may have been a factor in the relatively poor showing of the rural youngsters. Saer's critics, on the other hand, have always denied the validity of any experiment in which the socioeconomic variable was not controlled. Class status, they insist, probably had more to do with the results than language interference.

In a chapter entitled "The Background of the Problem," Arsenian (1937) summarized the results of 32 experiments or evaluations of bilingual situations. Of these 32, only 4 reported "no language handicap"

---

[1] Funds appropriated under the Bilingual Education Acts of 1968 and 1974 have been supportive of demonstration classrooms. An equally convincing argument has been made in favor of using such funds to identify and develop better instructional methods for use with children of limited English-speaking ability (cf. Troike & Saville, 1973).

among bilinguals tested. One of these "positive" reports was Ronjat's linguistic experiment with his own son, Louis (Ronjat, 1913). From the moment of Louis' birth, his father and mother addressed him in French and German respectively. Relatives on the father's side always spoke to Louis in French, while relatives on his mother's side always used German. In other words, *une personne, une langue*. Almost from the time he spoke his first words, Louis pronounced the two languages as well as any monolingual child with native fluency. The instances of language interference or dyglossia were so minor as not to affect grammatical perfection in either tongue. More significantly (from our point of view) was Ronjat's conclusion that his son's intelligence was in no way retarded by the learning of two languages simultaneously.

A prime example of the negative evaluations reviewed by Arsenian is the 1925 survey of 69,000 Puerto Rican school children in which bilingualism is singled out as a major factor in the lower scores recorded on the Stanford Achievement Test (SAT) using *American norms* as criteria (Survey on the Public Educational System of Porto Rico, 1926). Although the same children surpassed their own performance in the Spanish translation of test booklets, they still did not do as well as monolingual American children in any academic category except spelling. The commission refused, nevertheless, to blame bilingualism per se for these lower scores, attributing the difference in results to the shorter amount of time spent in Puerto Rican schools on the subjects tested and to a suspicion that any translation of the testing instruments could not rectify the subtle differences of cultural referents.

The existence of strong mitigating factors was confirmed a few years later by G. I. Sanchez (1932) in his study of intelligence tests administered to Spanish-speaking children. In his sampling, Sanchez found that verbal tests in English were an unreliable tool for measuring mental capacity of Spanish-surname school youngsters. This, at least, was the conclusion reached after testing 45 Mexican-American youths in New Mexico four times between December 1928 and April 1930, using the Haggerty Intelligence Tests, Delta 1 and Delta 2. The average gain in IQ during this 19-month interval was 20.5 points, an increase he believed could be traced to the intensified instruction these 45 subjects received in English language skills. As we shall see, this linkage between IQ and language training is by no means an accepted proposition among all educational psychologists.

Forewarned about the innumerable psychological and linguistic pitfalls awaiting any researcher in the bilingual field, Arsenian decided to follow the recommendations of the 1928 International Conference on Bilingualism and use a nonlanguage test of mental ability. In addition to the Hoffman (1934) questionnaire of bilingual background, he chose the Pintner Non-Language Test and the Spearman (1925) education or visual relationship test, possibly out of personal loyalty to Pintner, although it is also worth noting that the "culture-free" Pintner test had turned up evidence of cognitive retardation among the large group of Puerto Rican bilinguals given the SAT in 1925 (Arsenian, 1937).

Despite the awkwardness of administering two tests requiring mimed instructions, Arsenian selected over 2000 students aged 9 through 14 to take the Pintner and Spearman intelligence tests. Basing his decisions on their responses to the Hoffman questionnaire, he could then divide those students scoring 80% or higher into an experimental group and assign the bottom 20% to his monolingual control group. Because all pupils evaluated attended the same two New York City schools and had their homes in the same neighborhoods, Arsenian believed he had reduced the ethnic and racial variables to near zero. Furthermore, once the socioeconomic factor had been factored out—using a system of weighted scoring of all questions about home life and social class status—Arsenian declared he could detect no significant cause-and-effect relationship between bilingualism and IQ.

At the time, Arsenian was only one educator among many trying to probe the mysteries of cognitive style with relatively crude testing instruments. Contributors to the *Journal of Applied Psychology,* the *Journal of Educational Psychology, Psychological Clinic, Comparative Psychological Monographs,* and the *Journal of Genetic Psychology* routinely offered their own highly controversial evaluations while noting the skimpiness of hard data or uncontrolled variables in experiments leading to contrary hypotheses. Typical of these pre-Depression investigators whose clinical examinations invited strong criticism was Kathryn Ewart Serota (1925), who reported an experiment in which 100 Italian-Americans were tested along with a control group of 500 first-grade monolingual youngsters. Whereas the Italian-speaking group scored below the norm in intellectuality (embracing such cognitive skills as acquisition, organization, and retention of knowledge), in general intelligence, defined as the ability to solve any new problem, the bilinguals did as well as the monolingual control group. In order to soften the racist overtones of her research, Serota attributed the poor showing of the bilinguals to a language handicap, despite research by May Bere (1924) suggesting a very weak correlation between the increased use of English in the home by bilingual subjects and higher IQ scores on the Stanford–Binet IQ Tests. After examining 300 school-age Jewish, Italian, and Slovak immigrants, Bere (1924) concluded that intragroup cultural differences may have influenced the average median intelligence quotient more than any single factor. The IQ of the Jewish experimentals, she disclosed, was higher than that of the other groups tested, despite the fact that Hebrew or Yiddish was spoken as commonly in the Jewish homes as Slovak or an Italian dialect was by the other families. Her conclusion: "Lack of language ability does not imply ability with concrete tests, *nor the reverse*" (p. 7).

In a similar study of 658 Japanese-Americans living in California, Marvin Darsie (1926), cautioned his fellow specialists against drawing any hard and fast conclusions from the scores on the Stanford–Binet, SAT, and Army Beta (a nonverbal test, akin to the Pintner Performance Scale). In interpreting his data, Darsie noted that the mean Binet IQ of the Japanese bilingual adolescents came out to approximately 90, as against 99 for Anglo children from the same age group. The 9-point differentiation, he believed, could be explained in a number of ways. Since Japanese was the only language spoken at home by these students, the 1-year mental age superiority of the average monolingual over his bilingual classmate could have been a consequence of the native English child's hearing English more often outside school.

By the late 1940s and early 1950s, the case had been made so convincingly to treat linguistic fluency along with class background as a variable in IQ testing that many educators may be pardoned for losing interest in the subject. In this immediate postwar period, Natalie Darcy, an educational psychologist, conducted a series of research experiments with far-reaching consequences in preschool-age bilinguals. While noting the difficulties inherent in early childhood testing Darcy nevertheless believed that standardized tests of achievement and intelligence provided a reasonably objective means of measuring intellectual difference between polylingual and monolingual boys and girls (Darcy, 1946). She therefore decided to use the Stanford–Binet and Atkins IQ in her own investigation of 212 pre-K youngsters of Italian descent. After matching the two groups of monolinguals and bilinguals for age, sex, and social class, she reported that "in every age and sex division the mental age of the monoglots surpassed those of the bilinguals on the Stanford-Binet scale" (1946, p. 41) whereas the performance of the bilingual boys and girls surpassed that of the monolinguals on the Atkins object-fitting test. On the basis of such contradictory results, Darcy drew the cautious conclusion that although bilinguals probably had as great an intellectual capacity as monolinguals, they probably suffered from a language handicap that affected their verbal responses. In her view, however, such a disability at so early an age (from 2 to 6) was unlikely to persist after elementary school.

What studies like those of Darcy and Sanchez seemed to suggest was not only that verbal intelligence measurements were intrinsically unfair to bilinguals but also that some kind of performance test was a more satisfactory means for evaluating preschool youngsters. In either case, more controlled experiments were needed before any educator could be certain he or she was doing the right thing by recommending a bilingual program.

In retrospect, the turning point in bilingual research may have passed unnoticed with the publication of Dorothy T. Spoerl's article, "The academic and verbal adjustment of college-age bilingual students," in 1944. Based on tests given a group of bilingual freshmen at American International College, Spoerl could find no significant difference in their test scores and those of a control group matched for sex, age, intelligence, and social class. While bilinguals tested more poorly than monolinguals on five of the verbal items on the 1937 Stanford–Binet, she was surprised to find the bilinguals' grade-point average in high school consistently higher than that of the average monolinguals tested. Unable to attribute this improved performance to their higher IQ—since IQ scores showed no marked variance—Spoerl theorized that the bilinguals may have been pushing themselves harder, from a feeling of environmental insecurity. Thus, for the first time under approved testing procedures, bilingualism was recognized as a possible contributory factor to higher academic achievement!

These qualifications notwithstanding, Spoerl's work was evidentally too inconclusive to be included in the "favorable" category in Darcy's (1953) review of bilingual studies. Of the approximately 40 investigations commented on or listed in her extensive bibliography, only two were reported as showing a positive correlation between fluency in two languages and intelligence (Davies & Hughes, 1927; Stark, 1940). In the more important of these dissenting evaluations, J. Davies and H. G. Hughes (1927), two English social scientists, tested all pupils between the ages of 8 and 14 in three London schools. Analyzing the results of the Northumberland Standardized Tests in Intelligence, English, and Arithmetic, they found that the bilingual Jewish childrens' mean score on the verbal part was higher than the corresponding scores of monolingual Gentiles. As a result, the bilingual group was judged to be 1 full year ahead of those monolingual children taking the same test. Once other educators, however, were permitted to see the raw data on which Davies and Hughes based their conclusions, the experiment was judged worthless because the researchers had neglected to control such important variables as socioeconomic status and degrees of bilingualism.

This lack of control, in fact, was one of the more common criticisms of language research in the interwar period. Gradually, however, as more sophisticated methods were introduced, the number of studies favorable to bilingual education showed a proportional increase. In 1949, for example, W. F. Leopold brought out the third volume of his influential *Speech Development of a Bilingual Child*. As Ronjat had, a full generation earlier, Leopold used his own child as a subject, crediting bilingual training for having helped his little girl separate the sound of a word from its referent. That is, by force of habit—hearing the same things referred to by different words—she had learned not to confuse content with form.

A similar experience has been recorded by S. J. Evans (1953), whose data on Welsh school children must be set alongside that of his fellow countryman, D. J. Saer (1923). Evans, for his part, could find no evidence of fuzzy thinking among Welsh bilinguals. On the contrary, he welcomed bilingualism because learning two languages simultaneously "frees the mind from the tyranny of words" (p. 3). Any individual who can dissociate thought from words has an advantage, he believed, over people whose thinking is restricted by language.

Still, as long as monolinguals repeatedly outperformed bilinguals on standard intelligence tests, it was difficult to make a convincing case in favor of bilingualism without calling into question the whole testing procedure. And that is what Granville B. Johnson, Jr. (1953) finally did. Writing in the same issue of the *Journal of Genetic Psychology* that carried the Darcy article on bilingual literature, Johnson insisted there was no valid reason why ethnic minorities, "deficient in the culture of which English is reflective" (p. 4), should be given the same test as Anglos. In order, therefore, to determine the degree of cultural assimilation for each subject, Johnson developed his Reaction-Time Test of Bilingualism, to be used in place of the Hoffman Measurement of Bilingual Background. By having his subjects name as many words as possible in a given time span, a technique borrowed from the old Binet, Johnson imagined he had cleared at least one hurdle standing in the way of objective evaluation procedure. (The next step, logically, was to replace the verbal Stanford–Binet with a nonverbal performance test. Johnson's own choice, once he had discovered a coefficient of correlation between the two, was the Goodenough "Draw-a-man" Test.)

Two admirers of the reaction-time test were Robert Cooper and Lawrence Greenfield (1969), creators of the Word Frequency Estimation. The advantage of the Cooper–Greenfield method was its simplicity. Bilinguals were requested only to keep a record of the approximate amount of time devoted to each language at home and to compile a skills inventory in both languages. The degree of bilingualism could then be calculated on the basis of the subject's own responses.

The subject of bilingual measurements was obviously creating a lot of interest among educators. In the same year that Johnson's article appeared, Anne Anastasi and Fernando Cordova (1953) published the results of their research into the bilingual capabilities of 178 Puerto

Rican junior high students living in Spanish Harlem. All 178 were given the Cattell Culture-Free Intelligence Test, one half receiving instructions in English, the other half in Spanish. The languages were then switched for the second set of tests. Although the overall performance of the group fell below test norms—owing to the subjects' imperfect command of both languages—the two examiners reported a marked improvement from the first to second testing among the boys, regardless of language. Secondly, although the overall median scores of both sexes was approximately equal, it was shown that Puerto Rican girls performed better when the order of testing was Spanish–English, whereas the boys tested higher when it was English–Spanish, evidence of a stronger acculturation pull among the males.

Another name associated with modern bilingual studies is that of John Macnamara, a specialist in evaluation measurements and intellectual development. In one recent study, Macnamara (1967) reviewed reports of linguistic interference, with especial reference to the work of Uriel Weinreich (1953). Weinreich held there was a strong possibility of conflict between two languages as dissimilar as Russian and English or between a dialect and "standard" speech, Macnamara concluded that the causes of language interference must remain a puzzle until a plausible theory was found to explain why individuals with similar levels of intelligence demonstrated such widely divergent levels of language competency. Until some such satisfactory explanation is offered, the field work of Kolers (1966) and Lambert, Ignatow, and Krauthammer (1966) may serve as models for future research of this type.

On the basis of his own investigations into bilingual articulation, Kolers (1966) satisfied himself that interference is unlikely to occur under normal circumstances. In his judgment, repetition of items in translation is just as helpful for recall purposes as repetition in the same language, for the reason that humans are equipped with a nonlinguistic semantic storage space. In the Lambert–Ignatow–Krauthammer experiment, summarized in the same article by Kolers (1966), French–English Canadian bilingual subjects were given three types of word lists: unilingual, in each of their two languages, and linguistically mixed. With few exceptions, individuals taking the test reported no more trouble recalling items from the mixed list than from the unilingual set of words.

One of the reasons Canada has been in the forefront of those countries looking into the psycholinguistic links between bilingualism and intelligence is the presence of Wallace Lambert at McGill University. In collaboration with coworkers on the McGill faculty, he has also sought to dispel some of the misconceptions surrounding bilingual education by organizing an entirely bilingual elementary curriculum at the St. Lambert school in Montreal. That project, however, was not even in the planning stage when Elizabeth Peal and Lambert (1962) completed their investigation of 10-year-old Canadian youngsters in six middle-class French schools under the jurisdiction of the Catholic School Commission of Montreal.

In a clear reversal of earlier case histories, the Canadian team found that bilinguals, as a group, performed better than monolinguals on verbal and nonverbal intelligence tests. Based on their sampling in the six Montreal schools, Lambert and Peal concluded that the greater verbal fluency of bilinguals more than compensated for any confusions caused by knowing two language codes. In other words, once allowance has been made for class and sex, the key factor in explaining the relative success of the bilingual children over their monolingual classmates may have been those cognitive skills—especially mental flexibility and concept formation—commonly identified with bilingual speakers. Peal and Lambert were careful, nevertheless, to add one word of caution: Nothing in their own investigation had shed any new light on the vexing question of whether the more intelligent child became bilingual or whether bilingualism facilitated any child's mental development. The researchers also felt that perhaps the time had come to stop looking for favorable or unfavorable effects of bilingualism on intelligence and to start some systematic examination of what it is that accounts for achievement in school or fluency in languages.

Responding to his own manifesto, so to speak, Lambert published a progress report 7 years later, analyzing the initial results of what came to be known as the St. Lambert Project (Lambert & Macnamara, 1969). In certain respects, it was a disappointment to those looking for confirmation of bilingualism's positive impact on cognitive or mental flexibility. When compared with monolingual English and French control classes, the English-dominant experimental group did just as well as, but no better than, their monolingual classmates in tests designed for standard first-grade arithmetic. Although able to follow directions and solve simple mathematic problems in either language, the experimental children experienced relatively more difficulty on the Metropolitan Achievement Test, the Peabody Picture Vocabulary Test, and a Word Association Analysis.

A summary of that first experiment is included in a mimeographed report prepared by Bruck, Lambert, and Tucker of McGill University in May 1973. In it, one may trace the achievement records of the St. Lambert pilot class (and of a follow-up class) from Grades 1 through 6. Thus, at the end of the second year, despite changes in teachers, methods of instruction, and modes of testing, the childrens' academic evaluation showed no marked deviation from their 1969 test scores. A change, however, was observed in the next 2 years because, by the end of the fourth year, the experimentals were not only reading, writing, speaking, and understanding English *as well as the control group* but were performing satisfactorily in French. Furthermore (although most of the textbooks were the same as those used in French-speaking Quebec schools), there were no signs of cognitive or intellectual confusion attributable to this bilingual ambience.

In the fifth report, the St. Lambert experimentals, i.e., the original pilot class plus the follow-up group, were still testing out as well as the English-speaking control group in language arts, with but one exception: In punctuation and capitalization skills, the follow-up experimentals were inferior to the control group. In science and mathematics, on the other hand, the McGill team could find no intellectual difference between the bilingual students and those native speakers of English following a monolingual course of study.

Finally, on the basis of their six-grade English reading and vocabulary test scores, the pilot-group children appeared every bit as proficient as monolinguals taking the same written tests. In French language skills, they came within a few percentage points of the French control group, performing as well or better than 60% of their French-speaking peers taking the Grade 6 *Test de Rendement* in French. Although the experimentals made only the same number of grammatical and syntactical errors as upper elementary school French Canadians their compositions were judged inferior—i.e., less creative—to those in the French control group. In conclusion, the sixth-grade experimental was holding his own in relation to French monolinguals his age in spite of a reduced proportion of his school time being devoted to instruction in French. In terms of cognitive thinking, moreover, the pilot class ranked as high as both control groups on standard measures of intelligence and "significantly higher on measures of cognitive flexibility." Here, at last, was the hard data some educators had been waiting for, evidence that children can be taught to communicate as effectively in two languages with no adverse effects on overall academic achievement.

Needless to say, the last word has not yet been written on the subject of the bilingual child and intelligence. In many cases, ethnic Americans are not looking for any special favors or separate educational tracks for their children. What is good for mainstream America is good enough for them. In other cases, such as that of the Mexican-American, a pervading fear of ethnicide has raised the question of whether immigrant children perhaps should be tested against their own cognitive norms rather than against white middle-class American standards. This, in brief, is the salient message contained in Ramirez and Castañeda (1974). Owing to a different set of cultural values, Mexican-Americans are often placed at a severe disadvantage when taking norm-referenced tests of intelligence. In particular, the authors suggest that it is necessary to appreciate the role of the father in the Mexican-American family to understand why Mexican-American children need more supervision than the average Anglo child. Chicanos, it was noted, tend to personalize relationships more than native-born Americans, performing well for teachers they like but showing little enthusiasm for school subjects per se. In pedagogical terms, their test scores show that they are more field-sensitive than Anglo youngsters. Although it is by no means certain that all Spanish-speaking students react similarly to the same stimuli, the assumption is that an Hispanic child with little self-confidence will do better if encouraged by his teacher.

Ramirez and Castañeda also felt that many Hispanic pupils might have done better if some test questions were made more relevant to their own sociocultural background. That is, any test in which the content is more abstract than specific, more analytical than expository, is poorly suited to the cognitive style of field-sensitive children of any ethnic group.

The day, in fact, may not be too far distant when the monolingual or unicognitive child will be considered as handicapped as today's young immigrant fresh from rural Puerto Rico or mainland Portugal. For, as one educational writer, Von Maltitz (1975, p. 70), expressed it, "either bilingualism and biculturalism are feasible ways of life in the United States or they are not. One can't have it both ways." In the meantime, thanks to a handful of perceptive (and persevering) educational psychologists, anthropologists, and language teachers, it is possible to discount some of the earlier theories about the negative cognitive effect of bilingualism on scholastic achievement. While bilingual children occasionally have greater difficulty in expressing themselves than youngsters fluent in only one language, imperfect articulation would seem an insufficient excuse for denying children the broader intellectual horizons and verbal flexibility resulting from learning in two languages. In any case, there is no longer any basis in fact for assuming that a functionally bilingual pupil is academically disadvantaged simply because the language heard at home is not the same as that spoken in the classroom.

References

Anastasi, A., and Cordova, F. A. Some effects of bilingualism upon the intelligence and test performance of Puerto Rican children in New York City. *Journal of Educational Psychology*, 1953, 44, 1–19.

Arsenian, S. *Bilingualism and mental development: A study of the intelligence and the social background of bilingual children.* New York: Teachers College, Columbia University, 1937. (Reprinted by AMS Press, 1972.)

Beatty, W. H. (Ed.) *Improving educational assessment and an inventory of affective measures.* Washington, D.C.: National Education Association, 1969. Pp. 41–73.

Bere, M. *A comparative study of the mental capacity of children of foreign parentage.* New York: Teachers College, Columbia University Press, 1924.

Bruck, M., Lambert, W. E., and Tucker, G. R. *Cognitive and attitudinal consequences of bilingual schooling: The St. Lambert Project through grade six.* Montreal: McGill University, 1973.

Cooper, R. L., and Greenfield, L. Word frequency estimation as a measure of degree of bilingualism. *Modern Language Journal,* 1969, *53,* 163–176.

Darcy, N. T. The effect of bilingualism upon the measurement of the intelligence of children of pre-school age. *Journal of Educational Psychology,* 1946, *37,* 21–44.

Darcy, N. T. The performance of bilingual Puerto Rican children on verbal and non-verbal language tests of intelligence. *Journal of Educational Research,* 1952, *45,* 499–506.

Darcy, N. T. A review of the literature on the effect of bilingualism upon the measurement of intelligence. *Journal of Genetic Psychology,* 1953, *82,* 21–57.

Darsie, M. The mental capacity of American-born Japanese children. *Comparative Psychological Monographs,* 1926, *3,* 1–18.

Davies, J., and Hughes, H. G. An investigation into the comparative intelligence and attainments of Jewish and non-Jewish school children. *British Journal of Psychology,* 1927, *18,* 134–146.

Evans, S. J. Address of the conference of headmasters of grammar schools, Wales, 1906. In Central Advisory Council for Education, *The place of Welsh and English in the schools of Wales.* London: Her Majesty's Stationery Office, 1953.

Hoffman, M. N. *The measurement of bilingual background.* New York: Teachers College, Columbia University, 1934.

Jamieson, E., and Sandiford, P. The mental capacity of Southern Ontario Indians. *Journal of Educational Psychology,* 1928, *19,* 313–328.

Johnson, G. B., Jr. Bilingualism as measured by a reaction-time technique between a language and a non-language intelligence quotient. *Journal of Genetic Psychology,* 1953, *82,* 3–9.

Kolers, P. Reading and talking bilingually. *American Journal of Psychology.* 1966, *79,* 357–376.

Lambert, W. E., and Macnamara, J. Some cognitive consequences of following a first-grade curriculum in a second language. *Journal of Educational Psychology,* 1969, *60,* 89–96.

Lambert, W. E., Ignatow, M., and Krauthammer, M. *Bilingual organization in free recall.* Montreal: McGill University, 1966.

Leopold, W. F. *Speech development of a bilingual child* (Vol. 3). Evanston, Ill.: Northwestern University Press, 1949.

Macnamara, J. The bilingual's linguistic performance—A psychological overview. *Journal of Social Issues,* 1967, *23,* 58–77.

Peal, E., and Lambert, W. E. The relation of bilingualism to intelligence. *Psychological Monographs: General and Applied,* 1962, *546,* 1–23.

Ramirez, M., and Casteñeda, A. *Cultural democracy, bicognitive development and education.* New York: Academic Press, 1974.

Ronjat, J. *Le développement du langue observé chez un enfant bilingue.* Paris: Champion, 1913.

Saer, D. J. The effect of bilingualism on intelligence. *British Journal of Psychology,* 1923, *14,* 25–38.

Sanchez, G. I. Scores of Spanish speaking children on repeated tests. *Pedagogical Seminary and Journal of Applied Psychology,* 1932, *40,* 223–231.

Sanchez, G. I. Bilingualism and mental measures. *Journal of Applied Psychology,* 1934, *5,* 395–402.

Serota, K. E. A comparative study of 100 Italian children at the six-year level. *Psychological Clinic,* 1925, *16,* 216–231.

Smith, F. Bilingualism and mental development. *British Journal of Psychology,* 1923, *13,* 271–282.

Spearman, C. *The nature of intelligence and the principles of cognition.* London: Macmillan, 1925.

Spoerl, D. T. The academic and verbal adjustment of college-age bilingual students. *Journal of Genetic Psychology,* 1944, *64,* 139–157.

Stark, W. A. The effect of bilingualism on general intelligence: An investigation carried out in certain Dublin primary schools. *British Journal of Educational Psychology,* 1940, *10,* 78–79.

Survey of the public educational system of Porto Rico. New York: Teachers College, Columbia University, 1926.

Troike, R., and Saville, M. A handbook of bilingual education. Washington, D.C.: TESOL, 1973.

Von Maltitz, F. *Living and learning in two languages.* New York: McGraw–Hill, 1975.

Weinreich, U. *Languages in contact.* New York: Linguistic Circle of New York, 1953.

United States Commission on Civil Rights. *A better chance to learn: Bilingual–bicultural education.* United States Commission on Civil Rights Clearinghouse Publication 51, 1975, 103–104.

Subject Index

A

Acculturation and methods of transportation, 138
Aggression as a biological universe, 173
in childhood, 174
interference, 173
overcrowding, 175
relationship to life-space, 176
Albuquerque, New Mexico, 192
American education, conflict in, 43
American International College, 258
American language teaching, influence of World War II on, 229
Analysis of variance, definition of, 4
Anglo-Americans, 3–4, 7–8, 10–11
in immersion programs, 80–81
teacher expectations, 74
Anglocentric instruments, 133
Army Beta Test, 252
Assimilation
tradition of, 26–28
language as a means of, 28
Atkins IQ Test, 257
Attitudes
affective meanings in different languages, 157
aggression between linguistic groups, 125–126
attending school of other languages, 124–125
correct speech by French teachers, 119–120
Cross-Cultural Attitude Inventory, 8
Cultural Attitude Scale, 3, 7
Puerto Ricans, Anglo-Americans, and Black Americans, 3

returning to Navajo reservation, 136
semantic differential, 6
Situational Attitude Scale, 6
social distance, 5, 6
students in immersion programs, 80–81
teacher aides in Navajo schools, 135
toward French and English students, 127
Audio–lingual method, 144

B

Behaviorism, 47
audio–lingual method, 144
empiricism, 146
Bereiter–Engelmann Preschool Program, 197
Berlitz direct method, 147
Bicultural measurement, 6–7
Bilingual education
and kindergarten, 90, 92
and language arts, 91
and Navajo Indians, 131
Bilingual programs, failure of, 18
Bilingualism
analyses in the sociolinguistic perspective, 234
children and intelligence, 254
classroom environment, 183
cognitive mapping, 52
coordinate, 253
curriculum as enrichment, 233
definition, 46
ethnicity, 232
literacy, 17, 27
social significance of, 32